Design for Research

Design For Research

PRINCIPLES OF LABORATORY ARCHITECTURE

editor

Susan Braybrooke

technical consultant

Merle Westlake

contributors

Harrison Goodman, Bryant Gould,
David Loe, Joseph Loring,
Edward Rowlands, Newton Watson,
and John Weeks

A WILEY-INTERSCIENCE PUBLICATION
JOHN WILEY & SONS
New York • Chichester • Brisbane • Toronto • Singapore

Copyright © 1986 by John Wiley & Sons, Inc.

All rights reserved. Published simultaneously in Canada.

Reproduction or translation of any part of this work
beyond that permitted by Section 107 or 108 of the
1976 United States Copyright Act without the permission
of the copyright owner is unlawful. Requests for
permission or further information should be addressed to
the Permissions Department, John Wiley & Sons, Inc.

Library of Congress Cataloging-in-Publication Data:

Main entry under title:

Design for research.

  "A Wiley-Interscience publication."

  Includes index.
  1. Laboratories—Design and construction.
I. Braybrooke, Susan.
TH4652.D473 1985   727'.5   85-12075
ISBN 0-471-06260-X

Printed in the United States of America

10 9 8 7 6 5 4 3 2 1

ABOUT THE AUTHORS

SUSAN BRAYBROOKE is a writer, editor, and public relations consultant in architecture and design. She has published articles in a wide range of professional and technical journals. She edited the *AIA Metric Building and Construction Guide,* published by John Wiley & Sons in 1980, and is the author of *Print Magazine's Casebooks, 3, 4, 5, and 6—The Best in Environmental Graphics.* She was awarded an individual project fellowship by the National Endowment for the Arts for the research leading to *Design for Research: Principles of Laboratory Architecture.*

BRYANT P. GOULD, AIA, is a senior vice-president and manager of predesign services with The Eggers Group, PC., New York-based architects, planners, and interior designers. A leading authority on master planning, facility programming, and space planning, he is the author of *Planning the New Corporate Headquarters, A Guide for Architects and Executives,* published by John Wiley & Sons in 1983. Research and Laboratory facilities for which he developed the program include: Iona College Science and Technology Center, New Rochelle, New York; Air Products and Chemicals, Inc., Corporate Headquarters, Research Center, and Applied Research and Development Laboratories, Trexlertown, Pennsylvania; Downstate Medical Center, Health Sciences Building, Brooklyn, New York; Medical Science Building, University of Medicine and Dentistry of New Jersey, Newark, New Jersey.

JOSEPH R. LORING, PE., is president and chief electrical engineer of Joseph R. Loring & Associates, Inc., a major mechanical engineering firm based in New York City. A principal in his own firm for the past 28 years, Mr. Loring actively participates in all projects undertaken by the office. He has designed electrical power distribution systems, complex building electrical systems, communications systems, special lighting, building transportation, and materials handling systems for every building type, but has made something of a specialty of research and laboratory facilities. Among major installations for which he has designed the electrical system are: Bristol-Myers Pharmaceutical Research Facility, Wallingford, Connecticut; AT&T Bell Laboratory Facility, Lehigh Valley, Pennsylvania; numerous research centers for IBM; Exxon Research Engineering Office and Laboratory Complex, Clinton, New Jersey; Squibb Corporation World Headquarters, Lawrenceville, near Princeton, New Jersey.

HARRISON D. GOODMAN, PE., is a senior associate and head of the mechanical department of Joseph R. Loring & Associates, Inc., where he has been employed for the past 17 years. A teacher and writer as well as an engineer, he has contributed articles to *Air Conditioning* and *Heating and Ventilation*, and is review editor of *Co-Generation Handbook*. Major projects in which he has participated, include: Merck Microbiology and Radiochemistry Laboratories, Linden, New Jersey; Armed Forces Radiobiology Research Institute, Bethesda, Maryland; and the Sherman Fairchild Center for the Sciences, Columbia University, New York City.

NEWTON F. WATSON, B.Arch., RIBA
EDWARD ROWLANDS, BSc. C.Eng., MInstP., MIEE, FIOA., FCIBS
DAVID L. LOE, MPhil., MCIBS

Professor Newton Watson is currently Bartlett Professor of Architecture at the Bartlett School of Architecture and Planning, University College, London, and Dean of the Faculty of Environmental Studies. Edward Rowlands is a Senior Lecturer and David Loe a Lecturer in Environmental Design and Engineering at the School. Together they have engaged in consulting and research as well as teaching.

   Their pioneering work has earned them the following awards: American Illuminating Engineering Society Award, 1974 for the lighting of the London Stock Exchange; American Illuminating Engineering Society Award, 1980 for creativity in the design of the lighting of the Tate Gallery Extension, London (both with Professor R. G. Hopkinson); Medal of the British Chartered Institution of Building Services, 1984 for their paper, "Preferred Lighting Conditions for the Display of Oil and Watercolour Paintings."

   They are currently appointed lighting consultants for the building of a new Museum of Modern Art in Hong Kong, and serve on national and international committees on the subject of lighting.

JOHN WEEKS, AA Dipl., FRIBA., is a director of the London based international architectural and planning firm, Llewelyn-Davies Weeks, which he founded in the 1950s with Richard Llewelyn-Davies. A recognized international authority on hospital design, he has written and lectured widely on the subject. He developed and wrote about the concept of "indeterminate architecture" as a response to the twentieth century need for buildings that can accommodate rapid, but unpredictable growth and change. In addition to the design of major medical facilities such as The Medical Research Council Complex, Northwick Park, Middlesex, England, and medical laboratories for St. Mary's Hospital, the Institute for Cancer Research, the Rayne Institute, and the National Hospital for Nervous Diseases in London, Llewelyn–Davies Weeks were also architects for Rushbrooke Village in Suffolk, The

Tate Gallery Extension, the London Stock Exchange, and offices for the Times Newspaper Company in London.

MERLE T. WESTLAKE, AIA, is a senior vice-president and director of the Stubbins Associates, the Cambridge, Massachusetts architectural firm, well known in recent years for the design of Citicorp Center in New York City. In addition to his managerial and communications responsibilities within the firm, Mr. Westlake has directed many of the firm's key projects, including the Rowland Institute for Science and the Nathan Marsh Pusey Library at Harvard University. A talented graphic designer, he developed a mural for this library based on the structure of famous typefaces.

R.LL.D.   *In memoriam*

"With equal passion I have sought knowledge. I have wished to understand the hearts of men. I have wished to know why the stars shine. And I have tried to apprehend the Pythagorean power by which number holds sway above the flux. A little of this, but not much, I have achieved."

FROM THE AUTOBIOGRAPHY OF BERTRAND RUSSELL

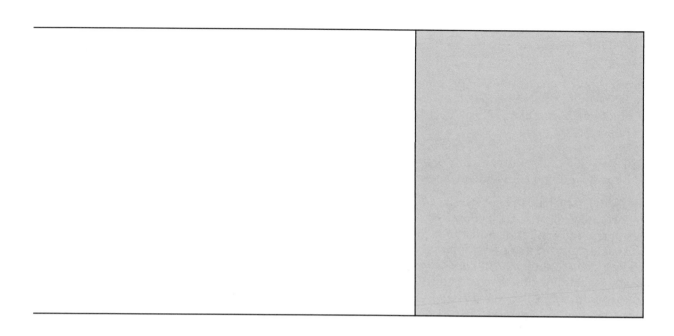

PREFACE

The research leading up to this book began with a suggestion from the late Lord Llewelyn-Davies that a volume published in 1961 by the Oxford University Press needed to be updated. That book, *The Design of Research Laboratories*, was written under his direction, and its nucleus was the report of a study of certain aspects of laboratory design conducted by the Nuffield Division for Architectural Studies while he was its Director. Essentially, this research was aimed at determining the amount of space and service facilities used by scientists at the bench; the proportion of time spent on reading and writing; physical characteristics of the laboratory environment; and rational lighting criteria. The research was thought to be the first systematic attempt to study laboratory design, and one of the early really detailed studies of how people actually use space. Some of the findings of the study were translated into a small building—an extension to the Animal Research Station in Cambridge, England, designed by the Nuffield team.

In reviewing the Nuffield study and the very scant literature on laboratory design produced since then, it became apparent that, while a number of the findings of the Nuffield study—in particular the anthropometrically derived dimensioning—remained valid, a totally new study of the state of the art and future directions in laboratory design was badly needed. The research was supported by an Individual Project Fellowship from the National Endowment for the Arts.

The research laboratory is an exceedingly important building type. It is the forum for advancement in very many areas of knowledge, the environment in which the most creative minds must function, the repository for enormously valuable equipment, and it represents significant national, corporate, and institutional investment in the future. It is also a substantial part of the practice of many architectural and engineering offices. Yet it has maintained a low profile as a design problem and vehicle for distinguished architecture. While there have been some famous tours de force, these have often raised serious questions of functional inadequacy. Efficient labs, on the other hand, have tended to be competent architecture, no more.

The research on which this book is based focused on three key issues in laboratory design: flexibility, safety, and quality of environment. For it was found that the design of the laboratory building is essentially a response to these three major challenges.

Flexibility: The nature of research can change in unpredictable ways. Research itself may uncover new approaches or points of emphasis. A corporation may decide to investigate new kinds of product manufacture. Educational programs may alter their priorities. Sophisticated electronic equipment may change the nature of task performance. Because laboratories are such heavily serviced buildings, the question of flexibility is a more technically demanding one than in many other building types. The key to flexibility in the laboratory is the way in which the services are introduced to the building and made accessible to the lab bench. The question of vertical or horizontal distribution or the employment of interstitial service floors must be examined in each case and resolved on the basis of life-cycle values. Since there is no such thing as total flexibility, it is important to assess the kinds and extent of flexibility that can be rationally planned for at the very beginning of the design process. The kind, number, size, and location of the fume hoods is thought by many to be the key element in establishing the overall building configuration.

Safety: The risk factor in laboratories is greater than in most other building types. People may be working with toxic chemicals. There may be danger of spills. There may be danger of biological contamination. There is danger of fire or explosion, or of exposure to radiation. Some parts of the building may have to be architecturally isolated or structurally reinforced. And in the individual laboratories, escape routes must be many and clear. The positioning of the fume hood must eliminate the possibility of trapping the worker within its confines; and must at the same time as far as possible contain the effects of a potential explosion within a limited area. The elimination of toxic wastes from the building must be handled with special care to prevent any hazard or pollution to the surrounding community.

Quality of Environment: Within the stringent functional and safety standards to which laboratories must be designed, the quality of the working environment becomes a major design challenge. The traditional picture of the absent-minded scientist working happily in squalid and cluttered surroundings, oblivious to all but his experiment, has died rather hard. Scientists, introduced to attractive, modern facilities, tailored to their real needs, have been known to comment that the surroundings were "too good for them."

Recent laboratories studied exhibit a great concern for the quality of the environment—and emphasize the value of the environment in promoting communication among scientists working in the same, or different, disciplines, who in the normal course of events may find it difficult to talk to each other. Access to color and natural light have been handled imaginatively—the use of atria or external corridors with informal seating and talking areas placed near windows to take advantage of the view. Color is often introduced within the laboratories themselves.

Furniture developed by the various manufacturers has generally proved handsome, functional and flexible enough to meet most needs, sometimes with specified modifications. But floor and counter surfaces demand careful testing to determine their potential penetration by chemical spills. Lighting is a key concern, since many of the tasks in the laboratory demand a high degree of accuracy, and the ability to read very small scales and observe minute or highly magnified phenomena.

At a time of architectural diversity, or "pluralism" as some prefer to call it, when so much attention is being given to stylistic and formal questions, it is encouraging to report that the design of the research laboratory, at its best, represents a serious effort to solve the environmental and functional questions of its genre without too much regard for fashionable allusion. The laboratories shown in this book have evolved from the need to create an appropriate framework and vehicle for the pursuit of knowledge. They are also good architecture.

One cannot research the research lab without thinking of the innumerable animals on whose suffering and death so much scientific endeavor still depends. The ethics of live animal experimentation lies outside the scope of this book, but the design of humane habitation for the unfortunate subjects of these experiments is properly its concern. Those whose work takes for granted the cruel exploitation of other species must never allow themselves to forget that they are dealing with living creatures sensitive to both fear and pain. And they must do their best to alleviate both; while to the scientific community at large falls the obligation to earnestly seek alternative avenues to knowledge.

SUSAN BRAYBROOKE

Manahawkin, New Jersey
October 1985

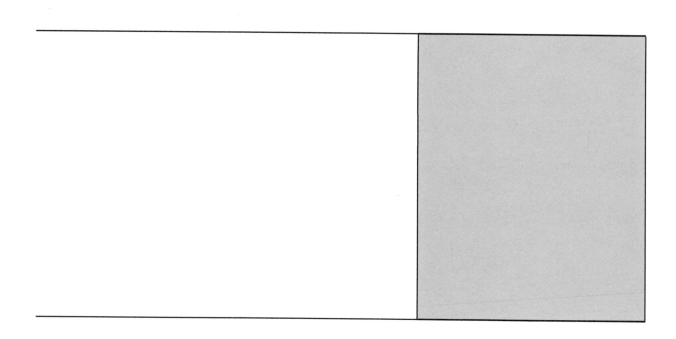

ACKNOWLEDGMENTS

I am deeply grateful to the authors, the publisher (in the person of Dudley Hunt), and to Merle Westlake for their commitment and patience, which have been exemplary through a very long gestation period. I also want to thank all the architects, scientists, and building administrators who showed us their work and working environments and talked frankly about the design process. In particular, I would like to mention Philip Berman, Samuel Brody, Lewis Davis, James Foley, Edwin Land, E. D. Shuster, Hugh Stubbins and Frank Weisenborn. I am grateful to the National Endowment for the Arts for funding the research leading up to this book; and to Richard Llewelyn-Davies, whose idea it was, but who died before the work was completed.

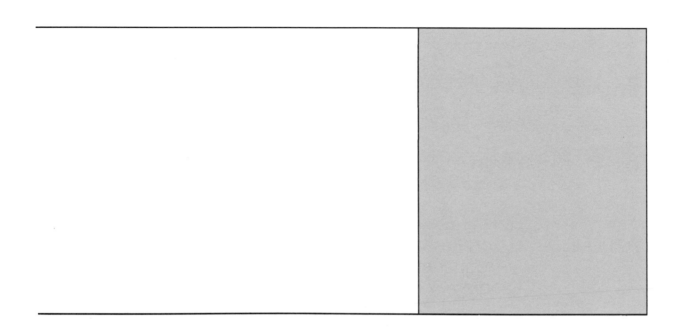

CONTENTS

Design for Research

1

A DESIGN
APPROACH

John Weeks, FRIBA

The history of the laboratory as a specialized building type begins with the alchemist's cell. Paintings of the alchemist at work often show a room in picturesque gloom with a furnace, giant alembics, flasks and crucibles on the floor, while the ceiling and walls are hung with mysterious clutter giving an impression somewhere between magic and madness. Most of the work seems to be done at the furnace by an assistant with bellows, while the alchemist is sunk in contemplation.

When chemistry began to appear as a scientific rather than a magical discipline, rooms for experimental work began to be depicted in a more objective way. In drawings of the first scientific laboratories in universities in the early eighteenth century, the apparatus can be seen clearly. Several furnaces were often grouped at the sides of the room, discharging into a common hood, and stout tables were provided to support the increasingly complex apparatus. In the famous drawing of Lavoisier's laboratory, shown in Fig. 1.1, the scientist is dictating notes on the progress of the experiment to his wife, seated at a writing table; mystery

has wholly given way to careful observation and exact recording.

In the 1850s coal gas began to be used as a local heat source, hotter than candles and spirit lamps and more flexible and controllable than the furnace. Thus piped services to benches appeared, and in new laboratories built in the nineteenth century, with sinks built into them and gas, water, and drainage laid on to them, benches became massive, teak-topped fixtures. Additional services became available as the century progressed, and by the mid-twentieth century the laboratory bench had become the base for often very elaborate arrays of apparatus using electricity, compressed air, steam, demineralized water, and suction, all available from a services manifold. Sometimes the controls were brought to the bench front so that it was unnecessary to reach through the equipment on the bench top to operate them. The laboratory was planned around the benches; they had become part of the building and immovable except by a construction crew.

The first laboratories were built as conversions

Figure 1.1 Lavoisier's laboratory. From Grimaux, *Lavoisier* (1888).

of rooms in existing buildings and purpose-built laboratories began to be designed much later; but even early laboratories began to exhibit the kind of planning geometry current today. In a drawing of Liebig's teaching laboratory at Giessen, around 1842, shown in Fig. 1.2, there are fixed benches along two walls, with cupboards and drawers under them as well as shelves over them, and in the center, two rows of heavy tables, also with drawers. The space between the benches and tables is about six feet; benches are about two feet deep and the tables are about three feet deep. Every horizontal surface is covered with apparatus; some stands on the floor and some on the tops of cupboards. The scene is very familiar to this day. And the bench layout, all the long sides parallel and about six feet apart, responds to clear ergonomic necessity; scientists can work at the benches, back to back, and someone can walk between them.

So long as most laboratory work was bench-based, the gradual evolution of the bench itself as a piece of fixed equipment was logical, but today new equipment and methods of work have made this principle obsolete. The development of electronic devices of all kinds and the continually increasing use of small computers and Visual (Video) Display Units (VDUs) requires much more flexibility than is provided by fixed benches. The scientist no longer works at a bench, attending a complex scaffolding of apparatus, but frequently sits at an array of VDUs, recording and calculating. The fixed, highly serviced benches have become obstructions and are often used only as storage surfaces, while much of the equipment in use stands in front of them.

The design requirements of laboratories have come full circle. The alchemist's cell, with a minimum of fixtures, gave way gradually to rooms with elaborately serviced fixed benches and cupboards occupying most of the wall space and often the floor space as well; but today many disciplines need a serviced room and, once again, the minimum of fixed equipment. The major area for design decisions is in the services and the means whereby these can be made available flexibly, usefully, and with the minimum of obstruction to the free use of the whole floor space available. The case studies in this book demonstrate ingenious servicing systems which are designed only to achieve this objective.

In the design of laboratories, the gulf in understanding, often remarked, between designers and

Figure 1.2 Liebig's teaching laboratory at Giessen, circa 1842.

the users of buildings is particularly clear. Whereas architects may wish to design a total, fixed environment, in which details are part of the whole concept, the users of a building attach far less importance to the whole than to the parts each uses intimately. The interior environment of a laboratory is not, in fact, controllable by architectural means; the essential requirement of the users is that, since their requirements inevitably will change, everything in sight should be movable. The architect is required to design and put into the hands of the client the means of transforming the environment himself; the architect is judged a success in direct proportion to the ease with which his client can alter his building.

The result of this has been twofold. First, laboratory design generally has not attracted star architects—those whose image is that of creative form-givers—since they cannot be in full control of the form. Most laboratory buildings, therefore, while exceedingly useful, are not architectural masterworks. Second, when by chance such architects have been commissioned to design laboratories, they find it helpful to articulate the functions into separate zones. Thus, Louis Kahn's Alfred Newman Richards Medical Research Building (see Fig. 1.3), although undoubtedly an architectual masterwork, has raised questions of function and flexibility. And in his beautiful building for the Salk Institute shown in Fig. 1.4, he designed separate

Figure 1.3 Alfred Newman Richards Medical Research Building by Louis Kahn (University of Pennsylvania Archives).

(a)

Figure 1.4a Salk Institute. (Courtesy Salk Institute.)

kinds of space, one an elegant, flexible workshop, and the other a range of highly specific spaces for retreat, writing, and thought, communal use, and offices. However, such physical articulation often tends to freeze the institution into patterns of organization of work which may not endure. A redeployment of staff, a shift in work patterns, a change in scientific attitudes, all produce space requirements which may not fit the physical shell built to the original program. Misuse of space will occur, expansion in one zone may not be required at the same time as contraction in another, and quite shortly the beautiful fit between function and architectural interpretation becomes a sham.

The unfortunate fact is that it is even more difficult to predict the growth requirements of parts of a dynamic organization than that of the whole—the parts have a different life cycle from the whole. Physical separation and architectural identification of the various functions in a plant are therefore more likely to lead to misfit, since the parts will certainly change in their spatial requirements even if the whole does not.

It has been said that the future is trumpet-shaped; that is, prediction now of requirements in $n1$, $n2$, $n3$, . . . years becomes progressively more difficult as the value of n increases. This may be a truism, but it is nevertheless one which is often ignored; but in the design of laboratories it cannot be ignored, because n is a very small number indeed if the prediction of change is to be reliable.

The architect must accept that his role in the de-

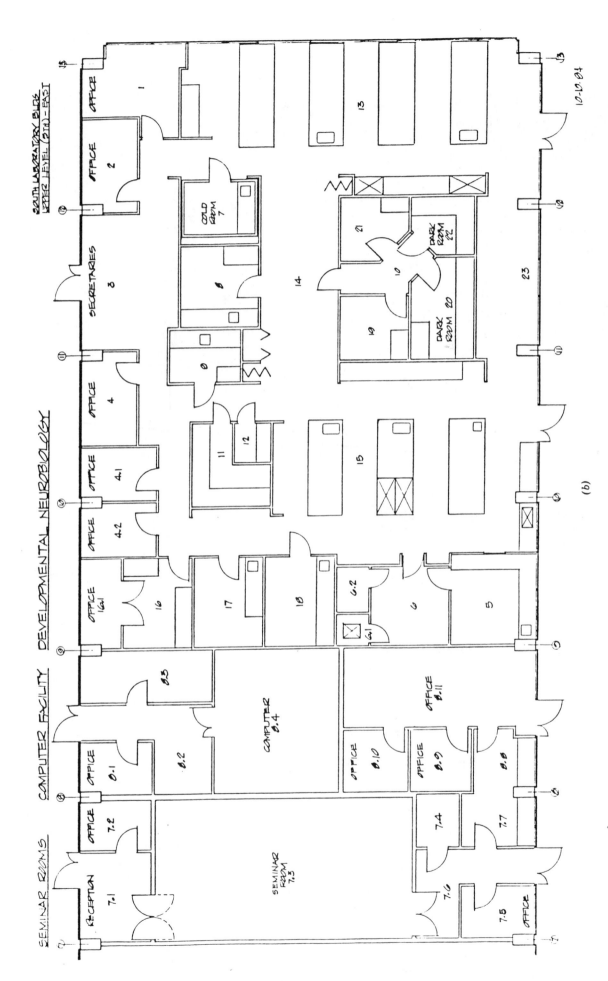

Figure 1.4b Plan of the South Laboratory Building, upper level—east. (Courtesy Salk Institute.)

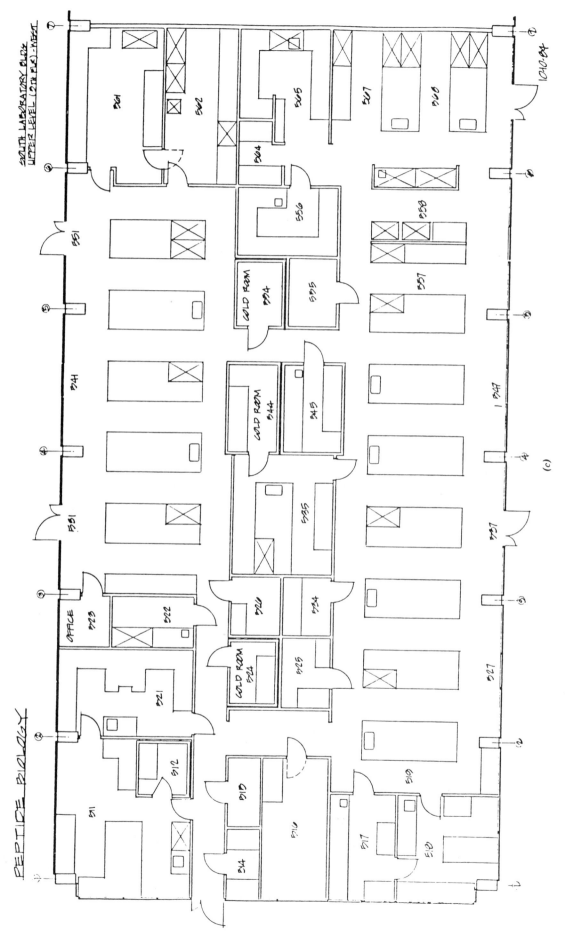

Figure 1.4c Plan of the South Laboratory Building, upper level—west. (Courtesy Salk Institute.)

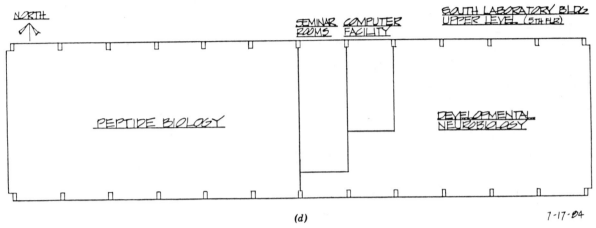

Figure 1.4*d* Detailed plan of the peptide biology laboratory. (Courtesy Salk Institute.)

sign of laboratory facilities should not be identified with that of the scientist. The architect's role is to design buildings for laboratory work, but the scientist cannot chart the future pattern of that work. One of the most important clauses in the architect's brief should be that the building must not be identified with any one pattern or even type of research work exclusively and permanently. Research is always changing the patterns of laboratory work, as techniques, once experimental, become routine. Developments are uneven and are dependent upon the presence of individuals' interest in particular areas, on changes in institutional policies, and on developments in the world scene. There is no universal pattern. The trap for the architect lies in purposeful identification of the building with the work of the moment. The architect has to design buildings which do not get in the way of research developments, yet do not demand development in order to justify their existence. Simple economics usually precludes construction of redundant spaces; thus most laboratory buildings must be designed for known requirements but be capable of expansion. A laboratory building can never be perfect and final; it must assume that the clients' program is only an incident in the whole life of the building, and is ephemeral.

There is a mismatch between the "natural" lifespan of a building and the work which goes on within it. At one time it was a canon of architectural education that "form follows function." This theory, which developed alongside the emergence of mainstream contemporary architecture, held that,

rather than the image of a building taking priority over the functions, a building should be designed as carefully as possible around an exact program of space, fitting exactly a program of activity. Such a building would be organic and naturally beautiful, as beautiful as a tree, which has internal systems that enable it to respond to external circumstances and be at peace with them.

Fortunately this is a false canon and a false analogue; if it were true, most of our stock of buildings would be useless, since every building is used in a way which is different from that for which it was designed. People, on the other hand, are intelligently flexible and can adjust to hostile environments much better and much more quickly than buildings can adapt to fit their changing functions.

The useful lifespan of a building does not have a single measure; different parts have different lifespans. The structure, that is to say the columns and slabs, is the most durable. Partitions are moved from time to time and furniture and equipment directly related to the work being performed are moved all the time. In a laboratory building the services are intimately connected with the functions, much more intimately than are the spaces. An awkward room size is a nuisance but will not usually prevent work being done, but the absence of services for a new piece of equipment will block activity in a particular area until the lack is repaired. Thus the lifespans of services are highly variable but more significantly related to the work being done in the laboratory than is the room size.

Laboratory work is often carried out in buildings which are unbelievably inappropriate to their functions, buildings which have survived through a century of changing use, yet in which many breakthrough findings have been proved experimentally. Workers may have to use idiosyncratically shaped rooms or work between immovable walls, and there are often flights of stairs connecting one part with another; still the work goes on. But this fact cannot be used as an excuse for permanent but irrational planning. The fact that such buildings work is a tribute to the fortitude of the human spirit, and not an indication that, since any kind of building can be made to work, the architect can indulge his personal fantasy.

If the architect is to be chiefly concerned with providing structure and services, a supportive structure for unpredictable work patterns, what kinds of rules should be followed? The structure is enduring and represents considerable capital investment. But, in being supportive rather than directive, it has to be designed so that it does not get in the way, and the rules for this game must be understood.

The most successful way of providing a wide use-range of space with flexible services and a minimum of structural interference is through the use of inter-floor service spaces. The column-free floors are spanned by deep trusses through which

services run, and these are accessible over the whole area of the building (see Fig. 1.5). In the typical laboratory at Ullèval Hospital, Oslo, designed by Harald T. Tørum and Odd Østbye (see Fig. 1.6), services are taken at modular intervals from the ceiling service void. Lighting, ventilation, and partitions may all be freely rearranged.

It can be argued that since this structural system provides a very high degree of flexibility, precisely according to the principles described, so it must be the preferred system. However, it is also arguable that the degree of flexibility provided through the use of this system may be unnecessarily high.

And it is expensive. The addition of a service floor to each served floor adds more than 20% to the volume of a building, and long-span structures are always more expensive than short-span structures. In effect, the argument for spending the money relies on a requirement for frequent changes to room sizes as well as services. Since planning modifications are less expensive to carry out in this kind of structure than in others, the high initial cost can be self-amortizing.

But how much flexibility is required? More than twenty years ago a study of the space required for laboratory work was carried out by the British Nuf-

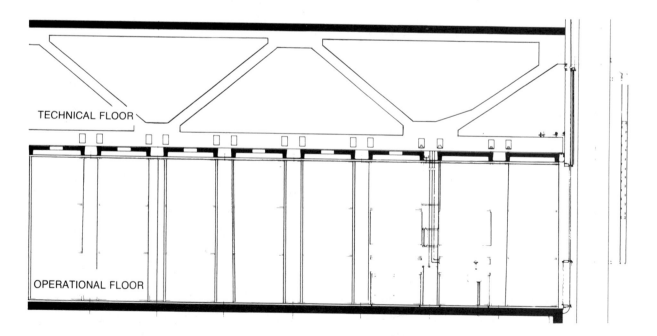

TECHNICAL FLOOR

OPERATIONAL FLOOR

Figure 1.5   Lab at Ullèval Hospital Oslo, Section showing inter-floor service spaces.

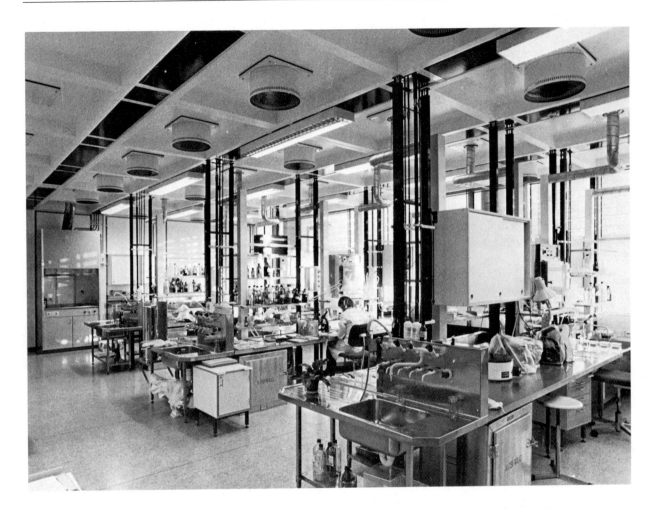

Figure 1.6 Typical lab at Ullèval Hospital.

field Foundation,* and time has shown that the planning dimensions developed as part of this study still have validity.

Laboratory tasks typically involve two elements, equipment and somebody to operate it. Sometimes two tasks occur with the operators back to back (see Fig. 1.7). Work tops are conveniently about 600 mm (23.622 inches) deep with 150 mm (5.905 inches)† behind them for wall-mounted services; an operator occupies a similar space. When these dimensions are added together, and circulation space is added as well, a working dimension

is derived which is a measure of most laboratory tasks.

An interval about 3.5 meters between the center line of laboratory partitions—and 3.6 meter (11.811 ft.) is a convenient, duodecimal number—will allow space in which two people may work back to back at equipment and a third person may pass between them. This is an ergonomic measure, and it is as true for the different sorts of equipment which nowadays make up the armamentary of the laboratory worker as it has always been (see Fig. 1.8). The fact that wall and floor space, once used for benches, is now often used for electronic equipment makes no difference. A planning module of 3.6 meters (11.811 ft) × 7.2 meters (23.622 ft) is available within the same plan discipline, and a room may be increased further in 3.6-meter steps.

---

*Nuffield Foundation Division for Architectural Studies, *The Design of Research Laboratories,* Oxford University Press, London, 1961.
†Metric to customary conversions given are not rounded.

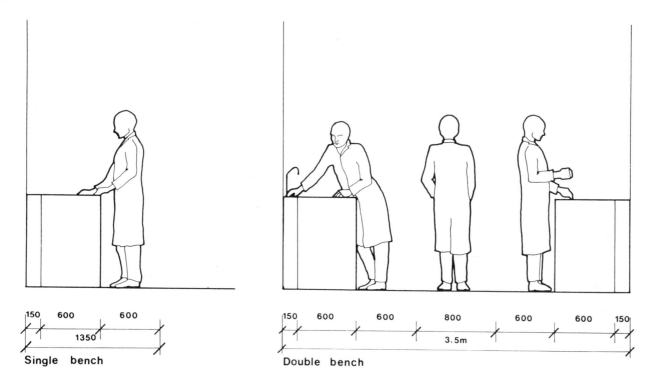

150   600   600
1350
Single bench

150   600   600   800   600   600   150
3.5m
Double bench

Figure 1.7 Ergonomic dimensions for laboratory work.

Buildings have been designed on this basis for many years; they are very simple, continue to be useful, and are continually being changed. They seem to provide a useful degree of planning flexibility.

Such buldings typically have vertical shafts for mains services risers on both sides of a central corridor. Structural spans are small (7.2 meters—23.622 ft) and the structure is therefore economical. Other than the structure and the services shafts, everything—benches, partitions services, lighting, ventilation, equipment—is movable. The laboratories provide the laboratory workers with the ability to change their environment themselves to fit their work, without the need to activate the institution and its administrative hierarchy.

A planning module which has been found to be useful is typically 7.2 meters (23.622 ft) × 3.6 meters (11.811 ft) with mains services risers (water, gas, electricity, and drainage) at 7.2-meter (23.622 ft) intervals and electrical risers at an intermediate 3.6-meter (11.811 ft) point. In a double module the center of a 7.2 meter (23.622 ft) × 7.2 meter (23.622 ft) room is free for floor or bench-mounted equip-

ment, with electricity available from ceiling mounted pendants. Movable benches can be of two heights, one for sitting, one for standing. Sinks are built into the benches where required, but these are connected to the main drainage risers by glass or plastic pipes with unscrewable connections; the sinks are as flexible as the benches in which they are placed. Drain lines are above the floor (under the benches) for ease of access. Service spines, running out from the main risers, are surface-mounted on walls at two levels: at low level, gases and water (drip cups may be provided in the spine), and at a higher level, electric outlets, computer links, and communication lines (see Fig. 1.9). It is important that this spine is at least 300 mm (11.811 in.) above the bench surface, so that it is possible to reach the outlets without disturbing the apparatus on the bench top. There are adjustable shelves on the walls, and above benches, and mobile blocks of drawers or cupboards are housed under the benches.

Partitions may be built parallel with the outside wall, where required, so that rooms may be provided, accessible directly from the corridors, for

Figure 1.8 The Rayne Institute, London (Photo Henk Snoek).

12

Figure 1.9 National Hospital for Nervous Diseases, London.

special environments, either cold, hot, dust-free, or dark. In the Nuffield laboratories there was no allowance for benches under the windows. Although it was argued that such benches are overlit and seldom used, it has been found in practice that they are often used for writing, since they are isolated from the experiments, some of which may be wet (see Fig. 1.10). An under-window spine can provide communications, electricity, and computer links. No water or drainage is supplied.

The vertical services shafts flank the corridors and have full-height doors to them, so that all services are available throughout their length. No pipes or cables are buried. The spines which run out from the vertical service shafts are demountable and additional services can be run in them where required (see Fig. 1.11).

It is sometimes necessary to isolate laboratories from each other for bacteriological reasons; pro-vision should be made for connection between adjacent modules so that any laboratory may be isolated from the corridors but remain accessible. The doors to adjacent laboratories provide fire exits.

Planning for energy conservation is now a recognized discipline, and a building should generally have as large an interior space within as small an external envelope as possible. To aid in this, corridors are sometimes planned along the outside faces of the building, and the whole of the laboratory accommodation is internal. Cultural considerations may require that laboratories have windows, but in some countries this is not thought particularly desirable. Where the corridors run along the outer edges of the building, a large duct at the center flanked by laboratories is very efficient (see Fig. 1.12). Such a duct can run through the height of the building and be sealed from the laboratories by fire-resistant walls. To some extent

Figure 1.10 Institute of Cancer Research Laboratories, London (Photo Henk Snoek).

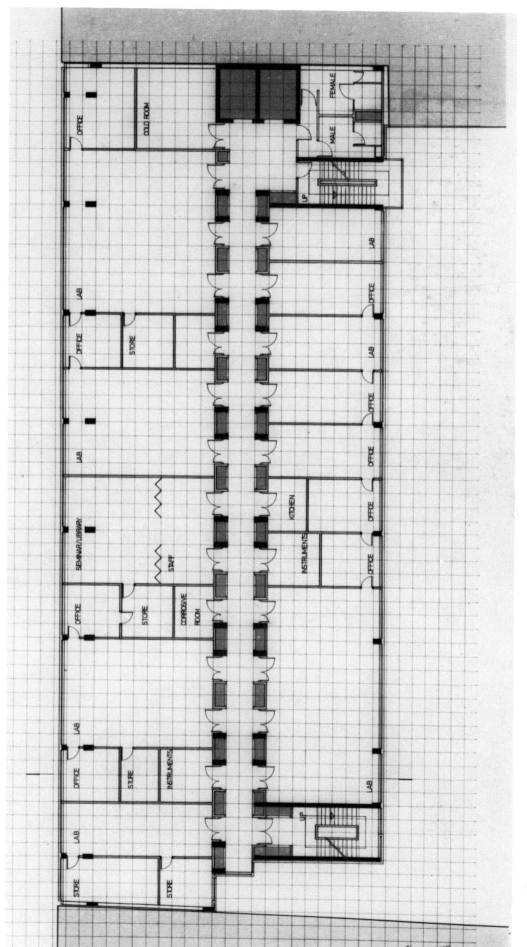

Figure 1.11 The Rayne Institute, London. Plan showing vertical shafts flanking central corridor.

15

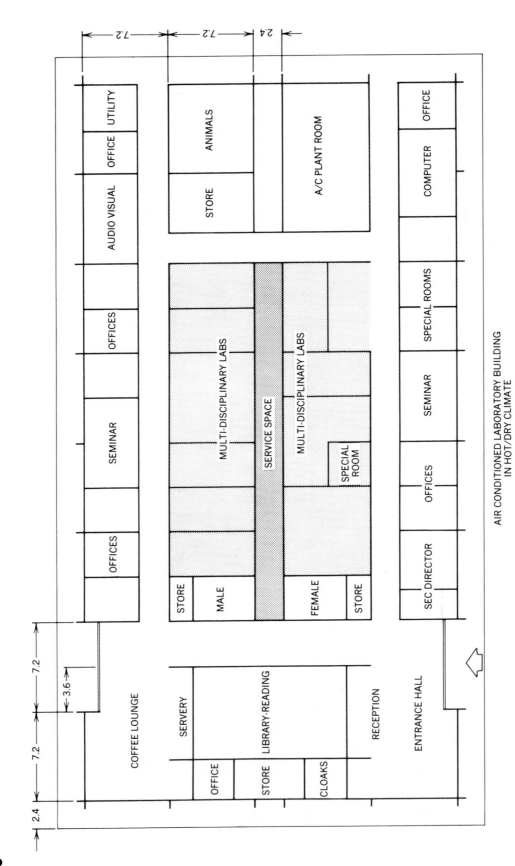

Figure 1.12 Plan of laboratory building with central duct.

AIR CONDITIONED LABORATORY BUILDING
IN HOT/DRY CLIMATE

such a duct affords the same flexibility characteristics as horizontal, inter-floor service spaces. Maintenance engineers may use it for servicing equipment clipped onto the duct side of the walls of adjacent laboratories, and additional services can be run or existing services changed without the need for the engineers to go into the working laboratories at all. The same ergonomic planning rules apply to this kind of laboratory building as apply to the ones described previously. The 7.2-meter (23.622 ft) module remains useful.

SUMMARY

The most enduring requirement for an architect in the design of research facilities is the maintenance of the ability of the users to use the facility in an ill-defined way. All programs for research facilities are out of date when the facility is brought into use. All work patterns will have changed to some degree. All briefs are wrong, to a greater or lesser extent. A laboratory building has to have a morphology which allows work zones to be allocated and reallocated easily and must provide easy internal connections between them. All equipment used in laboratories is obsolescent and will soon be changed. Nothing should be built into the structure, because the structure has a different life span from all the functions which occur within it. The working laboratory is an environment of clutter; that is the characteristic appearance of laboratory work. An architect with an obsession for visually neat order interferes with this uselessly and, if successful, to the detriment of the clients. The architect's success is to be noticed in the elegance of the shell he designs and by the degree of calm with which his spaces interact with the continually changing, cluttered environment. Where a building can accommodate change easily and gracefully, the architect has succeeded.

FACILITIES PROGRAMMING

Bryant Putnam Gould, AIA

2.1 THE FACILITIES PROGRAM

The facilities program is a complete statement of spatial needs. It serves as the primary medium for communicating design criteria from the future users of a laboratory to the professionals who will create its physical environment.

Complete and precise programming is necessary because of the program's long-term effect on the performance of facilities. Laboratories are costly to build and operate and are often subject to sudden growth and changes in technology. Moreover, a laboratory's design should afford a good working environment under stringent safety standards. The criteria which provide for compliance with these demands are defined and quantified in the facilities program.

The program is the keystone of the planning and design process, which is illustrated in Fig. 2.1. A later section of this chapter describes various applications of the program at several phases of project development.

The scope of the facilities program is influenced by the context in which it is developed. A detailed set of criteria must be prepared for the design of a laboratory, but how many of the criteria are included under the umbrella of the program and how many in a family of related documents may be largely a matter of timing. The content of a typical program as well as additional studies that may be included are given in a later section.

2.2 THE PROGRAMMING PROCESS

In general, the programming process involves the translation of abstract goals into specific spatial terms. Figure 2.2 shows the major steps in the process and how they interact.

2.2.1 Context

Every building program evolves under conditions unique to the project, and the planning of facilities is affected accordingly. For instance, a laboratory may consist of a new building on a bare site, be housed in both existing and new facilities, or occupy a building intended to be converted to some other use. Planning varies according to laboratory function and location and the policies and preferences of the owner. The context affects the process of programming, particularly in scheduling and in relationships to interactive tasks.

2.2.2 The Project Schedule

Programming must be completed within an allotted period of time in a project schedule. Often a

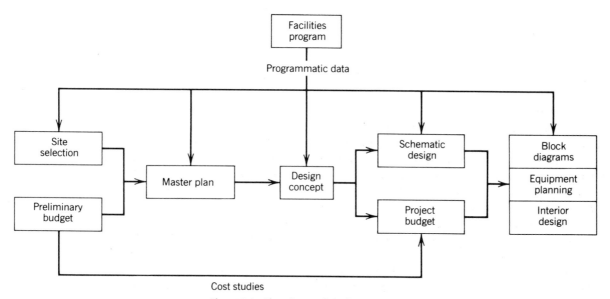

Figure 2.1 Planning and design process.

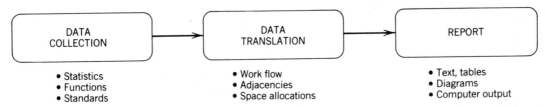

Figure 2.2 Major steps in programming.

laboratory is designed and built on an accelerated schedule, so the programming may be produced under considerable pressure. Other tasks in the project schedule (site selection, for instance) may rely on data generated by the program, so it may be necessary to quickly develop preliminary information and "feed" it to those engaged in parallel studies. It is advisable to identify the need for such exchanges of data when preparing a project schedule.

2.2.3 Major Phases in Programming

Programming involves the translation of needs into alphanumeric and graphic terms. The facilities program is usually produced in three major steps:

1. Data collection, in which the users' needs are systematically gathered, codified, and analyzed.
2. Data translation, in which the needs are converted into text, tables, diagrams, and detailed space allocations.
3. Program report, consolidating all criteria into a concise document or documents usable by the designers of a laboratory.

2.2.4 Initial Steps in Programming

Since facilities programming is often the first work undertaken in project development, the project team may be organized shortly before programming begins. The team usually includes a representative of the owner (functioning as project manager), the project architect, the leader of the programming staff, and (later) the construction manager or contractor's representative. Project engineers and specialists join the team at appropriate times in the schedule. Consultants in safety, environmental studies, lab equipment, energy analysis, and cost estimating may supplement the team.

Facilities programming may be done by the owner's staff, a consultant specializing in laboratory planning, or the architect. In either situation, the programming staff becomes involved in the project at its inception. If expansion or retrofitting of existing facilities is required, the staff responsible for making building surveys and evaluations also participates. These predesign professionals have a pivotal role in the early phases of the project.

A meeting of the project team is held to initiate the work. The meeting establishes policies, procedures, and responsibilities for managing the project and also sets in motion the predesign activities. An agenda should be prepared for the initial meeting and, preferably, furnished to participants beforehand. A typical agenda might include:

- Team responsibilities for programming and surveys.
- The schedule for predesign tasks.
- The persons to be interviewed.
- Years to which space needs will be projected.
- Review of format of questionnaires.
- Review of owner's space standards.
- General definition of project scope.
- List of preliminary data to be furnished by owner, such as personnel listings, organization chart, site survey, drawings of existing facilities, utilities data.

If the programming requires interviews and data preparation involving large numbers of users, it may be well to follow the initial meeting with an orientation presentation at which data collection procedures and interview agendas are explained to the users.

In all situations, data collection should be carefully planned and organized to make minimum demand on the time of the owner's staff. At the same time, the owner should recognize that the staff's participation in programming is essential and that it is wrong to eliminate or weaken the interaction between planners and users.

2.2.5 Scheduling the Facilities Program

As noted earlier, programming is done during a designated time period in the project schedule. The period will vary according to the size and complexity of the project and the number of users involved in data collection. The most accurate method of estimating time is to assign hours or days to each task in programming. Table 2.1 provides a task matrix which may be used to calculate total time and the number of personnel required to accomplish the work in a given period. The table may also be used in establishing the cost of program-

TABLE 2.1 Task Matrix for Scheduling

| | Staff (Hours)(Days) | | | | | | | |
| | | | | | | Other | | |
Task	Project Architect	Program Leader	Senior Planner	Planner	Graphics	Description	(Hours) (Days)	Total
A. Initiation								
1. Initial Meeting								
2. Prepare Schedule								
3. Prepare Forms & Questionnaire								
4. Review Owner's Data								
5. Orientation Meeting								
6. Visit Similar Labs								
7. Other								
B. Data Collection								
1. Review Completed Forms								
2. Interview Staff (No.)								
3. Write-Up Notes								
4. Summarize Input								
5. Review Summary w/Owner								
6. Other								
C. Draft Report								
1. Analyze Operations								
2. Establish Modules								
3. Prepare Text, Tables, etc.								
4. Prepare Graphics								
5. Calculate Net Area								
6. Review Draft w/Owner								
D. Final Report								
1. Make Revisions								
2. Coordinate Document Production								
3. Final Presentation								
4. Other								
Total								

| Summary | Hours or Days | | |
Task	Schedule	Required	No. of Staff
A. Initiation			
B. Data Collection			
C. Draft Report			
D. Final Report			

ming. The planner's staff may establish the schedule, in which case staff time is allocated in consideration of current personnel and workloads, or the time period may be pre-established, meaning that it may be necessary to hire additional staff or plan for premium time.

If the data collection procedure requires the owner's staff to assemble data, then a realistic period should be assigned for this task; one to three weeks is usually required. The time for interviews may be established on the assumption that an average of two to three individual interviews can be done by one planner in one day. However, it may be difficult for the owner's people to make themselves available in the desired period, so it may be necessary to allow extra time for out-of-sequence meetings.

Although there are many variables that can affect the time required to prepare a program for a laboratory, eight to fourteen weeks may be assumed for a typical programming schedule. It is stressed that planning and design is a nonlinear process and that a number of other events may occur while programming is under way.

2.2.6 Data Collection

It is suggested that data collection be accomplished by the following procedures:

1. Send forms and instructions for their use to designated administrators, department heads, key professionals, and managers of service operations.
2. Review completed forms prior to interviews.
3. Interview the designated users.
4. Organize and summarize the data obtained from forms and interviews.
5. Review all data with owner's project manager and/or lab administration prior to data translation.

2.2.7 Use of Forms and Questionnaires

Most planners rely on some combination of forms and interviews to elicit information from the owner. Forms and instructions for their use are sent to selected members of the owner's staff, after which interviews are scheduled to review the data entered on the forms and to discuss in detail the users' needs for their space. In general, the forms are used to record factual, quantitative data, while the interviews deal with qualitative issues.

The decision as to which information is best obtained through forms or questionnaires and which through interviews should be made on the basis of the combination that produces the necessary information with the least demand on staff time.

Forms or questionnaires should be simple, easy to use, and accompanied by instructions for entering information. Figure 2.3* is an example of a form used for an academic facilities program. Separate forms may be developed for special purpose, such as lab utilization statistics or equipment inventory.

2.2.8 Interviews

Ideally, an interview is held between a planner and an individual or a small group of users. Unless a planner employs a technique that involves extended sessions with large numbers of users, it is best to limit group sizes to eight or less people. An interview is most productive when the owner's staff has been notified in advance of the agenda. Table 2.2 provides a checklist containing many of the topics that are discussed in an interview for a laboratory program. In using such a checklist, it is necessary to adapt it to the type of facility. For instance, data for a program for an academic science building includes such information as class sizes, schedule, and instructional aids.

Suggestions for conducting interviews follow:

- The planner must be specific about the information that is sought and be well prepared for the interview. Most users resent fishing expeditions.
- It's best to find out the user's rank and correct title before the interview.
- Although an informal atmosphere is desirable, the planner should follow a regular sequence of topics and keep discussions on track as much as possible.
- The users should be tactfully steered away from issues unrelated to the program.

*This figure and certain other illustrations in Chapter 2 are courtesy of The Eggers Group, PC.

DEPARTMENT _____ DATA COMPILED BY _____ DATE _____

A. BASIC DATA

Teaching Program(s) _____

No. Student Stations _____
Total Students Taught _____
Remarks: _____
_____
_____

B. TYPICAL BENCH SERVICES

1. Piped Services (check)

_____

CW	HW	Gas	Air	Vac.	Other (Desc.)

2. Electric Services

Purpose	Volts	Phase	Load

3. Sinks per Stud. Sta. _____

4. Remarks: _____
_____
_____
_____

C. FUME HOODS

No.	Size	Type Bench	Walk-in

D. STORAGE

1. Students

Purpose	No. Drawers	LF Shelving

2. General Purpose

Purpose	LF Shelving

3. Remarks: _____
_____
_____
_____

E. SPECIAL CRITERIA

1. Temperature:
   More Than 70°F Winter _____
   Less Than 78°F Summer _____

2. Humidity:
   More Than 30°RH Winter _____
   Less Than 60°RH Summer _____

3. Live loads, excess of 60 psf _____

4. Noise and/or Vibration Control _____

5. Task Lighting _____
_____

6. Other: _____
_____
_____

Figure 2.3 Data collection form.

TABLE 2.2 Planning Considerations for Corporate Laboratories

A. SITE CONSIDERATIONS
    1. Special Considerations for Labs
        (a) Wind direction (dispersal of gaseous wastes)
        (b) Subsoil (consider in relation to disposal of toxic liquids)
        (c) Electromagnetic interference
        (d) Utilities
        (e) Security
        (f) Control of hazards
            • Blast
            • Radiation
            • Fire
            • Toxic fumes
            • Pathogens
        (g) Bulk supply delivery (trucking, rail spur, warehousing)
B. FUNCTIONAL RELATIONSHIPS
    1. With Other Components on Site
        (a) Brands management groups
        (b) Corporate engineering
        (c) Corporate manufacturing
        (d) Package design
        (e) Data processing
        (f) Purchasing
        (g) Personnel
        (h) Law and patents
        (i) Services (possibly shared)
            • Food Serving
            • Mail and messenger
            • Receiving
            • Maintenance
            • Security
            • Filing and microfilming
            • Library
            • Volume reproduction and copying
            • HVAC, light, power, communications
            • Waste disposal
    2. Interrelationships
        (a) Administration
        (b) Unit labs
        (c) Pilot plant
        (d) Research
        (e) Product development
        (f) Process development
        (g) Fabrication
        (h) Possible shared lab operations
            • Analytical
            • Physical testing
            • Mathematical analysis
            • EDP
            • Engineering
            • Microbiology
            • Other

Table 2.2 (*Continued*)

        (i) Lab support
- Sterilizing
- Glasswash
- Balance
- Preparation
- Storage
- Maintenance
- Other

C. ESTABLISHMENT OF MODULES
  1. Unit Labs
    (a) Number of professionals and technicians in typical lab
    (b) Work surfaces
- Standard benches
- Desks (height)
- Instruments (possible consolidation)

    (c) Atypical working clearances
    (d) Fume hoods
    (e) Cabinets and shelving
    (f) Safety provisions
- Hatches
- Showers
- Eye cups
- Blankets

    (g) Lab office
- Enclosed
- Semi-enclosed
- Integral with lab
- May be across corridor

    (h) Natural light in labs
    (i) Ceiling heights
  2. Administrative offices
    (a) Private office types and sizes
    (b) General office allocation
    (c) Files
    (d) Waiting
    (e) Conference

D. SPECIAL LAB REQUIREMENTS
  1. Microbiology
    (a) Measures against cross-contamination
- Zoning for sterile and nonsterile areas
- Positive and negative pressure

    (b) Sterilization
    (c) Controlled environment (culture growth, cold rooms, package units, standby power)
  2. Analytical
    (a) Possible service function
    (b) Instruments
    (c) Balance rooms
  3. Animal Labs
    (a) Location (including community aspects)
    (b) Primary relationships to other functions

Table 2.2 (*Continued*)

      (c) Species of animals housed

      (d) Animal housing
- Quarantine
- Isolation (ill animals)
- Isolation (by species or project)
- Long term

      (e) Circulation (clean and dirty)

      (f) Cross-contamination controls

      (g) Sanitation
- Autoclave (cages, equipment, food, bedding)
- Washing (rack-cage, bottles, waste can)
- Refrigeration (perishables, carcasses, waste)
- Incinerator and/or destructor

      (h) Special labs
- Surgery
- Special diets
- Diagnostic
- Radioisotope
- Infectious disease
- Behavioral
- Necropsy

      (i) Storage
- Food
- Bedding
- Supplies
- Equipment and cages

      (j) Outdoor runs

      (k) Administrative areas

   4. Explosive Hazards Labs

      (a) Separations and clearances

      (b) Revetments

      (c) Structure
- Reinforced concrete
- Frangible sections
- Escape hatches, ladders, chutes
- Steel plate doors and hardware
- Sparkproof finishes

      (d) Dust control

E. SUPPORT FACILITIES

   1. Chromatography and Electrophoresis

      (a) Separate ventilation w/purge system

      (b) Hoods

      (c) Corrosive media (chemical resistant materials, washable surfaces, drains, glass traps, lines for sinks)

      (d) Grounding and outlets

      (e) Varying current sources

      (f) Emergency showers, etc.

   2. Electron Microscope

      (a) Door opening size

      (b) Equipment and clearance sizes

      (c) Vibration control

      (d) Shielding

Table 2.2 (*Continued*)

(e) Dust control and A/C
(f) Light tight condition
(g) Washable surfaces, drain
(h) Variable illumination
(i) Plate processing
(j) Record-keeping
(k) Storage
(l) Specimen preparation room (equipment, services, controlled environment)

3. Dark Room
   (a) Light-proofing
   (b) Finishes (color, reflectivity, maintenance)
   (c) Electrical (outlets, rheostat, strip-plugs, in-use light)
   (d) Plumbing (sinks, print washer)
   (e) Counters and cabinets (chemical resistant)
   (f) Light-proof and refrigerated cabinets

4. Glass Wash

5. Sterilizing

6. Controlled Environment Spaces
   (a) Culture growth
   (b) Delicate instruments
   (c) Temperature, humidity, and dust controls
   (d) Vibration and shock controls
   (e) Radioactive materials
   (f) Standby power
   (g) Electromagnetic shielding

7. Light Rooms

8. Mock-ups for Product Development (in conjunction with sales and product staffs)

9. Data Processing
   (a) Central processing
   (b) I/O terminals
     • Data entry
     • Printer
     • CRT
   (c) Calculator system

10. Library
    (a) Control
    (b) Reader stations
    (c) Number of volumes
    (d) Integration with business-technical library

11. Storage
    (a) General
    (b) Spare parts and equipment
    (c) Bulk supplies
    (d) Chemicals (detached and ventilated space)
    (e) Refrigerated supplies
    (f) Outdoor storage (including petrochemicals)

12. Equipment Repair and Maintenance
    (a) Machine shops
    (b) Paint shop
    (c) Clean shop (electronics)

- The planner should ask the user to express an ideal space situation. It's sometimes difficult for a user to define optimal conditions when existing facilities hamper good use of space.
- It is appropriate to ask a user to justify a request for space if the request does not seem to be founded on actual need.

2.2.9 Data Analysis

After all information is collected, it should be organized and summarized. Data should be entered in a format that will be followed in later stages of programming. The format may follow the owner's organization or a computerized system for inventorying space.

2.2.10 Data Translation

Data obtained through the procedures described above are translated into specific spatial terms, including adjacency diagrams, space allocations, planning modules, and performance criteria. Later sections of Chapter 2 provide methods of translation.

2.2.11 Program Report

The program is usually presented in a report that consolidates all data and that may also include related studies. For very large projects, it may be desirable to divide the report into two parts; one being the *Functional Program* and the other the *Architectural Program*. The Functional Program provides statistical and operational data pertaining to the organization and use of the spaces in the laboratory. The data include the owner's goals for the project and the criteria governing the allocation and arrangement of space. The Architectural Program is mainly a listing of net areas derived from the Functional Program, together with detailed information about space relationships. The Architectural Program may include a breakdown giving detailed information about every room.

2.3 DESIGN ISSUES

Since the facilities program establishes optimal relationships between functional elements of a lab-

oratory, the programming process includes analysis of the issues, both subjective and objective, that influence the arrangement of space. Although siting and building form are established during design, it is during programming that the issues are defined and translated into guidelines usable for design.

2.3.1 Basic Concepts

The program should spell out the relationships between major elements of space, including standard labs, offices, corridors, and service distribution spaces. These relationships are a direct reflection of the type of laboratory and the manner in which it is operated. The users may have strong preferences concerning interior versus perimeter locations for labs and offices. The pros and cons of alternate concepts should be discussed with the users during interviews. Chapters 3 and 4 discuss these issues in greater detail.

2.3.2 Planning Module

The issues and constraints that determine the most suitable module, or modules, for a laboratory facility are properly addressed during programming. See Chapter 3 for information about modular design and examples of modules.

2.4 SPACE STANDARDS AND ALLOCATIONS

The establishment of adequately-sized spaces is at the core of the facilities program. This section of Chapter 2 suggests standards for the assignment of space and provides guidelines for allocating net square footage to specific functions.

2.4.1 Definitions

Space allocations are expressed in square feet of floor area. Net, or assignable, square footage (NASF) is measured from interior faces of exterior walls and includes all usable area, such as labs, offices, lab support, and ancillary spaces. Net area does *not* include:

- The space taken up by walls or partitions.
- Major circulation, including stairs, elevators, corridors, and principal aisles.
- Mechanical spaces, including mechanical rooms, duct shafts, and electrical closets.
- Public toilets and janitors' closets.

Gross area (GSF) includes all floor area within exterior faces of exterior walls.

2.4.2 Space Standards

The assignment of space or functions may be governed by consistent standards established by an owner. If no such standards exist when the planning of a laboratory is begun, the owner and planner should work together to develop a workable system for space assignments.

2.4.3 Planning Rules-of-Thumb

Although decisions about the location and financing of a laboratory are, ideally, made only after a facilities program has been completed, it is sometimes necessary to make broad assumptions of scope and cost well before any predesign investigations have begun. The following rules-of-thumb are presented for use in such a situation. They are not intended as a substitute for programming and should always be superseded by more accurate information as it becomes available.

should be noted that, unless an occupant has extensive administrative responsibilities, an office of 100–125 NASF is usually adequate.

2.4.5 Space Allocations for General Office Areas

Net area must be programmed for secretaries, clerks, and other personnel not assigned to private offices. Table 2.4 gives unit allocations for desks and equipment in open areas. All allocations include extra space for circulation and access.

2.4.6 Space Allocations for Office Support

- Conference or Seminar: allow 150 NASF for rooms with capacity of six or less, 20 SF per person for capacities of six to 20 and 18 SF per person for capacities of 20–30. Room sizes may need to be increased if extensive audiovisual presentations are made.
- Mail Room: Allow 100 NASF per mail room supervisor or messenger. Increase allocation if mail room is to also house central copier and duplicating equipment.
- Utility Rooms: In a large facility it may be desirable to provide small utility rooms in office areas for local copying, office supplies, and coffee-makers. Each such room should contain 80–100 NASF.

Assumption:	Rule of Thumb:
Gross SF for corporate lab (including lab support, ancillary and minimal pilot plant)	450–500 GSF/occupant
Gross SF for academic science building (natural & phyical sciences)	Full time equivalent (FTE) undergraduate enrollment × 17
Net SF of support for standard labs (storage, CTH, electron microscope, etc., not including central animal quarters)	1. Net SF of standard labs × .30 = support for corporate labs 2. New SF of research & teaching labs × .25 = support for academic science building

2.4.4 Space Allocations for Private Offices

Eligibility for fully enclosed private offices is usually determined by an individual's rank in an organization. Table 2.3 gives suggested standards and ranges of net area allocations for private offices. It

2.4.7 Space Allocations for Laboratories

The sizes of laboratories and support spaces are determined through the data collection process. Unlike offices, in which most space is assigned to accommodations for occupants, labs must be

TABLE 2.3 Private Office Assignments

Typical Position	Responsibilities (One or more of these conditions obtain)	Range NASF	Notes
Corporate Officer Administrator Dean Division Head	1. In responsible charge of major division or department 2. Two or more groups report to individual 3. Frequent, high-level visitors 4. Makes decisions regarding programs or commitment or acquisition of funds	225–300	Usually needs access to a conference room
Department Head Associate Dean	Highest positions reporting to above	150–225	
Manager	1. In charge of some strategic operation, e.g., computer, facilities, business, pilot plant 2. Manages a staff 3. Receives frequent visitors 4. Liaison with above positions	125–150	
Full-time Faculty Scientist Engineer	Mainly analytical principal work place in office	125–150	100 SF is smallest office using full-height partitions
	Principal work place in lab	100–125	

TABLE 2.4 Allocations for General Offices

Function	NASF per unit	Notes
Desk—one or two in area	75	Includes desk, chair, & circulation
Desk—more than two	60	Includes desk, chair, & circulation
File cabinet (standard)	8	
File cabinet (lateral)	10–12	
Open shelf unit (4 LF)	12	
Work table	40	
Shared Computer Terminal	30	CRT & console. Increase for printer
Film/fiche unit	30	
Local copier	30	
Central copier	65	Includes space for collating
Waiting area (per person)	15	

planned to also house equipment. As an aid to laboratory planning, formulas have been developed which may be used to estimate space for labs. The sizes obtained through application of formulas must be confirmed by analysis of need. The following guidelines and considerations may apply to space allocations for bench-scale labs.

- An allowance of 150 NASF per professional and technician working in a lab may be used to es-

tablish a preliminary estimate of area for research labs.

- A clear length of 15 LF of bench surface per person is ample for most labs. This allowance may be reduced in labs occupied by three or more persons.

- Space allocations for teaching labs are based on the number of teaching stations in a lab. The following schedule shows unit allocations used by a number of institutions and agencies:

Discipline	NASF/Station
Biology	50
Chemistry	60
Physics	50
Biochemistry	60

Additional space should be programmed if audiovisual instruction is carried out or if equipment such as incubators is required.

- Lab width is controlled by width of benches and aisles between them. Aisles are normally 4' 6" to 6' 6", with the greater dimension provided when large equipment must be moved through a lab or where hazardous procedures occur.

2.4.8 Space Allocations for Laboratory Support

Allocations for support spaces such as preparation rooms, constant temperature and humidity rooms (CTH), electron microscope, balance rooms, storage rooms, and glass washing depend on the scope of operations and other factors. These spaces must be individually sized according to the equipment that is housed, with allowance for clearances. (See also Chapter 3.)

2.4.9 Space Allocations for Ancillary Facilities

A large laboratory may require ancillary facilities, including library, cafeteria, maintenance shops, and other spaces not directly related to lab operations.

- Reception Rooms: Provide 15 NASF per person for seating, exclusive of aisles passing through the area. Assuming one person at a reception desk, allow 75 NASF for the desk. Provide additional desk or counter space if forms are filled out for badges.
- Libraries: A library for a laboratory may range from a single space presided over by a part-time librarian to a complete library with many thousands of volumes and a full-time staff. A preliminary estimate of the space required for a central library may be developed from the following guidelines:

1. Estimate the number of volumes in the collection and the annual rate of acquisition.
2. Provide one NASF for each 10 volumes in book stack areas.
3. Estimate the number of reader stations; not many may be needed if most readers withdraw books to read at their work locations.
4. Allocate 25 NASF for each reader station.
5. Assume ancillary space equal to 30% of the total of stack and reader space. This will provide for offices, circulation desk, catalog area, readers services, and technical areas.

- Lunchrooms and Cafeterias: The size of a lunchroom may be estimated by allocating 20 NASF per seat for rooms with capacities up to 15 persons and 15 NASF per seat for capacities of 15–50 persons. Add an allowance of 50–100 NASF for vending machines and/or refrigerator, sink, and warming oven.

A cafeteria serving meals may be programmed as follows:

1. Estimate the total utilization, which may range between 55% to 75% of building population.
2. $\dfrac{\text{Number of persons served}}{\text{Number of shifts}} + 10\% = $ number of seats.
3. Number of seats $\times$ 20 = total seating and serving NASF.
4. Number of persons served $\times$ 3.2 = NASF for kitchen and related facilities.

The area produced by the above formulas should be checked with the operator of the cafeteria

2.4.10 General Storage

It is important that storage space not be underestimated. While requirements vary according to the type of lab, the following preliminary assumptions may be made in allocating storage space:

1. Departmental storage space in direct support of and convenient to bench-scale labs (not including CTH rooms) 12% to 17% of lab area.
2. Local and central storage (nondepartmental) in

TABLE 2.5 Factors and Reciprocals for Estimating Gross Area

Type of Laboratory Building	Gross ——— Net	Net ——— Gross
Medical Teaching/Research	1.82	55.0%
Academic Science Building	1.67	60.0%
Corporate Research	1.54	65.0%
Clinical Pathology	1.54	65.0%
Commercial Service	1.47	68.0%

support of bench-scale labs 5% to 7% of lab area.

In the above rules-of-thumb the higher percentages would apply to labs that require storage for a large amount of materials or equipment (chemicals and physics labs, for instance).

2.4.11 Estimating Gross Area

Detailed allocations for labs, support space, and ancillary facilities are computed as *net area*. A factor is applied to the total net area to arrive at an estimate of *gross area* for a laboratory building. The conversion, or "efficiency" factor varies according to the type of lab. The more sophisticated facilities, such as medical research labs, requiring extensive mechanical/electrical services have a high net/gross differential. Labs with simpler procedures carried out in large, open spaces need less space for nonproductive purposes and therefore have a lower differential. Table 2.5 gives factors and their reciprocals for use in estimating gross areas.

2.5 CORPORATE LABORATORIES AND PILOT PLANTS

2.5.1 Types of Corporate Laboratories

Laboratories for private industry encompass a wide variety of products, including chemicals, plastics, pharmaceuticals, food, fabrics, and many others. Diversified companies may require labs for several products; the possibility of further diversification or mergers makes flexibility of lab design an important consideration.

Most corporate research is carried out in typical, bench-scale standard (or unit) labs, which may be adapted for special procedures such as microbiology and animal research. Space standards for such labs are given in Section 2.4. Corporate laboratory functions include applied research, product development, testing, applications, and process development, all of which may require heavy equipment, industrial-type spaces, and protection against hazards. The pilot plant, which provides for the final "scale-up" of a product under development, is unique to a company's operations, so few guidelines are available for design.

2.5.2 Planning Considerations

A corporate research center may provide facilities for several company products and operations ranging from "pure" research to process development. The center may be supported by ancillary facilities, such as a library and cafeteria, and may also use the central services of a corporate complex. Thus, the factors considered in programming may encompass a broad scope and involve facilities and activities outside of the boundaries of the research center.

Forecasts of growth and of new operations are very important in planning corporate laboratories. It may be ascertained that product departments will grow at different rates, so the program and the subsequent design should allow for this condition. Modularity in space and building systems can enhance the flexibility necessary to accommodate the growth and change. The research center that provides both unit laboratories and pilot plants should be planned to afford required modularity and work flow, while minimizing the effects of noise, trucking, and unsightly areas.

A common criterion of laboratory planning is that the physical environment should foster interaction and exchanges of views between professionals in different fields of work. This objective (which may be espoused more enthusiastically by a laboratory's administration than by the professionals) may be difficult to realize in a very large corporate complex. Some planners program informal seating areas for large facilities to encourage interaction.

Analytical labs usually perform a service for several departments and are therefore centralized relative to departmental labs. A facilities program should specify this relationship as well as any others involving common access to a particular area.

2.5.3 Programming of Corporate Laboratories

Effective programming requires a knowledge of the company's organization, products, and projections, both in terms of growth and possible new operations. A laboratory project may be designed only for a specific purpose, such as corporate research, or may encompass a complete range of operations including product development. These special facilities may need to be programmed for specific lab products and types:

Lab Type	Facilities	Notes
Chemicals	Storage for raw materials in bulk	Solvents or other hazardous materials may be used
Health, Beauty Products, Pharmaceuticals	Animal quarters Animal holding Sterilization	May involve biohazards and be subject to strict government standards
Foods	Microbiology labs Sterilization Consumer kitchens Taste testing	
Industrial Gases	Flame and flow testing Gaseous storage	
Cryogenics	Liquid nitrogen supply Freezers	

2.5.4 Pilot Plants

A program for a pilot plant is based on investigation of the procedures planned for the facility. Often, a pilot plant is intended for development of new products or even for future processes. Thus, a degree of flexibility is usually required.

A typical pilot plant is an industrial-type structure, all or part of which may require clear heights of 20 feet or more. Large, heavy equipment, such as molders and extruders, demand considerable floor space and clearances. Plants for chemicals and petroleum products usually involve hazardous procedures and must be designed for protection against fire and explosion.

The following information may need to be assembled in programming pilot plants:

- Sizes, clearances, and operating characteristics of process equipment.
- Process workflow.
- Weights and sizes of equipment or materials that must be conveyed mechanically.
- Amounts and types of materials to be stored and the methods of storage.
- Zoning and code requirements.
- Requirements for ancillary facilities such as shops, lockers, lunch rooms.
- Relationships to other facilities such as unit labs, warehouse, power plant, high pressure test, loading docks, and parking.

Programming for pilot plants usually involves extensive interaction between the users and the planners of the facilities. Because future operations are involved, a certain amount of brainstorming may take place. These considerations may need to be addressed in programming:

- Equipment requiring extended vertical clearances (stills, for instance) may be grouped together to consolidate high-bay construction.
- Procedures may involve set-up or demounting of equipment on modular pallets or movable platforms. Such a plant should be laid out on a grid encompassing service connections, drains, and structural members.
- Main circulation aisles must be wide enough and given vertical clearances for vehicles, which may include trucks, forklifts, or hydraulic lifts. Doors (interior and exterior) must be large enough to accommodate equipment moved within and out of the building
- Weight handling equipment may include conveyors, bridge cranes, monorails, and "A"

frame hoists. Certain machinery must be precisely positioned in relation to weight handling equipment for changing of dies or servicing.

- If feasible, equipment with the same power sources (steam, for instance) should be grouped together.
- Power loads may be reduced by scheduling operations to avoid simultaneous use of equipment demanding a heavy supply of power.
- Equipment should be positioned so that controls are easily accessible.
- Most pilot plants require a considerable amount of storage for bulk materials, stored in boxes, bags, or drums; government regulations may require separation of hazardous materials and other measures of protection.
- Safety requirements are basic to the planning of most pilot plants. Provisions may include relieving walls, blow-out panels, explosion-proof lighting and controls, spark-proof floors, decontamination areas, and special ventilation.
- Some operations, such as grinding, are very noisy and must be acoustically isolated.
- Opportunities for joint use of facilities should be explored. For instance, it may be feasible for the pilot plant staff to share shop equipment with other groups in a laboratory complex.

2.6 ACADEMIC LABORATORIES

Laboratories for colleges and universities provide facilities for both teaching and research. The laboratories vary widely in physical arrangement and complexity, depending on the number of occupants and the taxonomies involved.

2.6.1 Programming of Instructional Facilities

Academic facilities are usually programmed after a comprehensive analysis of an institution's academic program and utilization of existing facilities, and surveys of site and structure. Instruction is given in lecture halls, classrooms, seminar rooms, and so-called "class laboratories." The laboratories may be simple rooms provided with equipment needed for the courses given or "wet labs" serving a curriculum in science. The scope

of laboratories is determined by calculating the percentage of total class hours assigned to teaching in laboratories in particular disciplines. Thus, a planner must be able to project space needs for all types of facilities in order to program the laboratories.

Planners use different methods to calculate instructional space, but a common technique employs "contact hours" in formulas that produce space factors for different types of facilities. A relatively simple method has been developed using statistics normally kept by an institution. An example of the use of this method for a science curriculum is shown in Table 2.6.

This method yields the number of student stations in classrooms and labs. The division of classroom stations into individual rooms is based on a study of class sizes, possibly adjusted by anticipated changes in instructional patterns. When some portion of the total student stations represents existing classrooms, it may be desirable to plan for alterations to modify the existing room sizes; overcrowding or underutilization due to disparities between class sizes and available rooms is a common problem in utilization.

Establishing the number and capacities of labs calls for a different planning approach. The student station calculation obtained through statistical analysis must be supplemented by a study of the functional criteria for the courses offered in each discipline. Certain groups of courses have common requirements for equipment and environmental systems, so these courses may be taught in similar spaces. Other courses demand labs with special physical characteristics incompatible with other use. For instance, Microbiology and Aquatic Biology both require special equipment or environmental controls that make them unusable for other courses.

Certain labs, such as Instrumentation and Radiology labs, may have a service function for an entire department. Others (Biochemistry for instance) are interdisciplinary in nature. The study of functional needs, utilization data, and instructional practices will result in a fairly low utilization rate for some labs, with a corresponding increase in total student stations. The discrepancy between the totals reached by statistical analysis and by criteria study varies according to curriculum and other factors, but it can be as high as 30% in some cases. The probability of a limited enrollment cou-

TABLE 2.6 Example of Calculation of Student Stations in Classrooms and Laboratories

Given:
- Total FTE = 3,500
- FTE enrolled in science courses 20%, or 700 FTE
- Average credit hour/student = 15
- Credit hours by discipline and credit hour: contact hour ratio:

Discipline	Percentage of Credit Hours	Ratio
Biology	52	1.33
Chemistry	26	1.33
Geology	10	1.25
Physics	12	1.25

- Scheduled weekly hours:

Classrooms	30
Labs	24

1. Determine Contact Hours for Each Discipline

   700 FTE × 15 = 10,500 Total Credit Hours

Discipline	Credit Hours Percentage Total	Credit Hours Hours	Ratio	Weekly Contact Hours (WCH)
Biology	52	5460	1.33	7260
Chemistry	26	2730	1.33	3630
Geology	10	1050	1.25	1310
Physics	12	1260	1.25	1580
Total		10,500		13,780

2. Distribute WCH to Classrooms & Labs

Discipline	Classroom Percentage Total	Classroom WCH	Lab Percentage Total	Lab WCH
Biology	30	2180	70	5080
Chemistry	60	2180	40	1450
Geology	55	720	45	590
Physics	55	870	45	710
Total		5950		7830

3. Determine Number of Student Stations

Discipline	Classroom WCH ÷ 30	Lab WCH ÷ 24
Biology	73	211
Chemistry	73	60
Geology	24	25
Physics	29	30
Total	199	326

4. Determine Numbers of Classrooms & Labs
   - Classrooms—assign 199 stations to classrooms and seminar rooms. Individual room capacities determined through study of class sizes and room utilization statistics.
   - Labs—use 326 stations as minimum. Numbers and capacities of labs determined through study of course offerings and utilization statistics. Total capacity will exceed 326 stations due to special requirements of some labs.

pled with low utilization of expensive space may cause an institution to reassess its program planning.

2.6.2 Programming of Research Laboratories

The extent of research labs will depend on whether advanced degrees are given, the scope of grant-supported research, and the disciplines involved. The assignment of labs to individuals or departments is largely a matter of institutional or governmental policy. Most research is done in bench-scale labs, differing in layout and equipment according to the type of research. Procedures may be conducted by teams of faculty members and graduate students, in which case allowance should be made for record-keeping in the labs. A planner should be aware that some institutions and department heads try to "bank" unused lab space in expectation of research grants.

2.6.3 Programming of Faculty Offices

The sizes of faculty offices may be dictated by standards of the institution or a governmental agency. See Table 2.3 for typical allocations. Standards may also fix the number of secretaries serving the faculty. A ratio of one secretary to seven full-time faculty is specified for some institutions, with a departmental secretary serving each chairperson. The program should include allowance for files, copying, mail, and other office services.

Part-time faculty do not usually require offices, but should have access to a desk and file space. Unless specified by standards, one desk per three part-time faculty may be assumed.

Graduate students and post-doctoral staff are usually based in the labs and are assigned work surfaces or desks in the labs. They may also be given "home bases," consisting of modular units with provision for storage of clothing, books, and personal effects; the units are located remote from the laboratories.

2.6.4 Teaching Laboratories for the Natural and Physical Sciences

Total student stations for each discipline may be determined by the method described above, or by other methods as decided by the planner. The total student stations are divided into teaching labs, sized according to the number of students in a class. The following schedule shows typical sizes for the various disciplines:

Lab	Student Stations/Lab
General Biology/Microbiology	32–40
Other Biology	20–24
Chemistry	16–24
General Physics and Geology	24–32
Other Physics	16–20
Planetarium	20–50

2.6.5 Lab Support for the Natural and Physical Sciences

The support required for teaching labs varies, but most require preparation rooms for set-ups of demonstrations and experiments. Preparation rooms may serve two or more labs. Other typical support spaces are shown in Table 2.7.

2.6.6 General Planning Considerations for Science Labs

These considerations may apply in the programming of labs for the natural and physical sciences:

- It may be possible to share such support facilities as electron microscope and dark rooms, balance rooms, and CTH rooms.
- Audiovisual and computer-assisted instruction may be carried out in teaching labs, in which case the planner must ascertain equipment requirements, sight lines, viewing distances, and requirements for room-darkening.
- Space may need to be programmed in the lab proper for large equipment such as growth chambers and tanks.
- Chemistry labs require a substantial amount of stock storage, which may be centralized with access from several labs.
- The program should identify bench heights for sitting or standing. Usually labs using microscopes have benches arranged for seating (30" height). Stand-up benches are 36" high.

TABLE 2.7 Support Facilities for Science Labs

Type of Lab	Support Spaces
Biology	Live animals
	Herbarium
	Greenhouse
	Sterile transfer
	Growth chambers
	Electron microscope
	Dark room
	Instrument rooms
	CTH
	Storage
Chemistry	Stockrooms (near labs)
	Balance rooms
	Instrumentation
	Spectometry
	Chromatography
	Storage (remote)
Physics	Optics darkrooms
	Metal/woodworking shop
	Nuclear procedures
	Isotope storage/transfer
	Equipment storage
Geology, Earth Sciences, Astrogeology	Instrumentation
	Rock storage, thin section, polishing
	Observatory

- Student drawers are provided in benches for Chemistry labs. High utilization of labs may require an area in which tote boxes can be stored.
- Physics labs require storage rooms for large equipment. Portable units may be moved between labs and storage rooms. Floor loadings are higher than normal.
- In general, Biology and Biochemistry labs require the most services to the benches and Chemistry labs the most fume hoods. Physics labs have minimal requirements for services.

2.6.7 Programming of Medical Teaching Labs

A knowledge of the curriculum is necessary in programming teaching labs for a school of medicine. The first two years of the four-year course are largely devoted to instruction in the basic sciences and the remaining two years to the clinical sciences. This traditional concept has been changed somewhat in recent years by the introduction of interdisciplinary courses and by a trend towards an earlier exposure to the clinical experience. The basic sciences are taught in classrooms, lecture rooms, and teaching labs, while clinical science is learned in a teaching hospital. Although elective labs may be provided for upper-division students, most teaching labs in a medical school are assigned to the six basic sciences: Anatomy, Biochemistry, Physiology, Pharmacology, Microbiology, and Pathology.

Usually basic science labs are sized for multiples of eight-student units, up to a maximum of 24 student stations. An exception is the Gross Anatomy lab, which may have a capacity of 32, based on eight tables for cadavers, each serving four students.

Basic science labs may be planned for one of three concepts: conventional, multidiscipline, and multipurpose. Figure 2.4 illustrates these concepts.

1. *Multidiscipline* labs provide a stand-up and a sit-down bench position for each student, and all courses except Gross Anatomy are taught in the labs. Thus, the students are based in the labs and the teachers move between them.

2. *Conventional* labs are assigned to the departments and are either sit-down or stand-up according to the discipline. The teachers are based in the labs and the students move between them.

3. *Multipurpose* labs are either sit-down or stand-up and may be used for two or more disciplines by different set-ups of equipment. Both teachers and students travel between these labs.

Multidiscipline labs are larger than the other types because two stations are provided for each student. However, with this concept it is not necessary to provide separate study stations. Multipurpose labs can be utilized efficiently, but storage space is required for equipment not in use. Both the multidiscipline and multipurpose labs can be consolidated in one area, whereas the conventional labs are dispersed to department areas.

Traditionally, the basic sciences have been taught in large, "wet" labs equipped with either sit-down or stand-up benches. In recent years, however, some institutions have moved away from

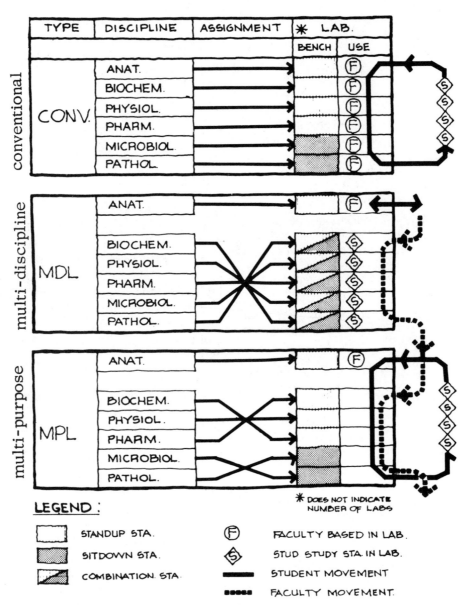

Figure 2.4   Teaching laboratory characteristics: three basic arrangements for teaching laboratories in the basic sciences.

the conventional lab setting and toward instruction in which electronic and computerized equipment, instead of individual experiments, is the principal medium for teaching. The rooms required for such instruction are similar to classrooms; students may sit at tables and individually operate equipment, or several students may be grouped around a unit. In one large institution in the United States conventional wet labs have been abandoned for certain disciplines in favor of the newer teaching format. Exceptions are Gross Anat-

omy, Neuroscience, and other courses requiring dissection.

Gross Anatomy labs are single-purpose spaces and cannot be used by other departments. Gross Anatomy must be directly accessible to an elevator or passage used exclusively for the transfer of cadavers.

Pathology labs may be related to the pathology services of the teaching hospital, if tissue staining and embedding for teaching and research are done by clinical pathology staff.

2.6.8 Medical Research Labs

The basic science faculty are more deeply engaged in research than are the clinical science faculty, because the latter also have staff responsibilities in the teaching hospital. Clinical science research is organized into the medical departments, i.e., medicine, surgery, obstetrics, pediatrics, and so forth. Medical research relies heavily on procedures involving animals, so a medical school contains central animal quarters as well as holding rooms for small animals in the departments. Ideally, each clinical science department should be located near its counterpart in the teaching hospital so that the professional staff can quickly reach nursing and intensive care units in an emergency.

2.7 ANIMAL LABORATORIES

Facilities in which live animals are housed range from rooms for small species (mice, rats, hamsters) to central quarters for small and large animals including cats, dogs, primates, sheep, and cows. A central animal facility, such as is needed for a medical school, may include:

- Receiving and examination areas for animals, food, and supplies.
- Quarantine area.
- Housing of animals with provision for separation of species and isolation for individual projects.
- Facilities for washing, sterilizing, and storing cages and equipment.
- Storage rooms for food, supplies, and bedding.
- Laboratories for surgery, radiology, necropsy, and other procedures.
- Administrative offices.
- Showers, lockers, toilets, and lunch room for personnel.
- Incinerator for animal waste and refuse.

2.7.1 Planning Considerations

Figure 2.5 shows the relationships between functional elements in animal quarters. It may be seen that a separation is needed between ''clean'' and ''dirty'' areas and that circulation schemes must be

planned to effect this separation. Positive/negative air pressures are used to further control contamination and odors. Additional considerations include:

- The receiving area should not be easily seen from areas in other facilities visited by the public or nonprofessional staff.
- Because of the need to provide outdoor exercise for dogs, animal quarters are often located on the highest or lowest level of a building housing other functions.
- Proper separations must be provided between clean and contaminated areas and between personnel areas and spaces housing animals.
- Because of the danger of interspecies infection, animal species must be separately housed.
- All doors and corridors should be wide enough to allow passage of racks and equipment. Minimum widths of 3'6'' and 7'0'' are recommended for doors and corridors respectively.
- Acoustical separation (especially for areas housing dogs) is necessary.
- Special controls are necessary for experiments involving hazardous agents. Safety measures specified by regulatory agencies provide for different levels of containment. Positive/negative air pressures, high-efficiency particulate air filters, air locks, decontamination areas, closed and ventilated cage systems, double-door autoclaves, and other measures may be required to maintain the necessary containment.
- Facilities for aseptic surgery are planned with separate areas for preparation, surgery, radiology, recovery, and support, including storage, washing/sterilizing, and lockers. The facilities must comply with all codes, including those applying to safety measures for use of anesthetic gases.

2.7.2 Space Allocations

Animals are housed in cages or pens, usually in rooms sized according to species. The rooms typically provide for a row of cages on either side of an aisle wide enough to transfer cages in and out of the room. A 10-foot-wide room is suitable for small animals, and 15' may be used for dogs housed in cages. Guidelines prepared by the In-

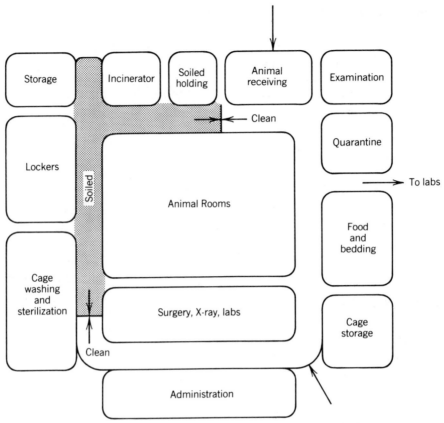

Figure 2.5 Functional relationships for central animal facility.

stitute of Laboratory Animal Resources, National Research Council provide recommended floor area and height per animal, based on the animals' weight and type of housing. Ranges of floor area per animal given in the guides are summarized as follows (unless otherwise noted, all allocations apply to housing in cages; numbers pertain to square inches or square feet):

> Mice, 6"–15"
> Rats, 17"–40"
> Hamsters, 10"–19"
> Guinea Pigs, 43"—101"
> Rabbits, 1.5'–5.0'
> Cats, 3.0'–4.0'
> Dogs, 8.0'–12.1'(cage)
> Dogs, 18'–24'(pen or run)
> Primates, 1.6'–25.1'
> Pigeons, 115"
> Quail, 36"
> Chickens, 36"–256"
> Sheep & Goats, 10'–20'(pen)
> Swine, 6'–30'(pen)

> Cattle, 16'–27'(stanchion)
> Cattle, 24'–151'(pen)
> Horses, 44'(tie stall)
> Horses, 144'(pen)

Other spaces in animal laboratories must be sized according to the activities and equipment in each space.

2.8 ENGINEERING LABORATORIES

Laboratories used for teaching, research, or corporate development in engineering are usually planned to be similar to physics labs. Space may be needed for large, heavy equipment, which may be moved in or out of adjacent storage rooms or other labs. The labs are supported by shops, possibly including "clean rooms" for instrument repair and shops for woodworking, machining, and metalworking. Engineering testing requires equipment for assessing chemical and molecular properties and strengths of materials. Large, heavy equipment may be needed for such tests, requiring an industrial-type space at ground level, with overhead doors, high ceilings, and adjacent storage rooms.

2.9 CLINICAL PATHOLOGY LABORATORIES

Hospitals require laboratories for analysis of gross specimens, blood, urine, tissues, and other materials involved in diagnosis, treatment, autopsy, and research. Facilities for a clinical pathology area in a hospital may include:

- Autopsy suite, including autopsy rooms, solution/utility, morgue, radiology room, photography and dark rooms, cold rooms, offices, showers, and locker rooms. If the suite is in a teaching hospital, the autopsy rooms may be arranged for demonstration and videotaping or CCTV broadcasts.
- Administrative offices for the pathology department.
- Facilities near a public entrance for blood donation.
- Blood drawing area and urine specimen toilets accessible from out-patient department.
- Laboratories, which may include chemistry, bacteriology, mycology/TB, hematology, histology, clinical microscopy, and anatomic pathology.
- Lab support, including tissue staining and embedding, CTH rooms, chromatography, instrumentation, glass wash, sterilizing, preparation, and storage.

The procedures are carried out mainly in large, open areas with typical benches and cabinetry. The labs contain considerable equipment capable of a high volume of analytical procedures. The procedures are computerized and results are a part of a hospital's systems for patient data registry and central records.

Labs requiring special environmental controls, such as bacteriology, toxicology, virology, and immunology must be separated from nonhazardous areas and provided with positive/negative pressures, filters, air locks, and other measures for preventing cross-contamination.

Although there are formulas for establishing the area of clinical pathology facilities based on the number of beds in a hospital, the space allocations should be based on a study encompassing staffing projections, annual procedures, and demand for specific services. Allocation for bench-scale labs and support may be estimated using the guidelines given in Section 2.4

Autopsy suites may be planned on the assumption that one table is sufficient for 500 annual procedures; a table and its associated equipment requires 300–500 NSF. A suite servicing a major medical center will require up to 3,500 SF.

2.10 CONTENT OF THE FACILITIES PROGRAM

The point was made earlier in this chapter that the content of the facilities program may vary according to context and timing. Normally, the program will include at least:

- A statement of the owner's goals.
- Personnel census and projections to a given year, or years.
- The overall functional relationships between major elements of a laboratory; if the laboratory is part of a complex, the relationship to other facilities on a site is also diagrammed.
- General planning issues and objectives, possibly including lab/office relationships, interaction of users, desired workflow, and flexibility.
- Statistical data for the program; for instance, academic programs, utilization analyses, forecasts of growth.
- Functional requirements for each department, describing organizational units, interrelationships, operations, and special criteria. The requirements are developed for all functions, including lab support and ancillary services.
- Planning modules, possibly including general layouts of typical spaces.
- Space standards.
- Schedule of services supplying the labs.

- Net area summaries, divided into departments and phases of development.
- Detailed net area breakdowns, identifying space allocations for every room and area.
- Estimates of gross area, using appropriate conversion factors.

Predesign investigations include a number of studies that are closely related to the facilities program, or which are believed by some authorities to be an integral part of programming. Depending on the project and the timing of the predesign tasks, it may be desirable to produce a set of predesign documents, or to include all, or a part of the predesign studies in a comprehensive program statement. It may be feasible to include in the statement, in addition to the basic content outlined above, such studies as:

- Analysis of the site.
- Traffic study.
- Surveys and evaluations of existing facilities.
- Environmental criteria, including temperature, humidity, energy-conservation standards.
- Studies conducted by behavioral scientists on physiological and psychological responses to interior environment.
- Equipment and furniture listings, possibly indicating re-use.
- Outline specifications.
- Budget estimates, possibly projected to future phases.

2.11 USING THE PROGRAM

The facilities program is a discrete document produced in the initial phases of project development. Nevertheless, the program is used for several purposes and at a number of points in a project's schedule.

- The gross area projections are used in preliminary budgeting and for site evaluation/selection.
- If an existing laboratory is to be expanded, the projected gross area may be compared to existing space to define the scope of new construction.

- The space allocations and functional criteria form the basis for conceptual schemes for site and building.
- The programmed criteria are used to make an optimal distribution of departments and services to floors and wings of the new or expanded facility.
- The partition layouts and typical space arrangements made during design are based on the net area space allocations and functional relationships specified in the program.
- Detailed furniture and equipment layouts are developed at a later stage of design from the data given in the program.
- The program serves as a permanent record of design-basis decisions, and as such may be a reference for post-occupancy evaluations.

The program may well be an essential element in the exploration of planning alternatives involving existing structures in a complex of buildings. The functional relationships and space allocations specified in a program enable a planner to assess the feasibility of alternative courses of action. Figure 2.6 illustrates alternatives that might be considered in planning for a college campus that requires new space for both science laboratories and for other academic functions.

2.12 PRESENTING THE PROGRAM

The facilities program should be produced as a bound report. If, because of the size and complexity of the project, it is desirable to provide both a Functional Program and an Architectural Program, these two elements may be contained in separate volumes. The program should be presented in concise terms and in a format that is convenient for the users. Much of the information can be tabulated or shown in diagrams and charts. This section provides suggestions for presenting each section of a typical program report for a laboratory.

2.12.1 Introduction

The introduction includes a description of the owner's goals for the project. It is well to also in-

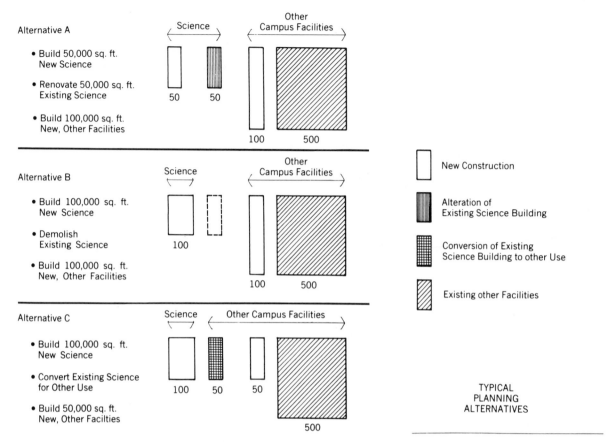

Figure 2.6 Alternatives in planning for academic science facilities.

clude a summary of basic findings, including number of personnel and net/gross area totals.

2.12.2 Data Summary

It is a convenience for the users to include a schedule giving staffing and net area for each department, divided into functional categories of space and phases. Table 2.8 shows part of a schedule such as might be prepared for a corporate research center.

The data would be shown for each function and totalled at the end of the schedule.

2.12.3 General Functional Relationships

This part of the program report defines the essential relationships between major elements of space in a laboratory. A "bubble diagram" is a good way to show these relationships. Figure 2.7 shows such a diagram. Note that the intensity of the relation-

TABLE 2.8 An Example of Format Scheduling

Function	Year	Staff	Office	Std Lab	Pilot Hi-Bay	Pilot Low-Bay	Pilot Total	Ancillary	Total
Corporate Research	84	63	3,390	8,000	2,000	1,500	3,500	3,000	17,890
	89	132	8,250	13,450	2,000	2,500	4,500	3,600	29,800
	94	245	14,930	25,550	2,000	3,620	5,620	5,500	51,600

FOOD PRODUCTS

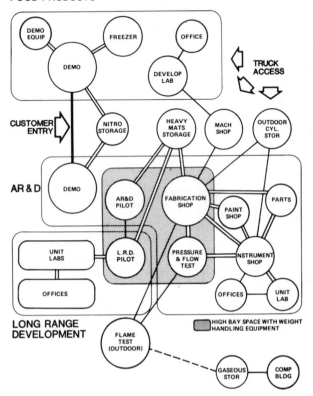

Figure 2.7 Functional relationships for an applied research and development laboratory.

ships is indicated as well as adjacency to major entrances.

Other diagrams may be prepared to show the pattern of circulation for the various categories of occupants and for the movement of materials. When a laboratory building is one component of a complex, the relationship between the lab and other buildings may be diagrammed. Figure 2.8 shows relationships within a medical center, which includes a proposed building containing teaching labs for a medical school.

- Statistical data may be presented in tabular form or as charts or graphs. Figure 2.9 shows enrollment trends for a college and Fig. 2.10 a utilization analysis for instructional space.

- Functional requirements for each department are described in narrative or outline form and are supplemented by graphics illustrating relationships or workflow.

- Functional groupings may need to be identified by department. Figure 2.11 shows relationships within a college science building.

- Lab services are scheduled in tabular form. The format shown in Fig. 2.12a was used in a program for an academic science building.

- Detailed net area space allocations are provided for every room and area. Because many

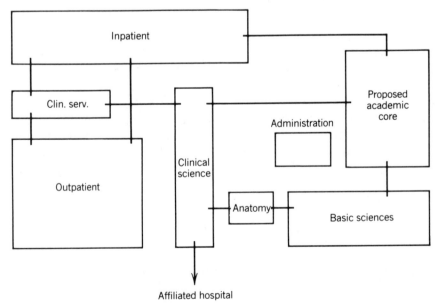

Figure 2.8 Functional relationships for a medical center.

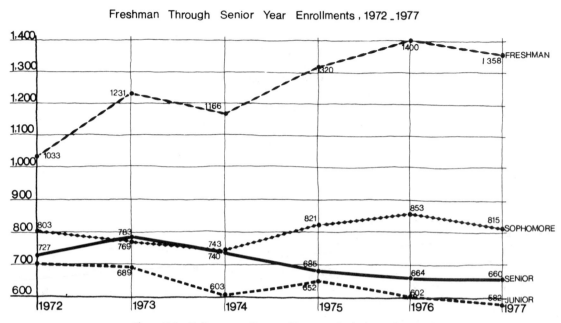

Figure 2.9 College enrollment. (Does not include unclassified.)

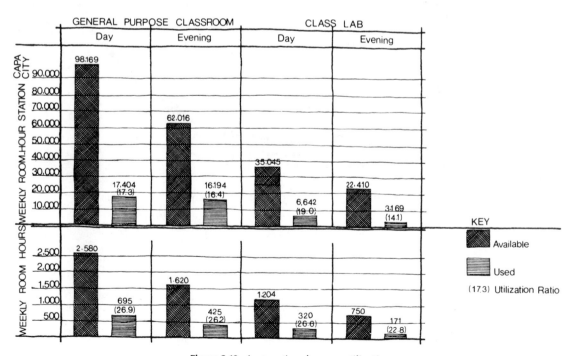

Figure 2.10 Instructional space utilization.

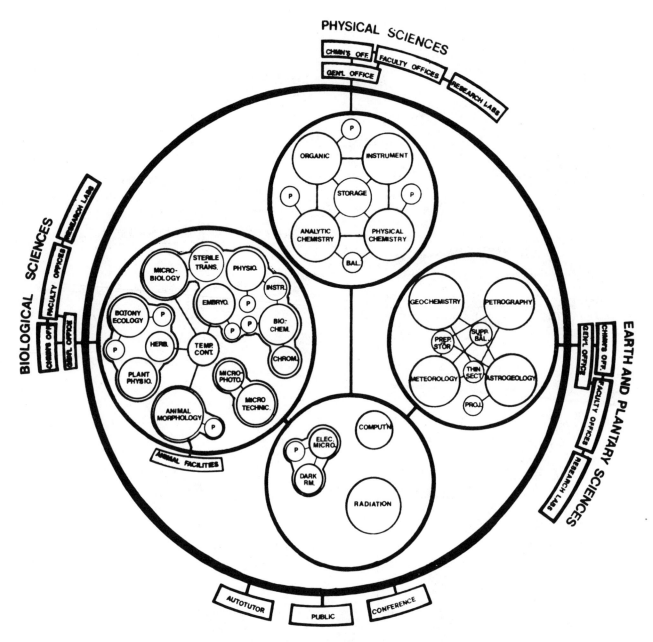

Figure 2.11 Functional relationships for a college science building.

LAB SERVICES AND EQUIPMENT SUMMARY													

DEPARTMENT: _____

LABORATORY	PIPED SERVICES						ELECTRICAL SERVICES				FUME HOODS		SPECIAL CRITERIA	NOTES
TYPE	HW	CW	G	A	V	OTHER	PURPOSE	VLT	FHS	LD	NO.	SIZE		

NET AREA ALLOCATIONS									

FUNCTION	OFFICE			LAB			SPECIAL		NOTES
	NO.	UNIT	SQ. FT.	NO.	CAP	SQ. FT.	DESCRIPTION	SQ. FT.	

Figure 2.12 Program formats. (*a*), Lab services; (*b*), space allocations.

pages may be required for the breakdowns, it may be desirable to include them in an appendix, or even a separate volume. Fig. 2.12*b* shows a typical format.

2.13 COMPUTER-ASSISTED PROGRAMMING

The many analyses, calculations, and tabulations of statistical data involved in programming can be greatly facilitated by the computer. Software can be developed or obtained which will provide for the inventorying of existing space and for the listing of personnel data, space units, and net area calculations. Computerization will enable sorting and summarization of data under various categories. Computer graphics may also be used to show optimal arrangements of functional elements based on the adjacencies specified in a program. (See Chapter 3 for information on computerized design aids.)

LABORATORY DESIGN CONSIDERATIONS

Bryant Putnam Gould, AIA

3.1 INTRODUCTION

This chapter will focus on those considerations that govern the design of laboratories, and will provide examples of the graphics used in formulating a design. In attempting to point up issues and constraints that an architect must consider in designing laboratory facilities, Chapter 3 is mainly concerned with decisions made in the conceptual and schematic phases of design. The later phases of project delivery, including design development, construction documents, and construction management, are well understood by design professionals and clients and are not considered here. Specific design criteria are given in other chapters of this book: Chapter 1 includes data concerning modules, ergonomics, and design approach. Chapter 2 discusses planning considerations applying to a number of different laboratory types, while Chapter 4 shows the effect of servicing methods on the arrangement of space. Chapter 5 provides detailed criteria for lighting. Finally, Chapter 6 gives examples of significant laboratories in the United States and Great Britain.

The design of a laboratory, as of any type of facility, must accommodate function, offer a pleasant and safe working environment, and afford a suitable balance of short- and long-term costs. Superimposed on these universal demands are the special requirements of laboratories. It is the uniqueness of these requirements that makes laboratory design so challenging and exacting.

As Chapter 1 makes clear, laboratory buildings, though designed for known requirements, must be capable of expansion. It is the near-certainty of change and the difficulty of predicting its nature that is the hallmark of nearly every laboratory project. The facilities program can establish with some precision functional criteria based on current operations, and can define (to the extent possible) probable future growth and change as perceived by the users. The design of the facility must provide for present methods of operation without blocking future change. The design must, in most cases, also allow for expansion, preferably under alternate scenarios of growth.

3.2 SITE SELECTION

Selection of a site for a laboratory involves factors applying to any type of facility, such as access, size of site, zoning, utilities, and environment. Factors specific to laboratories include:

Personnel

A location in an employment market that provides access to high-caliber professional and technical people can be an advantage. Proximity to a university brings a laboratory close to such people and provides opportunities for advances in education and for interaction with the scientific community.

Community Acceptance

A community may or may not be eager to accept a laboratory. Some local governments seek to attract research, while others have a bias against such land use. Electronics and other labs considered ''high-tech'' may be acceptable to a community, while chemical or petrochemicals facilities may not. Pilot plants are often a target for resistance. Zoning ordinances and environmental regulations should be carefully considered in site selection. If a variance is necessary to permit the construction of a lab, the prospects for its passage should be realistically assessed as well as the time and costs for applications, hearings, and negotiations.

Site Characteristics

Such factors as space for facilities and parking, topography, vegetation, subsoil, and the like will be considered as a matter of course. Special considerations may include:

- Topography and climatic conditions as factors in dispersal of gaseous wastes.
- Electromagnetic interference.
- Vibrations, including seismic disturbances.
- Topography as a factor in the location of high-pressure test facilities.

Utilities

Usually a laboratory is a heavy user of electric power, water, and energy sources, so adequate utilities are of great importance in selection of a site. Provision for waste disposal is, of course, a critical factor.

Site Environs

The character of the neighborhood, traffic conditions, and access to community services should be considered. Noise, dust, and vibrations due to traffic or industries may be detrimental to lab operations.

Environment

A site with a superior environment can be a positive factor in the recruitment of professionals. Attractive natural features, pleasant views, and opportunities for outdoor recreation can aid in recruitment of staff at all levels.

3.3 DESIGN CONCEPT

A concept evolves through analysis of site and program and consideration of a number of issues, both objective and subjective. The process, while intuitive to a large extent, must take into account the constraints and special needs arising from the nature of laboratory facilities.

Program Analysis

A designer must become familiar with all aspects of the facilities program. It may be helpful to summarize essential data, if the program does not provide this information. Simple graphics to rough scale may be used to show comparative sizes and relationships of functional areas. Figures 3.1* and 3.2 are examples of graphics used in program analysis.

Site Analysis

Factors considered in site analysis include:

- Access from local roads or highways.
- Need for street widenings, extra lanes, traffic signals, or other improvements to local roads.
- Zoning regulations, including required parking, land coverage, height limitations, setbacks, and buffers. If parking spaces must be computed on the basis of gross floor area per space

*This figure, and certain other illustrations in Chapter 3, are courtesy of the Eggers Group, PC.

for all occupancies, the number of spaces for a lab may be unduly high.

- Other constraints, such as flood plains, environmental regulations, easements, or rights-of-way.
- Climatological data, including prevailing winds, solar angles, temperatures.
- Other natural features such as topography, vegetation, watercourses, views, soils and subsoils.

The analysis will determine buildable areas on the site, the most suitable points of entry for vehicles, the best building orientations, the amount of land covered by buildings and parking, and other data relevant to planning a site. Additional factors may include safety separations for high-pressure testing, security, and isolation from sources of vibration. Figure 3.3 shows the relationship between facilities, road systems, and parking for a corporate research center. The scheme orients labs and offices toward landscaped areas and pilot plants to a central court; the lab–office wing may be expanded independently.

Building Form

Building form derives from programmatic criteria, zoning and code requirements, and site-related factors, together with architectural and engineering considerations, such as proportions, modules, scale, context, and servicing methods. The case studies in Chapter 6 show architectural solutions for several laboratories, each encompassing a range of functions, programs, and site conditions.

Block Planning

Conceptual design involves the distribution of large functional elements rather than detailed layouts of rooms and areas. These "blocks" of space must be located to maintain the relationships specified in the facilities program and to allow for expansion as required. Some architects present to their clients block diagrams consisting of color-coded plans on which all departments and services are located. The functional areas fall within the modular scheme adopted for the building. Approval of a scheme is obtained before layouts are

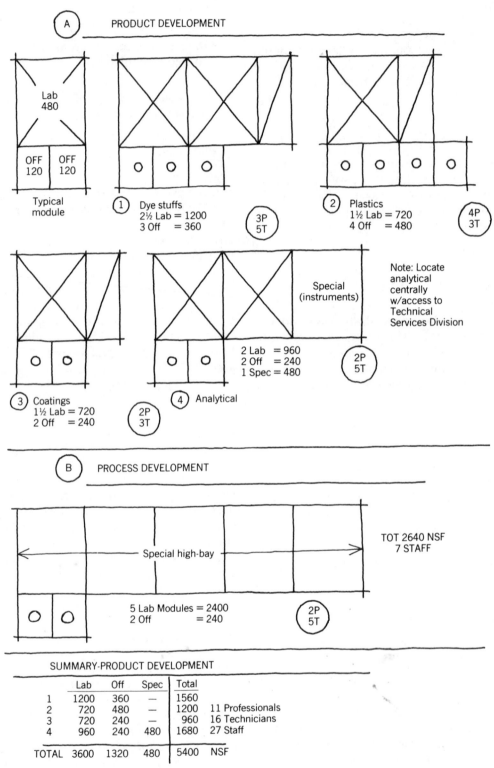

Figure 3.1 Program analysis. Modules for a corporate research facility laid out to rough scale.

52

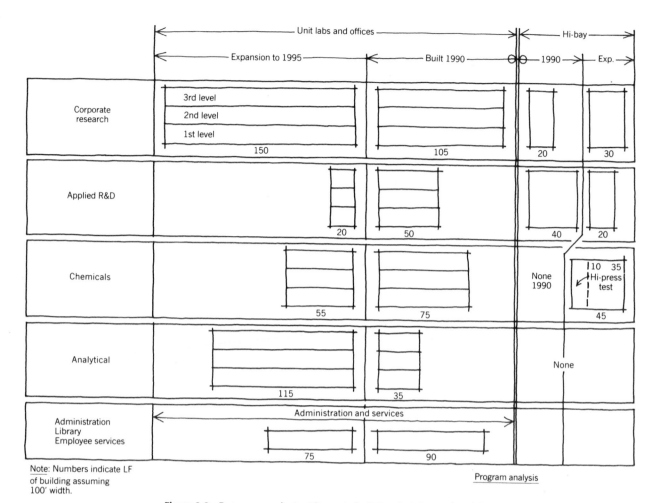

Note: Numbers indicate LF
of building assuming
100′ width.

Program analysis

Figure 3.2 Program analysis. Alternate building heights and widths.

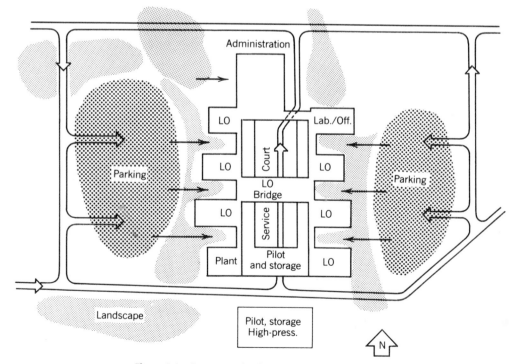

Figure 3.3 Conceptual scheme applying site analysis.

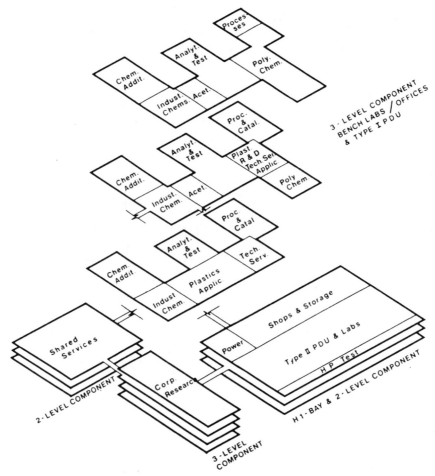

Figure 3.4 Block diagram. Departments and services distributed to floors and building elements according to the space allocations and adjacencies specified in the program.

begun. Figure 3.4 shows a block diagram for a corporate lab.

The Approval Process

It is during programming and the development of the design concept that the client (and the users, if client and users are different entities) participate most deeply in the project. Usually a client will appoint a team to work with the architect during design; formal presentations may be made to larger groups of users at specific points in the project. The development of a concept should involve close interaction between the architect and the client's team. Usually a number of alternatives are explored by the architect and reviewed with the team in a series of meetings. The meetings may involve considerable brainstorming, particularly if

the lab is to be used for new programs. Approval by a client should, within practical limits, represent a consensus of the users.

3.4   BUILDING HEIGHT CONSIDERATIONS

Zoning regulations that limit the height of a lab building require an essentially horizontal scheme. Alternatively, a site of limited area may force a vertical solution. Given a choice, a low-rise facility is usually preferable for a laboratory. However, the decision should be based on analysis of all factors. Seemingly obvious solutions, such as a one-story building on a large site, may not prove to be best for a particular project. These considerations may apply in determining the number of stories for a laboratory:

Space Requirements

The minimum area on a level may be controlled by the size of the largest department to be accomodated in a lab. It may not be desirable to divide the large area on separate floors.

Vertical Clearances

Usually offices and bench-scale labs will have a common story height. However some high-bay spaces, as for pilot plants or warehouses, may be required. How the low- and high-bay spaces are accommodated will affect building heights.

Modular Design

A lab designed according to consistent modules gives the opportunity for stacking of rooms and services. The economies gained by stacking may warrant a multilevel scheme.

Scale

Extended walking distances and massive forms may result if very large areas are distributed in a low-rise structure. While a facility may be divided into smaller components to preserve human scale, it may also be feasible to create higher buildings or to vary building heights.

Floor Loadings

Heavy equipment, as in pilot plants and engineering or physics labs, may call for a low-rise building so that as much space as possible will be at ground level.

3.5 FLEXIBILITY

A facilities program should specify the degree of flexibility required for the particular laboratory. Ideally, functions requiring the highest level of flexibility should be differentiated from those for which little or no future changes are projected. With the need determined, a mode of planning should be selected giving the required degree of flexibility without undue costs and without forcing a planning solution.

The following points should be considered:

- Functions requiring flexibility should be grouped together and not mingled with relatively static elements.
- It may be better to settle for minimal flexibility than to build in elaborate provisions for dimly perceived future needs.
- A space may have to integrate with another, expand, be subdivided, or alter its function. Any one or several or these contingencies may occur in the life of a facility.
- Planning for flexibility, to be effective, should extend to all of the building systems.
- It is desirable to consolidate fixed building elements, such as shaftways, stairs, and elevators.
- Across-the-board provisions for flexibility, as against selective application, may be prohibitively costly.

3.6 EXPANSION

Since providing for expansion is an integral part of a design concept, a building's ultimate form must be defined even though future elements may be developed only diagrammatically. Structural, mechanical, and electrical systems may be designed to accept future loads, or space may be provided to accomodate additional services. As noted in the preceding discussion of flexibility, provisions for expansion should be made selectively to avoid undue costs. Consider the following in planning for expansion:

- Individual departments may grow at different rates. Complete confinement of any function should be avoided, if possible.
- Small increments of expansion are best made horizontally, since stacking of small additions is costly.
- Vertical expansion is costly and disruptive of operations.
- If vertical expansion is the only method possible, consider locating mechanical equipment on an intermediate floor instead of on a roof to minimize relocations.

- Core elements may be located to serve future space. Consider distance to exits, maximum mechanical runs, etc.
- Modular planning permits more effective expansion.
- Curtain walls may be designed for dismounting and re-erection.
- The possibility of shell space should be considered as an option to future construction.
- Graduated-term lease arrangements can enable a client to move into space vacated by tenants on a phased basis.

3.7 DISTRIBUTION OF MECHANICAL/ELECTRICAL SERVICES

The manner in which services are brought to the labs is an architectural consideration of major importance, since it directly affects the arrangement of space. Chapters 1 and 4 include discussions of several basic types of distribution. The decision on the best method for a particular lab should be based on analysis of a number of related considerations, including the desired office/lab relationship, degree of flexibility, whether natural light is required in labs, life cycle costs, and building height. There are many arrangements possible, including central shaftways serving clusters of labs, outboard shafts, and roof monitors. However, many systems fall into one of the three basic categories illustrated in Fig. 3.5. They are:

A. Vertical service cores along a corridor serving labs (vertical system).
B. Continuous central shaftway or service corridor separating banks of labs (horizontal system).
C. Interstitial floors (horizontal system).

There are, of course, many variations possible within these categories. In each scheme, services may be up-fed or down-fed to benches. Ductwork for hood exhaust will be carried to the roof in enclosures, according to code. Chapters 1 and 4 may be referred to for the relative advantages and disadvantages of each basic scheme. Additional considerations include:

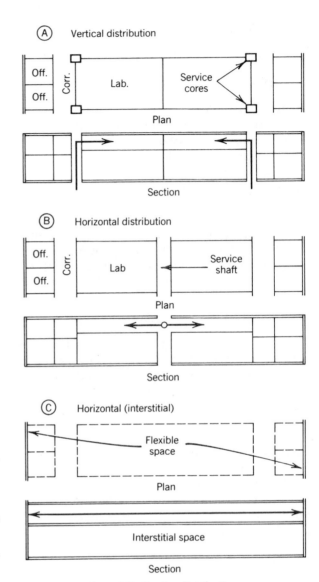

Figure 3.5 Service distribution.

For the *Type A* (vertical) scheme:

- Depending on hood location it may be necessary to provide escape doors or utilities between labs.
- Offices may be situated within the lab proper, or they may be located across the public corridor.

For the *Type B* (horizontal) scheme:

- The central service shaft may be widened so that it becomes a service corridor. Doors would then be provided at both ends of the labs leading to public and service corridors.

- Daylight may be admitted to labs by the use of borrowed lights at offices and labs.

3.8 LIFE SAFETY CONSIDERATIONS

A laboratory may house operations involving such hazards as carcinogens, pathogens, and radiation. Each such hazard requires special protective measures. All laboratories must comply with fire protection regulations. Many jurisdictions, including (in the U.S.) the National Fire Protection Association, local fire bureaus, building codes, and insurance underwriters, govern the design of labs, so it is not possible to provide other than a general overview of life safety considerations here. It is essential that a client identify operations requiring protection from fire and other hazards before design is begun so that the design will comply with all regulations. The degree to which safety requirements affect design depends in part on the hazard classification which, in turn, is influenced by the amount of flammables, combustibles, or explosives stored in the labs. Determining such storage will, therefore, be one of the first tasks in compiling data for design. Table 3.1 gives a general checklist of life safety considerations; this table should not be considered all-inclusive.

Fire Protection

Such criteria affect building form, materials of construction and all mechanical and electrical systems.

Explosives Hazards

Procedures involving highly reactive materials are normally confined to pilot plants or high-pressure test areas. The effect on design depends on the amount of overpressure generated by an explosion. Although explosive forces are inconsistent, the following effects can be anticipated:

Over 0.25 p.s.i.   glass breakage
Over 0.50 p.s.i.   some damage to building
Over 2.0 p.s.i.   human casualty or fatality
Over 3.0 p.s.i.   steel frame building collapse

Design considerations include:

- Explosive forces are usually equated to equivalent pounds of TNT. Overpressures may be calculated at specific distances from ground zero. Damage is caused by missiles, shrapnel, or the effect of the shock wave; dynamic pressures are similar to high winds.

- Laboratory buildings with normal construction will need to be separated from high-pressure facilities by a distance sufficient to avoid damage from blast.

- Pilot plants or other such structures may need to have nonrelieving walls designed for 100 p.s.i. to deflect initial shock wave, and frangible or "blowout" wall and roof panels to relieve the remaining forces. The relieving panels usually detach from the structure at 20 p.s.i. One edge of a blowout panel may be secured to the structure by chains so that the panel will not act as a dangerous projectile after release.

- High-pressure cells are built with massive concrete walls and roofs. One wall of a cell is a relieving surface beyond which are blast mats, revetments, or concrete walls that contain blast and fragments. Special venting and other measures are provided for cells. Usually the cells are directly adjacent to a work area, with access to the cells by steel-plate doors. Heavy glass or plastic vision panels between work area and cell permit observation of pressure vessels. Controls, including valve wheels, are located in the work area.

- Additional provisions may include sparkproof floors, special electrical outlets, purging systems, and dust collection systems.

- Safety standards applying to explosives hazards are less well defined than, for instance, fire protection codes. Thus a designer may need to conduct research or use the services of a consultant.

Radiological Hazards

The design of labs with X-ray or other radiological equipment is controlled by stringent safety criteria. Requirements for storage and handling of isotopes, and for the shielding, monitoring, and disposal of nuclear waste are too specialized for inclusion in this book. It is essential, however, that

TABLE 3.1 General Safety Checklist

Consideration	Possible Governing Factors
Floor area	Type of construction and hazard classification.
Location of building	Zoning restriction or required fire or blast separation.
Height of building	Zoning restriction. Requirements for sprinklers or standpipes.
Shape of building	Locations of cores. Compartmentation of areas.
Type of construction	Required ratings. Fireproof rooms for storage of hazardous chemicals, flammable liquids.
Number of occupants	Exitway facilities.
Number of stairs (normally minimum of two per story)	Specified length of travel. Capacity/Unit of egress.
Compartmentation by fire-rated partitions and doors	Floor area. Hazards. Whether sprinklering provided.
Stair and corridor widths	Unit of egress and capacity. Doors swinging into corridors.
Length of dead-end corridors	Limited by codes.
Length of travel to exit ways	Limited by codes.
Number of doorways	Units of egress. Required second means of egress.
Size of doors	Minimum sizes specified by code.
Type and construction of doors	Fire ratings. Code requirements for operation (self closing, automatic, etc.). Required vision panels.
Stair construction and details	Code requirements for treads and risers, handrails, door swings, etc.
Roofs	Required ladders, stairs, enclosures. Roof parapet. Extension of hood exhausts.
Second means of egress (escape) within labs	Fume hood location. Hazard classification. Size of lab.
Arrangement of benches and equipment	Ready access to exit.
Provisions of typical unit labs	Requirements for safety showers, eyecups, fire blankets.
HVAC system	Provision of fire dampers in ducts.
Automatic fire extinguishing system	Hazard classification. Height of building. Floor area. Reduction of damage due to water. Fire extinguishers.
Fire standpipes (usually required for buildings over two stories)	Building height. Building area.
Detection and alarm systems	Provision of sprinklers
General ventilation	Location of intakes. Air distribution and pressures (to prevent airborne spread of flammables, explosives, or toxics). Duct materials and construction.
Location ventilation	Location of hoods to avoid turbulence affecting hood efficiency. Hood face velocities. Capture velocities for local exhaust systems other than hoods.
Fans, motors, and controls	Special design depending on hazards (flammables, corrosives, explosives).
Electrical	Location of controls. Flame and explosion-proof lights and outlets.

safety requirements be thoroughly analyzed before design is begun.

Contaminants

Microbiology labs and other labs conducting procedures involving pathogens or carcinogens must be designed to eliminate cross-contamination between experiments and the environment and among the experiments themselves. Measures for maintaining a safe environment include positive pressure for clean rooms, negative pressure and prohibition of recirculation of air from contaminated areas, adequate ventilation, and high-efficiency filters. Air locks at entries to the areas and decontamination facilities for personnel may also be required. Cleanable, impervious finishes are usually provided as well as sterilization and glass-washing equipment.

Any research involving recombinant DNA requires provisions for containment, under strict National Institute of Health (NIH) controls. The NIH classifies containment labs as P-1, P-2, P-3, and P-4, with P-4 having the most stringent criteria. (See also Chapter 4.)

3.9 ENERGY CONSERVATION

Laboratories are high consumers of energy because of the demands for services and requirements for special interior environments. Chapter 4 includes techniques for energy conservation in the design of HVAC systems. Architectural considerations, particularly the use of passive systems, can greatly affect the form and appearance of a laboratory building. Such considerations include:

- Building geometry. Shapes affording the least ratio of surface to volume are energy-efficient.
- Orientation, according to solar angles and prevailing winds.
- Insulating values of the building envelope.
- Introduction of daylight into interior areas via skylights, clerestories, or borrowed lights.
- Fenestration, including insulating glass, heat-absorbing or reflective glass, solar shading measures, operable sash.
- Natural cooling.

3.10 SECURITY

Security may be an important consideration, especially for laboratories involved in corporate research or in classified government contracts. A laboratory building may need to be planned for controlled access, guard stations, TV surveillance central monitoring systems, and destruction of classified material. Security measures are nearly always provided for computer hardware areas. Site security may involve fencing, security lighting, alarms, TV systems, and guard patrols. A client may require a system of identification for service and delivery vehicles.

Building security measures include anti-intrusion alarms at doors and windows, special hardware, and card access or digital codes for controlled areas. Vandalism and theft, particularly of vehicles, may be a problem for facilities in or near urban areas. Nearby pedestrian traffic and visitor control are security problems for city projects.

3.11 MODULAR DESIGN

A module represents the smallest repetitive unit of space. It may be combined with other like units to form typical elements of space (also called modules) that accommodate a variety of functions. Because many operations in a lab are carried out in spaces with similar equipment, there is considerable opportunity for modular planning. During design the modular "blocks" of space are extended to form structural bays. The basic modules influence fenestration, lighting, ceiling systems, and other aspects of design. Among the factors that affect the establishment of a lab module are:

- Number of persons working in a lab.
- Required continuous length of work surfaces.
- Width of aisles between benches.
- Number of fume hoods.
- Provision for record-keeping in lab proper.

By careful study of functional needs, it may be possible to plan an entire building around a basic lab module of, say, 12' × 24'. Other spatial elements, such as offices, service shafts, and corridors, can be planned to fall within a basic module, or modules, so that a high degree of flexibility and interchangeability is attained. Figure 3.6 shows an application of a five-foot horizontal module.

3.12 COST CONSIDERATIONS

A laboratory is one of the most expensive types of facilities in terms of both initial and long-term costs. Building construction costs in the United States in the fourth quarter of 1984 ranged between $100.00 and $150.00 per gross SF, with some specialized facilities reaching $200.00 per SF.

Because of the many mandatory functional and safety criteria governing lab design, there are rel-

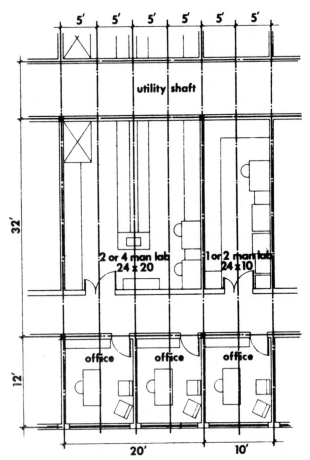

5' 5' 5' 5' 5' 5'

utility shaft

32'

2 or 4 man lab
24 x 20

1 or 2 man lab
24 x 10

12'

office   office   office

20'   10'

Figure 3.6   Application of module. A five foot horizontal module based on window spacing. Multiples of the module determine partition spacing and structural framing.

atively few opportunities for cost cutting. Such cost saving measures as reductions in space allocations or compromises in the quality of environmental systems can lower the cost of construction, but will add to life cycle costs and probably create future problems in utilization. Thus life cycle cost studies, such as those that appear in the appendix to Chapter 4, should be a part of the design process for laboratories. In deciding on space arrangements and the selection of materials and systems, factors other than cost should be given due weight. Such factors may include functional efficiency, comfort, and employee morale.

Project Budget

Ideally, a project budget should be the product of teamwork between client and architect and be based on a known scope of facilities. In actuality,

the budget may be drawn up to secure a capital appropriation made well before project needs are defined. Adjustments to the budget are necessary as design proceeds. Analysis of the facilities program and the site may disclose that either the budget or the scope of the project needs to be adjusted.

The following should be considered in developing the "ballpark figures" that may be required in such a situation:

- Unit costs per gross square foot are useful in establishing a general estimate, but only if they are adjusted for locale, current market conditions, type of project, and special conditions such as site or substructure.
- When possible, separate unit prices should be created for different functional elements of the project (e.g., labs, offices, pilot plant).
- Include escalation in cost covering period between budget preparation and estimated time of construction.
- Site costs are usually estimated by applying unit allocations to assumed number of parking spaces, linear feet of roadways and utilities, area to be landscaped, and other elements of site work. The resulting costs are only gross approximations and must be qualified by substantial contingencies.
- It is important that the initial budget be supplanted by more accurate estimates as soon as a design concept has been established. Adjustments to scope or budget are best made in the early stages of design. The development of alternate solutions during conceptual design should include comparisons in cost between the schemes as well as to the budget.

Cost Control in Project Development

Estimates should be frequently monitored and refined as design and construction documents progress. Either an architect (possibly assisted by a cost consultant) or a construction manager may have primary responsibility for cost control. The control process may be computer assisted; since the schedule is closely allied to project costs, computerized scheduling may be coordinated with a cost control system.

3.13   UNIT LAB DESIGN CONSIDERATIONS

The most common facility in many laboratories is the bench-scale "standard" or "unit" lab. Most research is carried out in such spaces, which can be designed to accommodate the needs of various disciplines. Since similar space arrangements can serve a variety of operations, there is considerable opportunity for modular design; in fact, when there are many unit labs, the lab module becomes a major design control. It is noted that a unit lab may be a "one-man" space for the exclusive use of a professional or a larger space, perhaps made up of several modules.

Lab, Office, and Service Shaft Arrangements

The arrangement of the unit lab is directly affected by the desired location of office space and by the method by which services are brought to the labs. A private office is usually needed for the professional in charge of an operation. Figure 3.7 shows a number of possible arrangements within a similar module. The office may be fully enclosed, defined by low space dividers, separated from the lab, or contained within it. The decisions among these alternatives depend in large part on the work patterns and preferences of the users. A basic consideration is whether windows are to be provided in the labs. If they are, then offices must be across

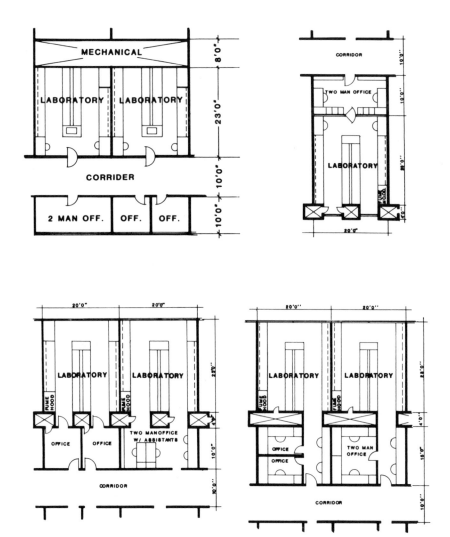

Figure 3.7   Alternate arrangements of labs and offices.

a corridor or somehow accommodated within the lab. The latter alternative may pose problems in access, hood locations, and emergency egress. Considerations in lab/office relationship include:

- Windows in labs reduce the wall area available for benches unless sill heights are kept about five feet above the floor.
- Temperature and humidity control is easier to maintain in interior labs.
- Some professionals want to keep visual surveillance over lab operations from their offices at all times; others prefer a separation.
- Work surfaces and file storage are usually needed in the lab proper for record-keeping by technicians or graduate students. Full-size desks are not always required; provision of a knee-hole station at a lab bench may suffice, or an approximately four-foot length of bench top may be dropped to 30" height to serve as a desk.
- The provision of fully-enclosed offices should be justified by a requirement for visual and aural privacy. Most professionals demand such an environment because of the need for intense concentration in reading, writing, and computation.

Figure 3.8 shows a unit lab plan which utilizes a central service core and places offices on the building perimeter. The plan provides for subdivision or enlarging of the labs if future changes are necessary.

Bench Arrangement

Typically, benches may parallel a partition containing lab services, extend from the partition at a right angle (in peninsular form), or be free-standing (island-type). Services can be easily extended when benches parallel or abut a partition. Island benches, which are used when access is needed from all sides (as in some teaching labs), are more difficult to service. They must be up-fed from below or down-fed from the ceiling, in a suitable enclosure.

Dimensions and Clearances

Lab widths are determined by the dimensions of benches and the spacing between them. Chapter 1 includes data based on ergonomic considerations. Wider spacings may be appropriate in a large, open lab occupied by several professionals and technicians or for safety reasons. In the U.S., modules of of 10 or 12 feet are usually suitable to maintain desirable bench spacings. A depth of 24 or 25 feet for the lab proper is often used for research labs in the U.S.

Floor-to-floor heights are governed by clear height of suspended ceiling (or lighting fixtures, if ceilings are omitted) and the space required overhead for structural members, ductwork, and piping. A minimum height of nine feet should be provided to fixture or finish ceiling. Three to five feet more may be needed depending on type of structure and mechanical/electrical systems.

Equipment

The traditionally designed and arranged unit lab accommodates the space needs of professionals and technicians, but may not be adequate if a large number of instruments is kept in the labs. In recent years electronic equipment and computer terminals have proliferated in research. Often, benches provided with expensive piped services have been given over to equipment that needs only normal electrical services. The loss of bench-top space can hinder lab operations, and the equipment may be placed in a location or at a height that is inappropriate for its operation. Alternatively, the equipment is sometimes placed in available spaces, such as storage rooms, that are not easily accessible. Before layouts are begun, a planner should obtain operating characteristics, sizes, and clearances for equipment used in lab procedures. Considerations in providing for instrumentation include:

- A counter or table with normal electrical service, rather than a bench and expensive cabinetry, may suffice for equipment.
- Consider a central equipment room to serve a group of labs, with services, lighting, and layout designed for the equipment.
- Design considerations may include lighting (for dials, gauges, CRTs, and digital readings), vibration-free location, controlled temperature and humidity, clearances for access or loading of equipment, and ideal height.
- Computer terminals may need to be accessible to several professionals and technicians or lo-

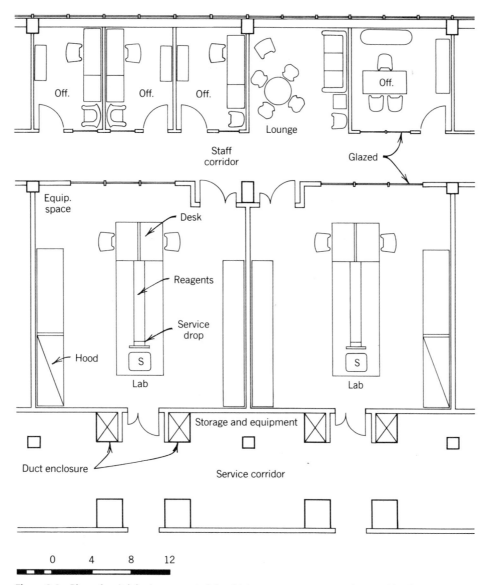

Figure 3.8 Plan of unit lab. A corporate lab which uses a separate service corridor for storage and servicing.

cated in individual offices. Acoustical treatment may be necessary for printers.

3.14 LABORATORY SUPPORT FACILITIES

The types of facilities needed to support lab procedures vary widely according to the nature of operations and must be determined during programming. It is important that the possibility of sharing

facilities among departments be explored. The concept may be resisted by a department's staff, but it is sometimes found that sharing involves, at most, a minor inconvenience. Design considerations for support spaces often found in laboratory buildings follow.

Regulated Temperature and Humidity Rooms

Cold rooms, constant temperature and humidity (CTH) rooms, and growth chambers are often required. Prefabricated units made of insulated panels may be suitable for these spaces.

- Allow space for work carried out in the rooms and for equipment clearances.
- Separate space may be needed for compressors or other equipment.
- Critical procedures, such as culture growth, may call for standby power or even redundant environmental systems.

Dark Rooms

Film processing is required for a number of lab procedures and for electron microscopes. Light-proofing, special ventilation, lighting, and cabinetry must be provided.

Electron Microscopes

Electron microscopy requires a suite of spaces including EM room (or rooms), dark room, preparation room(s), and space for transformers. If used for teaching, the EM area will require additional space to accommodate students. The EM suite must be located and designed for control of vibration, electromagnetic interference, and dust.

Glasswashing and Sterilization

Depending on the size and types of procedures carried out in a lab, glasswashing may be done in the labs or centralized. Small units similar to residential dishwashers may be provided for a lab or group of labs. Large, central glasswashing facilities contain equipment for washing, drying, and sterilizing.

Equipment Maintenance and Repair Shops

Facilities can range from relatively simple shops for machining, electrical repairs, and routine maintenance to sophisticated clean rooms for servicing of instruments. Shared use of shops for laboratory services and building maintenance may be considered, although the concept may not prove feasible because of the specialized and exacting work needed for the labs and the potential difficulties in joint use of equipment by technicians of different grades.

Storage

Storage spaces for a laboratory may range from cabinetry in a unit lab to warehouses containing bulk supplies in bags, drums, or crates. It is important that storage requirements be thoroughly researched with attention given to the following consideration:

- Safety provisions for hazardous materials.
- OSHA regulations governing storage of materials deemed to be health hazards.
- Pattern of distribution of materials, i.e., from long-term to short-term storage spaces and thence to work locations.
- Desired holding times for materials stored in labs, local storage rooms, central supply spaces, and detached buildings.
- Methods of storage, i.e., shelving, racks, pallets, bins.
- Methods of handling, such as carts, hand trucks, hydraulic lifts, conveyors, and cranes.
- Required aisles, maneuvering space, and doorway openings.
- Security requirements.
- Separation of incompatible materials.
- Special requirements, such as ventilation, washable finishes, dust collection.

Ancillary Facilities

Facilities such as maintenance shops, locker rooms, receiving, office services, and reception will be required as for any type of project. Additional functions, including technical library, computing center, cafeteria, and training may also be required. Chapter 2 provides guidelines for planning certain of these ancillary facilities.

3.15 HUMAN FACTORS IN DESIGN

Many of the considerations given above involve constraints on design—rules that cannot be bent by a designer. Moreover, a laboratory that is safe, economical, comfortable, energy-efficient, and functional is not necessarily a place which scientists and skilled technical people will consider pleasant or conducive to creative work. One challenge of laboratory design is to attain a humane environment inside what is, in many respects, a package for intricate systems and equipment.

Men and women engaged in research or teaching usually need an environment which can permit both intense concentration and interaction with others. Professionals and technical people may work long hours standing at benches, often involved with intricate processes and delicate instruments. Proper attention to ergonomics, colors, lighting, acoustics, temperature, and humidity is essential in the design of laboratories. Moreover, consideration should be given to spaces other than the labs themselves, so that the total environment will provide a sense of unity and human scale.

The following measures should be considered in designing for a humane environment.

- Site planning that preserves and enhances desirable natural features.
- Outdoor amenities, such as jogging trails, recreational areas, and terraces.
- Breaking down very large facilities into several smaller components.
- Creating informal seating areas, possibly as niches or corridors, for work breaks and unscheduled meetings.
- Introducing natural light to corridors and interior spaces by skylights or borrowed lights.
- Adequate ancillary facilities, including cafeterias, lunchrooms, lounges, and libraries.
- Imaginative and tasteful interior design concepts, including colors, finishes, graphics, equipment, furniture, and furnishings.
- Giving the users opportunities for expressing their preferences within the work environment.

3.16 COMPUTER-AIDED DESIGN

The computer is used extensively in all of the design disciplines for development of designs and construction documents and for cost and schedule control. Graphics systems are available for conceptual design, three-dimensional modeling, and preparation of working drawings and specifications. The computer, as an analytical tool, is used in engineering analysis and calculations. Many computer applications are appropriate for the design of laboratories. While it is not within the scope of this book to explore the many available systems and programs, the following applications are considered particularly useful in laboratory design:

- Exploration of modular schemes for typical labs. The graphics capabilities of a system may be used to test various modules and arrangements of space.
- Development of a system for inventorying space and equipment. The computer's ability to codify, sort, and update information makes it possible to keep a constant record of status, reflecting space changes, additions, and replacements.
- Use of graphics capabilities in a space management system to keep floor plans current.
- Use of generic listings of equipment and furniture in budgeting and cost control.

While all of the above applications do not occur in the design process, it is necessary to plan for them. Certain of the tasks entailed in developing systems for space management and inventory control (equipment surveys, for instance) may be done during design. Thus computerized operations may need to be integrated with design, whether or not the computer is used directly as an aid to design.

SERVICES FOR RESEARCH BUILDINGS

Joseph R. Loring, P.E.
Harrison D. Goodman, P.E.

with
John O. Samuel
and Richard F. Humenn, P.E.*

4.1 GENERAL

The design of the mechanical and electrical systems for laboratory buildings can be separated into two basic components:

- Central utility distribution systems.
- Individual laboratory distribution systems.

Ideally the design of a laboratory building, including plan configuration, laboratory arrangements, and utility systems, should be a symbiotic process in which the best possible solutions for each key design issue are developed at the same time. In actual practice, however, a hierarchy of priorities eventually evolves in which the physical arrangement of the laboratories predominates. Other factors and constraints which ultimately have a pronounced influence on the selection of the utility distribution system for the laboratory include:

- Floor-to-floor heights.
- Number, size, and shape of floors.
- Structural system.
- Building location (urban versus suburban).
- Types of laboratories and services.
- Number of fume hoods.
- Degree of flexibility desired.
- Provisions for expansion.
- Energy recovery systems.
- Environmental considerations.
- Budget limitations.

The impact of each of these factors on the selection of a utilities distribution system is discussed below.

Floor-to-Floor Heights

The amount of clear, unobstructed ceiling space in a laboratory is related to the floor-to-floor height as well as the structural system. If the laboratory building is constructed as an extension or wing of an existing building, floor-to-floor heights may be pre-established. Limited floor-to-floor heights will tend to favor vertical distribution systems.

---

*The authors are members of the firm of Joseph R. Loring & Associates, Inc. Consulting Engineers.

Number, Size, and Shape of Floors

As the number of floors in a laboratory building increases and as the size of the floor decreases, the factors favoring vertical distribution tend to increase. One reason for this is the obvious temptation to cut down on the "cube" of the building (since horizontal distribution generally requires greater floor-to-floor heights), thus reducing first cost as well as the operating cost of the fan systems. Another reason would be that, with fewer floors, the individual floor area tends to increase raising the cost of horizontal distribution.

Structural System

The design of the mechanical and electrical systems for a laboratory building are directly affected by the type of structural system and the number and location of the columns. On the surface, it might appear that column-free space is desirable in order to permit greater flexibility in the arrangement and re-arrangement of the laboratories. However, column-free space implies a greater depth of structure, which imposes further constraints on the mechanical and electrical distribution systems. Fortunately, however, the permanent corridor circulation system required in all laboratories offers ample alternatives for the placement of columns without interfering with the future relocation of laboratory partitions. Vertical service riser locations are often made to coincide with the structural column locations. The addition of columns, which permits the depth of the structural system to be reduced, also facilitates the distribution of the mechanical and electrical systems.

Building Location

The location of a laboratory building in an urban environment will impose greater restraints on the design of the mechanical and electrical systems than if the building were located in a suburban environment. The following building elements would have to be treated differently in an urban environment as opposed to a suburban environment.

1. Air intakes and exhausts.
2. Gas cylinder storage.
3. Location of incoming electric service and service equipment can be treated more flexibly in a suburban environment.

4. Toxic or acid waste treatment or dilution.
5. The location of the central heating and cooling plant, including cooling towers, can be treated more flexibly in a suburban environment.
6. A suburban site generally implies a low-rise structure, while an urban site generally implies a high-rise structure.
7. A suburban site, which is generally larger than an urban site, permits the physical separation of special areas, such as pilot plants and test cells, thus simplifying the design of the basic laboratory building.

Types of Laboratories and Services

The degree of sophistication of the laboratory program directly affects the magnitude of the building services. Generally speaking, teaching laboratories in a university undergraduate environment are least likely to require unusual provisions for flexibility and expansion; nor are they likely to require permanent provisions for distribution of various gases. Graduate science laboratories, laboratories devoted to sophisticated research projects with changing programs, and industrial research laboratories, depending upon the specific program, may require more flexibility and a large number of services for any given task.

Special laboratories, such as containment laboratories, animal research laboratories, radiation research laboratories, electronics research laboratories, microbiology laboratories, pilot plants, and the like, each have special requirements which will be touched on later in this chapter.

Number of Fume Hoods

Of all of the elements of laboratory equipment which require mechanical and/or electrical services, the fume hood has the most profound effect on the design of the HVAC system, and indeed of the laboratory itself. Fume hoods are large cabinets or isolated work stations in which sensitive or hazardous experiments are carried out, most of which require special dedicated exhaust ducts. The mechanical distribution system must therefore be designed with the understanding that the total system can accommodate a specific maximum number of hoods. Limitations in regard to the maximum number of hoods that can be accommodated

on a single floor and within a single lab must be clearly defined.

Degree of Flexibility Desired

The subject of flexibility and the degree to which it is required on a specific project must be addressed at the earliest stages of design. In projects where flexibility is a requirement, the utility distribution system, whether vertical or horizontal, should be designed to accommodate changes in laboratory dimensions (width) and, equally important, to accommodate changes within the laboratory itself.

Provisions for Expansion

Where a laboratory design program specifies that the project must be designed to permit the addition of future laboratories, the extent and nature of the expansion should be clearly defined.

Energy Recovery Systems

Laboratory buildings where 100% of the lab air is exhausted are prime candidates for energy recovery systems, such as glycol loops or air-to-air heat wheels and central heat pump systems. If economic studies justify the inclusion of this type of equipment, the mechanical systems must be specially configured to obtain the optimum results. Recent developments in volumetric control systems have permitted the introduction of variable air volume systems in laboratories. The section, later in this chapter, which describes "volumetric control systems for fume hoods" offers still further opportunities for energy recovery.

Environmental Considerations

There are a number of codes, health department regulations, and other environmental criteria which govern the point of emission or prior treatment of the laboratory air. Laboratories producing toxic fumes or occupied in viral or animal research fall into this category and require careful study of the wind characteristics around the exterior of the building as well as the required internal provisions for decontamination and odor-control.

Budget Limitations

Since features such as energy conservation equipment and provisions for flexibility and/or expansion involve additional cost, it is important that the cost of the mechanical and electrical systems be correctly assessed during the design stage.

4.2 LABORATORY DISTRIBUTION SYSTEMS

4.2.1 Basic Laboratory Arrangements

Basic laboratory arrangements impact on the selection of the mechanical and electrical distribution system as follows:

Arrangement	M&E Distribution Systems
1. Single loaded corridor, continuous service core	1. Vertical mains and horizontal sub-distribution along core walls
2. Double loaded public corridor	2. Vertical distribution – interior or exterior
3. Double loaded service corridor	3. Horizontal distribution along service corridor
4. Interstitial floors	4. Horizontal distribution

The above list is not intended to be all-inclusive. There are many variations possible and necessary for the multitude of special laboratory types, such as animal research labs, containment labs, microelectronic labs, and pilot plants.

4.2.2 System Selection Process

Many factors influence the selection of a specific laboratory arrangement and its associated utilities distribution system. Assuming that other factors have determined the general laboratory arrangement, there still remains the problem of selecting the most favorable utilities distribution system. This is generally done by comparing and evaluating the pros and cons of the various alternative methods of utility distribution. The comparisons, which should be carried out on a life cycle basis, are especially significant where the laboratories are subject to frequent rearrangement and where flexibility is a primary design requirement.

4.2.3 Typical Utilities Distribution Schemes

1. Continuous End-Wall Service Corridors

With this system, the various mechanical and electrical services are distributed horizontally along the entire service core wall. Each of these services is fed from a main vertical service feed. Each laboratory has direct access to the utilities.

The continuous end-wall service corridor concept has many advantages, including flexibility, ease of maintenance, and the ability to make service modifications and rearrangements without affecting the operation of the other laboratories. This concept usually implies the following:

- Circulation corridor is at the perimeter.
- Reduced floor-to-floor heights.

2. Vertical Distribution

This method introduces the required laboratory utility services into each laboratory by means of a series of vertical utility zones located so as to be able to supply either one or more laboratories by tapping the vertical risers within, or immediately adjacent to, each laboratory, and extending these services to the respective laboratory tables, hoods, and so on.

The horizontal runouts from risers to the remote equipment may run above or below the floor slab. The disturbance factor with above-slab runouts is less, but usually interferes with interior layouts during initial design.

The primary advantages of this approach are lower first cost of installation and the ability to design a system with minimum floor-to-floor heights. This system has the disadvantages of being relatively inflexible unless the service risers are spaced closely, and comparatively costly to maintain and modify. This concept usually implies the following:

- Minimum total volume occupied by the services, compared to any other scheme.
- A central mechanical room occupying a full floor to accommodate the horizontal distribution of the major services from which the risers are tapped. Is should be noted that the lab ser-

vices can only be activated vertically, that is, individual floors cannot be shut down.

3. Horizontal Distribution

This term describes the organization and method of routing of mechanical, electrical, plumbing, and gas services for a series of laboratories on a specific floor. These services can be grouped and run at the ceiling of a double loaded service corridor. The services for each laboratory are then tapped off the respective mains run at the corridor ceiling.

The basic advantage of this type of distribution is the added flexibility and comparative simplicity with which laboratories can be re-arranged or expanded in the future with a minimum of time lost, cost, and disruption. The main disadvantage is higher first cost of mechanical and electrical systems (the system offers the lowest life cycle costs in a facility which changes laboratory layouts often). This concept usually implies the following:

- Double loaded service corridor.
- Higher floor-to-floor heights.

In this type of distribution, labs can be controlled on a floor-to-floor basis, except for gravity flow systems, such as drains. Hoods can be grouped for energy conservation purposes. Mechanical rooms can be remote (although this is true for other types as well).

The basic advantage of horizontal distribution is the ability to group systems horizontally in order to control their safety, energy consumption, hours of operation, security, and so on.

4. Interstitial Floors

This type of distribution is one in which the laboratory floors are alternated with floors containing the various utility services installed on a modular basis. If properly planned and executed, this approach should represent the ultimate in flexibility, ease of maintenance, and ability to make service modifications and re-arrangements without affecting the operation of the other laboratories. But the concept does involve a significant increase in the "cube" of the structure and therefore in its cost. Because of the added cost of this method of distribution, the Public Health Service (PHS) has taken

a position recommending against its use for PHS laboratories.

The system selection process can best be illustrated by citing the case study of a recent project in which three major alternatives—horizontal distribution (double loaded service corridor), interstitial space, and vertical distribution—were compared and evaluated by means of a 15-year life cycle cost analysis; see the appendix.

4.2.4 Special Laboratory Arrangements

The previous discussion described a number of typical laboratory arrangements that can use utility distribution systems which are applicable to many different laboratory types. The following laboratory arrangements are highly specialized and require specific utility distribution schemes dictated by the special purposes of each laboratory, or by governmental regulations:

Electronic Laboratories

A variation of the interstitial floor type of distribution has been employed to serve large single-level laboratory and/or laboratory/manufacturing facilities involving Class 10,000 or higher levels of atmospheric purity, as well as cryogenic gases. In special situations involving the manufacture of microelectronic devices where the manufacturing process involves the use of tools that require laboratory-type conditions as well as considerable flexibility because of rapidly changing technology, the air and electric services are run overhead in large accessible ceiling plenums and the various gases, liquids, and drainage lines are run below in large accessible basement areas. In this case, the single-level laboratory or manufacturing floor is sandwiched between spaces carrying services and utilities.

Containment Laboratories

This highly specialized type of laboratory has been developed for work in new areas of knowledge, such as genetic research (recombinant DNA molecule), new strains of viruses, etc. These laboratories are designed with a high degree of isolation and require totally dedicated mechanical systems with redundant features.

Nuclear (Radiation) Research Laboratories

Laboratories which conduct experimentation involving radioactive materials must be specially designed to protect the research scientists from exposure to these dangerous materials. In addition, they are usually subject to regulatory laws and constraints which make their design more demanding than other laboratory types. For this reason, it is advisable to consult the guidelines issued by the Nuclear Regulatory Commission, or other Federal Agencies which conduct this type of experimentation; particularly the various recommendations of NIH. Air exhaust decontamination usually involves special filtration, scrubbing, and/or dilution.

Microbiology Laboratories

These laboratories are used essentially for research on pathogenic organisms to assist medical science in finding cures for various diseases. Their principal function, therefore, demands a safe work station environment; this normally involves biological safety hoods which are described in Section 4.5. Due to the need to filter exhaust air from these hoods, it is not advisable to tie their exhaust into the general chemical-exhaust systems.

Animal Rooms

Mechanical systems for Animal Rooms are highly specialized and must be designed to provide anywhere from 12 to 25 air changes per hour with air distribution devices providing laminar, or near laminar, flow. A high degree of control of temperature and humidity is also essential. The exhaust system should be provided with multiple outlets located near the floor. The exhaust system should be equipped with varying levels of filtration depending on the specialized requirements of the specific animal types housed within the laboratory. Special water supply and drainage systems must be provided for purposes of flushing animal wastes. Potable and non-potable water supplies should be provided. For more detailed requirements consult the American Association of Laboratory Animal Care Standards, various booklets published by the National Institutes of Health, and the ASHRAE Guides, and see Chapter 2 for programming guide.

Pilot Plants

Mechanical services for these specialized areas will vary with the type of facility the pilot plant is intended to support. Generally speaking, a pilot plant should be provided with a full complement of utilities sized to provide for maximum loads and utilization. Since experiments within these areas are generally temporary, and may vary in location, the utilities should be distributed in such a way as to provide ready access at any point in the pilot plant.

4.3 DESIGN CRITERIA

4.3.1 Heating, Ventilation, and Air Conditioning

Indoor Design Conditions

Indoor design conditions are generally governed by special processes, equipment, or occupants. For example, animal research requires slightly higher or lower temperatures and/or humidity levels than the normally accepted levels for human comfort.

When the indoor design conditions required for any process become significantly different, the use of the so-called "environmental room" becomes mandatory, both for the purpose of isolating these spaces from other comfort-controlled zones, and in order to exert more precise control over the special temperature and humidity ranges required within these controlled environments.

Incubator rooms, cold rooms, and so on, fall into this category of rooms in which the temperature and humidity conditions are produced by special refrigeration/air conditioning equipment, dedicated to this task for year-round operation. Environmental room temperatures ranging from 100°F to minus 60°F are not uncommon in ordinary laboratories.

Laboratory Ventilation

Laboratory ventilation design criteria are affected by the following:

- The minimum exhaust air required by the fume hoods.

- Pressure relationship with respect to the surrounding areas or to outdoors.
- Removal of the chemicals, odors, toxic fumes, etc., generated by particular laboratories and the required degree of dilution with outdoor air when exhausting.

Laboratories in which toxic, corrosive, radioactive, explosive, and pathogenic materials are regularly used should always be provided with 100% exhaust to outdoors. However, when the entire building functions as a laboratory, it becomes impractical to exhaust the entire building's air since a significant portion of the exhaust quantity has to be brought in from outdoors as "make-up" air. At this point, several alternatives have to be evaluated with respect to the type and operation of the fume hoods, the partitioning of the work spaces, and the zoning of the heating/cooling systems and equipment.

The discussions of fume hood types, auxiliary make-up air systems, and exhaust air heat recovery systems which follow set out the remaining criteria to be established with respect to the ventilation system design.

Internal Heat

The internal heat generated by laboratory equipment is another factor affecting the load calculations for a laboratory.

Electrical equipment loads, such as centrifuges, ovens, glass washers, dryers, computers, and so on, which are found even in undergraduate teaching laboratories, will range from 2 to 10 watts per square foot of lab area and exceed 25 watts per square foot in more sophisticated labs such as those used in biochemistry and electronic research and in many industrial labs. Therefore, even with the most flexible kind of air distribution system, the accurate assessment of the equipment heat load during early stages of the design is critical in laying out an economical system of ductwork and its related air diffusion system.

Air quantities in institutional labs vary from 1.2 CFM/SF to 2.5 CFM/SF under ordinary heat gain conditions. In laboratories employing large electrical equipment and requiring 3.0 to 5.0 CFM/SF, air transport problems may become insurmountable; therefore, extraordinary heat rejection sources should be treated separately to avoid unduly penalizing the overall plant and equipment capability.

Exhaust Air

Exhaust air containing toxic material, viruses, radioactivity, or undesirable (animal) odors should be chemically treated, incinerated, or filtered before being released to the atmosphere. These gases should be discharged as far away from air intakes as possible.

The usual practice in laboratory design is to discharge exhaust air upwards, by means of fans located in penthouses or above the roof, and to induce outdoor air into the air supply systems near the ground level, preferably from the windward side. Analysis of the wind currents, secondary eddies, and fume dispersion characteristics around a building will avoid mislocation of intake and exhaust outlets and avoid cross-contamination during operation.

4.3.2 Laboratory Services

Central Services

Here we consider all the services a particular laboratory needs in addition to the ordinary building services, such as electricity, water, storm and sanitary sewers. These central laboratory services usually include compressed air, vacuum, natural or propane gas, acid waste, distilled water, and demineralized water systems. Many other services are centrally distributed or locally dispensed depending on the particular type of laboratory in question. Among these, the most prevalent are nitrous oxide, nitrogen, oxygen, nonpotable water, hydrogen, carbon dioxide, mineral recovery, and other specialized systems.

The basic criteria governing the decision to centralize or locally dispense any of the liquid or gas services are: (1) code and fire regulations governing the use of toxic and inflammable liquids and gases, and (2) the economic benefits in respect to the cost of distribution piping that would result from centralizing the supply sources.

For example, the choice between a central acid dilution system, serving a multifloor laboratory, and local acid dilution pods is strictly a matter of economics governed by the number of sinks required for disposing of acid waste and the overall extent of the piping system necessary to interconnect them in a centralized system. In the case of pure and treated water systems (free from organic matter, minerals, bacteria, pyrogens, and dissolved gases) the cost of distribution via special piping system (glass, stainless steel, tin, polypropylene) may be higher than local distillation, demineralizing, and filtration units.

Design Considerations

Standardized laboratory services, such as vacuum, compressed air, hot and cold water, and gas, should be designed so that the lines can be installed in parallel with a minimum of joints and elbows, but appropriately equipped with valves to permit rearrangement of individual spaces without shutting off large areas of the building.

Valves in piping systems should be accessible to permit extension of the system as required by future changes in equipment and space layout.

Waste piping material should be selected to withstand corrosion and erosion by the types of waste anticipated from each laboratory. The upstream side of the potable water system should be protected against backflow (from contaminated sources) either by use of air gaps or by a separately vented storage water system assigned for direct use in equipment, such as closed tube condensers, vacuum jets, and so on.

Gas Storage

Liquified and compressed gases are usually governed by local codes requiring them to be stored outdoors, above ground. Storage areas should be protected against overheating, and should be away from electric power lines and combustible liquid lines or material. Storage of similar gases in cylinders is usually permitted in "manifold rooms" when these comply with the NFPA rules, other local ventilation codes, and fire regulations governing such applications.

4.3.3   Electrical Systems

The design criteria for laboratory building electrical systems can be categorized as follows:

- Load density assignments
- Demand and diversity factors.

- Distribution flexibility and accessibility.
- Special considerations.

Connected Load Design Capacity

The assignment of unit loads to establish load density and design capacity is based on the functions and equipment to be served, as follows:

- Academic facilities (Science, Chemistry, Physics, etc.): Allow 20 to 30 VA/sq. ft.
- Research facilities (Pharmaceutical, Petrochemical, Electronic, etc.): Allow 30 to 50 VA/sq. ft.
- Special facilities (equipped with ovens, steam generators, etc.): May reach or exceed 100 VA/sq. ft.

Except where heavy electrical loads are encountered, approximately 80% of laboratory space can be served from the 120/208 volt system, and the remainder from the 277/480 volt system.

Demand and Diversity Factors

The selection of suitable demand and diversity factors is governed by analysis of data from similar existing facilities, the type of equipment to be employed, and the degree of noncoincident loading that can be expected.

Demand and diversity factors are generally not applied to an individual laboratory module where virtually all the equipment within the space could be in operation at the same time.

The following is a representative example of selected demand/diversity factors for a research building:

1 module	100%
2 to 10 modules	100 to 80%
10 to 40 modules	80 to 50%
40 to 100 modules	50 to 30%
over 100 modules	30 to 25%

Distribution design should be arranged to serve large groups of laboratories in order to take advantage of the lower factors in sizing transformers and feeders.

Flexibility and Accessibility

For optimum flexibility, a dedicated appliance panel is assigned to each laboratory module of 400 to 600 square feet. It contains a minimum of 30, and up to 42 poles as dictated by the unit design load, and is equipped with a variety of 120 and 208 volt circuits to serve the scheduled equipment, plus a minimum of 25% spares.

For ease of servicing and to minimize disruption to the laboratory equipment served, quality grade plug-in branch circuit breakers and a main disconnecting device are recommended for each appliance panel. Where applicable, branch breakers may be ground fault interrupters and the main disconnect may be a shunt trip device controlled by emergency power cut-off stations within the laboratory space.

The appliance panel is best located outside the laboratory space in the adjacent service corridor or equivalent electrical equipment space, and served by an individual feeder originating from a power distribution panel or plug-in bus duct. The use of fully accessible wireway from the panel into and throughout the laboratory space facilitates installation of initial branch wiring and future changes and additions.

Where a group of laboratories require 277/480 volt branch circuits, three options generally apply:

1. Serve a group of laboratories from a single 277/480V branch circuit panel via wireway.
2. Provide a 277/480V power panel and run a dedicated power circuit to each laboratory, terminating in a small branch circuit panel.
3. Extend a 277/480V plug-in bus duct down the service corridor to enable circuit taps as required.

The same methods are applicable for circuits served from an emergency or clean power supply.

The method of distribution should favor the separation of laboratory loads from all other building loads, especially mechanical equipment and elevators. Further separation may be advisable to isolate sensitive laboratory equipment from motors, rectifiers, electromagnets, and similar equipment that generate line disturbances.

Special Considerations

Low Voltage Wiring. Distribution of telephone, communication, signal, and data transmission wiring is best served via wireways and cable trays where the runs are suitable for consolidation. The

use of steel, rather than aluminum, will minimize the effects of electromagnetic interference.

Line Disturbances. Where instruments may be sensitive to line disturbances, consideration should be given to the following corrective measures:

- Line filters.
- Isolated grounding.
- Isolating and/or shielded transformers.
- Static voltage regulation.
- Battery inverter system.
- Uninterruptible power supply (UPS) with on-line battery.

If selective separation of distribution facilities is exercised, the need for correction of line disturbances would be kept to a minimum.

Emergency Power. In research facilities dealing with biological and similar experimentation, there is often a need for a back-up power supply to serve culture and bacteria freezers, incubator shakers, etc., in order to prevent destruction or contamination during a utility power failure. Where a reasonable time interval is permissible, as in the case of a freezer, the emergency circuits can be served by the same standby generator required for life/safety. If, however, no interruption can be tolerated, only the introduction of an uninterruptible power supply with battery backup will guarantee continuity of power until the emergency generator is on line.

Hazardous Conditions. In facilities where explosive or ignitible liquids, gases, and materials may be present, applicable codes and standards must be implemented to guarantee the safety of electrical systems in hazardous environments. Further, special precautions must also be taken in providing grounding methods to prevent electrostatic discharge where metal containers are moved or stored.

Future Changes. A research laboratory building is subject to significant and frequent changes. Consequently, the design approach for the electrical systems must allow for growth and change with reasonable ease and without major disruption to operations during alterations. Selective pre-investment in the initial design can prove to be in-valuable in the future; for example:

- Minimum of 25% spare capacity in service and distribution facilities.
- Spare duct banks in service runs for future re-inforcement.
- Reserved space to add equipment and to run additional distribution feeders, including sleeves in electric closets.
- Fan cooling and dual insulation ratings for transformers to boost capacity.
- Selection of equipment and material readily adaptable to modify and expand.
- Distribution runs arranged to be accessible over entire length.

4.4 ENERGY CONSERVATION TECHNIQUES

A laboratory building designed with an energy-efficient envelope and equipped with systems min-imizing energy consumption (i.e., low illumination levels, minimum air ventilation) would readily meet the current criteria on energy *conservation* and al-low for further energy *reclamation* through con-ventional recovery equipment, such as the split condensers (central heat pump) plus thermal stor-age and computerized operational programs. These may further enhance the building's energy budget by overcoming certain inflexibilities in its system design or prevalent utility rates.

The following conditions may require addi-tional and more sophisticated energy reclamation techniques in order to keep overall energy con-sumption to acceptable levels:

1. Requirement for exhausting most or all of the space air resulting in a heavy outdoor air load to be handled by the building's heating and cooling systems. Criteria for odor removal (an-imal research) or contamination control (ra-dioactive or infectious) and for make-up air for fume hood exhaust systems usually result in 15 to 25 air changes per hour, far exceeding the $\frac{1}{2}$ to 2 air changes required in comfort control.
2. High degree of internal heat gain from elec-trically driven equipment (ovens, compres-

sors, motors, computers) and from hot pro-cesses (sterilizing, boiling of liquids, steam baths, glass washers) which impose an extraor-dinary burden on the cooling systems of the building.

4.4.1 Energy Reclamation Techniques

A great variety of energy reclamation techniques have emerged in recent years to cope with the ex-cessive energy requirements of the laboratory pro-cesses described above:

- Rotary air-to-air heat exchangers.
- Plate heat exchangers—air to air.
- Runaround system with coils and pumps.
- Runaround—multiple tower and dessicant spray systems.
- Single tube—capillary or gravity-return type heat pipe.
- Central double circuit condenser water, using central refrigeration chillers.

Rotary Air-to-Air Heat Exchangers

Commercially known as "heat wheels," "enthalpy wheels," or "total energy wheels," these devices have the capability of recovering heating as well as cooling energy at efficiencies up to 80%, and are best suited where the space air is not suitable for recirculation. Thus, a laboratory which does not use a large number of fume hoods or other equip-ment requiring exhaust but, nevertheless, re-quires a constant supply of fresh air can greatly benefit from this wheel's ability to transfer energy between the conditioned (temperature and hu-midity) space air and the incoming outdoor air. A laboratory exhausting air via hoods, or an animal research laboratory requiring direct removal of space air to outdoors, would not risk contamina-tion of the incoming fresh air through a heat wheel, thus ruling out its application for energy recovery.

Plate Heat Exchangers

These devices permit indirect heat transfer be-tween two air streams of different temperature by passing these streams through completely isolated compartments while transferring heat from one stream to the other. But the usual plate heat exchanger transfers only sensible heat, and even at that the efficiencies do not exceed 60%. Due to its ability to seal the supply air passage from the exhaust air passage, its application to heat recovery from toxic, corrosive, or even infectious air is feasible, although its overall cost may prohibit its frequent use.

Runaround Systems

In these systems, the heat transfer coils are located in the exhaust and supply air streams. Heat is then transferred from one air stream to the other by means of a liquid (or antifreeze solution) circulated between the coils. As in the case of plate heat exchangers, heat transfer is sensible and will not exceed 60%. The main advantage of runaround coils is the flexibility in the location of coils. The supply and exhaust streams need not be adjacent to each other, as must be the case with rotary wheel and plate heat exchangers.

Multiple Tower and Dessicant Spray Systems

These systems are similar to the coil and pump runaround systems except that they use an absorbent (such as lithium chloride/water) in place of the water or antifreeze solution, and a spray system (such as a cooling tower) in place of the heat transfer coils. The absorbent liquid is sprayed counterflow to the air streams in order to transfer heat from one air stream to the other. Recovery efficiencies in this system may run up to 70% since it recovers both sensible and latent heat; however, it will cost substantially more than the ordinary runaround coil and pump system.

Heat Pipes

Heat pipes have no moving parts. They are reversible isothermal devices strictly for sensible heat recovery. A heat pipe consists of a sealed metal tube lined with a "wick" that is saturated with a volatile fluid, such as a refrigerant. Heat applied to one end of the pipe vaporizes the refrigerant. The vapor flows to the opposite or cold end where it condenses and is absorbed by the wick. The liquid returns to the warm end through capillary action. When a bundle of such tubes is placed with one

portion in the exhaust air stream and the remainder in the supply air stream, heat transfer takes place between the air streams. Typical efficiencies range from 60 to 65%. Installation in a conventional HVAC system requires that the supply and exhaust air streams be adjacent to each other.

Double Circuit Condenser Water Systems

These central heat pump systems use a chiller with two separate condensers. One of the condensers is piped to the cooling tower circuit for direct heat rejection to the outdoors, and the other one is piped to the building's heating system. The second condenser usually operates at higher condensing temperatures, providing 110 to 120°F water. This recovered water can be circulated through the building's heating coils or domestic water preheaters whenever the chillers are in operation. This type of recovery system is most suitable for extracting heat from areas containing equipment (such as motors, computer equipment, ovens, and sterilizers) via local cooling equipment and using a central refrigeration system. The heat thus extracted can be transferred to other areas of the building for re-use in preheating domestic water and outdoor air, or in reheat systems.

4.4.2 Energy Management Programs

The increased use of centralized building automation systems to supervise a building's mechanical and electrical systems has gradually opened the field for energy management using automated hardware and ever-developing software systems. Among the most commonly specified standard energy management programs are the following types, applicable for both laboratory and non-laboratory buildings:

1. *Demand Limiting*—A KW monitoring and control program that automatically limits the building's electric power demand to a predetermined limit by turning off nonpriority electrical loads for short periods of time.

2. *Duty Cycling*—Lowers electrical energy consumption by cycling HVAC equipment. Cycling should be interlocked with space temperature to prevent uncomfortable conditions. In laboratories where condi-

tioned space air is used as make-up air for fume hoods, duty cycling is not appropriate.

3. *Utility Profile* (Energy Totalizer)—Will calculate various characteristics of a building's energy usage on a daily and/or billing period basis. Program output might be actual energy consumed, project energy consumption, actual peak demand, projected peak demand, calculated billed demand, energy savings, or totalized BTUs consumed.

4. *Chiller Optimization*—Will control condenser water temperature and select the correct number of chillers for a particular load as well as optimizing chilled water temperature.

5. *Enthalpy Control*—Optimizes the use of air with the lowest enthalpy by selecting or blending the return air/outside air streams. Again, the varying amounts of outdoor air will not permit the application of this control cycle to systems requiring constant volume make-up air.

6. *Supply Air Reset*—Optimizes supply air temperatures based on measured zone loads while maintaining consistent space temperature and relative humidity requirements.

7. *Optimum Start/Stop*—Optimizes mechanical system start times by calculating the optimal cooling system pulldown time and heating system warmup time based on inside building mass temperature. Also shutdown is optimized by taking advantage of the the "flywheel," or thermal inertia effect of the building.

8. *Chiller Profile*—Summarizes each chiller's operation by calculating instantaneous BTU rate, totalized BTU, totalized KW consumption, coefficient of performance, as well as chilled water supply and return temperatures and chilled water flow rate.

9. *Program (Timed) Start/Stop*—Will automatically initiate start and stop commands based on a preselected time schedule. This will allow preprogramming of desired run schedules for holidays.

10. *Maintenance Totalizer*—Will automatically record run times and print a maintenance message alarm when a predetermined limit is reached.

4.5 FUME HOODS

4.5.1 The Role of Face Velocity in Fume Hood Applications

Regardless of their discipline or function, science laboratories must provide an environment that is safe from toxic chemical fumes, dangerous microbes, odoriferous vapors and dusts, carcinogens and radioactive materials, all of which may be generated during a given experiment. This broad spectrum of hazards is best handled by the researcher in a locally enclosed and ventilated environment, known by the generic term "fume hood." The degree of danger to the health of the research scientist usually dictates the type of hood and the design considerations surrounding it.

The purpose of any hood is to capture the offending fume or gas by an exhaust air stream of sufficient velocity to entrap it and carry it away safely into the atmosphere. Unlike hoods used for industrial ventilation, which carry off undesirable products for an established chemical or industrial manufacturing process, the fume hood must enable the scientist to carry out his experimental procedures, which are often very fragile and difficult to control, with both safety and dexterity. The fume hood accommodates this dual requirement by providing a heavy flow of air into the enclosure's face opening, through which the scientist can readily work and observe, but from which he or she is protected by the "face velocity" of the air flow into the hood.

The fume hood's face velocity is therefore crucial to the protection of the scientist; this is the shield that prevents hazardous fumes from reaching the face or breathing zone. For this reason, it was once thought that the higher the face velocity, the better the protection; however, this has subsequently been shown to be incorrect. The upper limit of the face velocity is about 150 feet per minute (fpm); above this, the air turbulence generated by the head, arms, and body of the scientist causes a negative pressure in front of the scientist, which actually induces the fumes back into the breathing zone. Some authorities, moreover, dispute the upper limit of 150 fpm and strongly recommend a maximum face velocity of 125 fpm.

The lower limit of face velocity depends on several factors: the toxicity level of the fumes, the quantity and velocity of the fumes generated inside the hood, the air patterns in front of the fume hood (such as drafts from open doors), and the protective apparatus worn by the scientist. In 1965, the U.S. Department of Health, Education, and Welfare (HEW) published a table of recommended face velocities based on the degree of hazard. These varied as follows:

Degree of Hazard	Minimum Face Velocity
Low toxicity levels	50 fpm
Average toxicity levels in research involving a wide range of materials	75 fpm
Low-level radioactive tracer with nominal toxicity hazards	100 fpm
Significant chemical toxicity levels and moderately radioactive materials	150 fpm

Recent experience in fume hood application resulted in revision of these recommendations; however, they are still the minimum face velocities used by some Federal agencies. For this reason, it is extremely important to inquire if the client for which the system is designed has specific minima and maxima for fume hood face velocities. For example, the National Cancer Institute, a Federal agency, uses 100 fpm as a design parameter for chemical fume hoods (with limits of 90 fpm for low and 110 fpm for high). Most research laboratories have similar criteria for chemical fume hoods

Most fume hood applications for undergraduate teaching laboratories can be safely designed with a face velocity of 75 fpm. This is due to the rather limited hazards and short-term exposure to them at university teaching laboratories.

Finally, attempts have been made to provide a more rational method of selection for the proper design face velocity in a given laboratory situation. The American Society of Heating, Refrigerating, and Air Conditioning Engineers (ASHRAE) has published a table of recommended "average" face velocities, with minimum limits based on 80% of the "average" or design value. Prior to 1978, the three ASHRAE classifications for hazard gave rise to the following fume hood classifications: Class A (Se-

vere/Critical Usage—125 to 150 fpm); Class B (Moderate Usage—80 to 100 fpm); Class C (Minimum Usage—75 to 60 fpm). In 1978, ASHRAE modified Class C to 60 to 50 fpm. As of 1984, ASHRAE no longer classifies hood face velocity based solely on toxicity of materials handled. The 1984 recommendations for face velocities are based on recent experimental data which involved several variables. It must be noted that rational approaches to design face velocities may be, and often are, superseded by codes, governments agency regulations, or the local safety rules of the research laboratory staff.

4.5.2 Types of Fume Hoods

Because each hood must be an adequate size and shape to permit the researcher safe access to the experiment, several standard hood configurations have evolved and may be purchased as catalog items from laboratory furniture manufacturers. The basic assemblies of these fume hoods are summarized below.

Bench Hood

This hood is so named because its working surface is at bench height. It is by far the most common fume hood configuration, because most laboratory experimentation fits into this basic hood type.

Walk-in Hood

The walk-in hood, as its name suggests, has a face opening generally high enough to permit a person to walk into the hood; since the hood rests on the floor, the bottom of the hood is generally the floor itself.

Because of the large face area of the walk-in hood, it is often necessary to use "snorkel" or "elephant trunk" flexible local exhaust ducts to catch the more toxic fumes generated within the hood.

Distillation Hood

This hood is a special-purpose type well suited to large vacuum distillation set-ups; this is made possible by high vertical dimension, with the work surface generally about 18 inches above the floor.

California Hood

The California type is used where large, controlled, and vented work areas are required. It is a hooded lattice, with horizontal sliding sash on both sides of the hood.

Special Purpose Hoods

A number of special-purpose hoods are available to cover the following services: radioisotopes, perchloric acid, "glove boxes" for very dangerous experiments, biological safety cabinets, etc.

4.5.3 Air Flow Arrangements

Fume hoods are also subtyped into several air flow arrangements:

Vertical Sliding Sash

These hoods have long been the "standard" hoods of the industry. They have a sash which opens by sliding upward to a fixed open position; hence, they are variable volume and variable face velocity hoods. While these hoods are energy conserving in that very little air flow occurs when the sash is closed, the air velocity becomes very high as the sash is raised, and hence may blow chemicals and papers into the exhaust system. This hood also destabilizes the room air balance and may place the room under a positive pressure, which is generally undesirable.

To overcome this complaint, hood suppliers have designed an air inlet bypass which bypasses the exhaust air when the sash is closed. This has become the more acceptable type of vertical sliding sash, because it maintains a stable air balance in the lab space and does not increase face velocity as the sash is raised or lowered. Unfortunately, the bypass type vertical sliding sash is energy inefficient because it requires that minimum face velocity be maintained across the full face opening, and compounds the problem by constantly exhausting the same amount of air, regardless of actual need.

Horizontal Sliding Sash

In order to offer the scientist superior protection from hazardous emissions in the hood, the hori-

zontal sash hood has been specified, especially for larger hoods. In fact, the smallest commercially available hood size equipped with a horizontal sliding sash is six feet in length.

Sliding sash hoods generally come with four or five panes of sash in two tracks so that the panes can be horizontally slid into any position to form face opening(s) through which the scientist can comfortably work. Unlike the vertical sliding sash, the scientist can arrange the opening to permit his or her arms to extend behind the sash that shields the sensitive areas of the face. This affords excellent protection, while reducing the "cubic feet per minute" of exhaust air, often by as much as 60% of that required for a vertical sash. It also offers the potential for great energy savings provided that the conditioned air requirement to maintain thermal comfort does not exceed the needed air flow for fume hood exhaust.

In order to guarantee good air movement in the laboratory when the sash is closed, a permanent air foil opening under the sliding sash will permit about 95% of the rated air flow to be exhausted. This assures that the room air balance will not be destabilized during closed sash; it also is useful to exhaust chemical spills, etc., by simply closing the sash.

Auxiliary Air Fume Hoods

Due to the exorbitant rise in energy costs for heating and cooling room air used for thermal comfort, applications precluding the recirculation of room air (100% outside air), such as fume hood exhausts, demand that energy-conserving measures be taken where possible. One such attempt has been the development of the auxiliary air fume hood.

This hood uses exhaust air from two sources: the room supply air and an auxiliary supply air system which furnishes tempered outside air in winter and raw outside air in summer. The proportion of this auxiliary air mix may vary from 30 to 70% of the total amount exhausted through the hood.

This design would seem to save considerable thermal energy, particularly in the warmer months of the year. However, experience with these hoods has proven otherwise. A cautionary view of these hoods suggests the following:

1. Energy consumption is frequently about as high as with the horizontal sash hood, due to

the generally larger amounts of air needed to accomplish the same task. This requires more fan horsepower and more heating energy. Before using an auxiliary air hood, the designer should carefully determine the real air flow required to do the job and then make a thermal and electrical energy analysis for annual operation of the hood. This may approach or even exceed the energy requirements for a hood which exhausts only room air.

2. These hoods generally require that supplementary air be introduced across or in front of the opening. This has led to several undesirable effects: poor thermal environment for the scientist (both in temperature and humidity); condensation on cold surfaces; turbulent air motion in the hood face opening (almost invariably driving air out of the hood at one point or another). For these reasons, some agencies which handle very toxic or carcinogenic substances have prohibited the use of auxiliary air hoods.

3. The initial cost of the auxiliary air system generally makes these hoods higher in first cost. For this reason, the system designer should make a life cycle cost study before recommending their use.

Special Application Hoods

These hoods must be designed to handle very specific requirements, such as:

1. *Perchloric acid fume hoods.* These hoods are built to guard against potential explosion of the perchloric acid fumes by assuring that they cannot concentrate inside the hood.

2. *Radioisotope fume hoods.* Selection of these hoods is based on planned isotope utilization, which is usually in three radiation categories:

   - Low level, short half-life.
   - Moderate level.
   - High energy level.

   The "hot laboratory" hoods are usually highly specialized and require customized construction. They also require approval of the Nuclear Regulatory Commission.

3. *Biological safety cabinets.* These are special hoods for various degrees of safety performance in NIH containment room categories P-1, P-2, P-3, and P-4, as shown in Table 4.1

4. *Snorkels.* Where local exhaust is required on an open lab bench, "snorkels" are used. They are simply flexible ducts, generally made of metal which can be hooked into the laboratory exhaust system with a balancing damper; the terminus is then placed at the point where the exhaust is required. They operate on the principle of any local exhaust hood, that is, the capture velocity and distance from the terminus to the emission are both crucial to the success of the snorkel.

4.5.4 Exhaust Duct Materials and Construction

Historically, exhaust duct materials for fume hoods have been selected to withstand attack from corrosive chemicals and fumes. Invariably, this has led to a broad selection of possible candidates for exhaust duct construction, which generally fall into four broad categories:

1. Steel with coatings which can withstand specific types of chemical corrosion.
2. Stainless steel:
   - Type 304 for mild chemical attack.
   - Type 316 for more aggressive chemicals.
3. Reinforced plastics.
4. Uncoated metals where chemical attack is limited to very mild or no corrosivity:
   - Galvanized steel
   - Black steel
   - Aluminum

For many years, some of the favorite materials of construction involved materials or coatings made with asbestos. Recent rulings by Federal agencies that asbestos is a carcinogen have completely ruled out these materials as duct materials. Two such materials that were widely used into the 1970s were asphalt-asbestos coated steel and asbestos cement board; neither are now commercially available.

One of the most recently developed coated steel products is a patented vinyl bonded-to-metal material, known commercially as "PVS." The great advantage of this material is the ease with which it can

TABLE 4.1 Biological Safety Cabinets: Safety Performance Requirements and Specifications.

| Cabinet | Use Classification NCI[a] | | | | Performance Requirements | | | | | |
	Virus	Carcinogen	DNA[b]	CDC[c]	Face Velocity Lin. fpm	Exhaust Air CFM 4 ft. Hood	Exhaust Air CFM 6 ft. Hood	Leak Tightness	Exhaust Filter Efficiency (%)
Class I	Low–Moderate	No	P1–P3	1–3	75	200	300	Not applicable	99.97
Class II Type A	Low–Moderate	No	P1–P3	1–3	75	200	400	Gas tight; leak rate <1 by; 10^{-5} l/s at 2″ of water	99.97
Class II Type B	Low–High	Yes	P1–P3	1–3	100	250	360	Pressure tight; No air/soap bubble at 2″ of water	99.97
Class III	High	Yes	P4	4	d	d	d	Gas tight; leak rate <1 by 10^{-9} l/s at 3″ of water	99.97

[a] National Cancer Institute (U.S. Public Health Service).

[b] For work with recombinant DNA molecules.

[c] Center for Disease Control (U.S. Public Health Service).

[d] Not applicable.

be worked by standard sheet metal equipment, due to the flexibility of the vinyl coating. The coating is U/L Listed (Specification 181—Class I) and has therefore wide acceptance by the various regulatory agencies having jurisdiction. The corrosion resistance of the coating covers a wide range of chemicals; in addition, the steel is galvanized before being coated.

To determine what duct material is best suited for a given exhaust application, it is necessary to know which chemicals will be used, what their actual service conditions are (concentration, temperature, etc.), and the life safety concerns of the materials, particularly the qualification of the material to meet U/L Class I. Given several materials which can meet the above requirements, the selection is usually based on economics, including both material and fabricating costs.

To assist in the selection of suitable material for fume hood exhaust ductwork, information indicating the corrosion resistant qualities of each ductwork material is set out in the Sheet Metal and Air-Conditioning Contractors National Association, Inc. (SMACNA) *Manual for Industrial Ventilation*, and in the ASHRAE Guides.

Round ductwork offers enormous advantages over ductwork with a rectangular cross section when subjected to external pressure (as is the case with fume hood exhaust systems).

1. The round duct is structurally the ideal shape for resisting external pressure and hence can be made with thinner gauges of metal and less reinforcement.
2. It is highly resistant to "drumming" or "panting," and is thus much quieter than rectangular shapes.
3. Its fittings are commercially available in any number of configurations for good aerodynamics.
4. Its ease of construction makes it simple for the sheetmetal installer to handle.

If the duct construction is galvanized sheet steel or plastic coated steel, flat oval ductwork can be used in lieu of round in those cases where height clearance for round ductwork would be a problem. Flat oval configuration is also very strong in resisting external pressures.

Rectangular construction is usually more difficult and expensive to fabricate. In fact, only re-

cently has there been a recognized standard of any sort for this ductwork, SMACNA's *Industrial Duct Construction Standards*. Class I of these standards is suitable for fume hood exhaust.

It is essential that the designer specify the external static pressure which the duct walls must withstand. This is true for both round and rectangular ductwork. For each static pressure grouping in the SMACNA standards, there is a minimum gauge of sheet metal required, as well as other features, such as reinforcement.

In terms of duct construction, a word of caution about the application of fire dampers. NFPA Standard 90A mandates fire dampers or fire doors to arrest the spread of fire through rated walls or floors. NFPA Standard 45, on the other hand, deals with hazardous chemicals and recommends against the use of fire dampers for "local exhaust." Moreover, Standard 45 makes it clear that chemical fumes are a greater hazard than fire, and therefore mandates that in event of fire, all dampers in the fume hood exhaust must go to an open position. For this reason, the designer would be well advised to check with the local authorities having jurisdiction before equipping a fume hood exhaust duct with fire dampers or doors.

4.5.5 Fans for Fume Hood Exhaust Systems

The selection of a fume hood exhaust fan should take into account the following parameters:

Corrosion Resistance of the Fan Materials

For material selection for fume hood exhaust fans, the same considerations that apply to ductwork also apply to the interior areas of the fan which are exposed to the fumes. Generally, however, stainless steel fans are expensive and do not provide much greater protection than fans with several epoxy coatings, each baked on to the fan housing and wheel. To be sure of the correct number and thickness of these coatings, the designer can specify color-coded layers. This coating technique, commonly called by the trade name of *Heresite*, is an extremely reliable method of corrosion-resistant coating, with an excellent record of performance.

Where corrosion conditions are particularly severe, the fan construction should be FRP (fiberglass reinforced plastic). These fans, however, may be as much as double the cost of coated metal fans, especially in the larger sizes.

If the danger of explosion exists due to the nature of the fumes being handled, it is mandatory to construct the all-metal fan according to the following AMCA spark-resistant standards:

- *Type A Construction:* All parts of the fan in contact with the air or gas being exhausted shall be made of nonferrous material. This should completely preclude any sparks if the moving wheel touches the fan housing, due to any shaft or bearing failure or to any other mechanical failure of the fan.
- *Type B Construction:* The fan shall have an entirely nonferrous wheel and nonferrous ring about the opening through which the shaft passes. This construction covers the vast majority of potential explosions due to volatile fumes.
- *Type C Construction:* The fan shall be so constructed that a shift of the wheel or shaft will not permit two ferrous parts of the fan to rub or to strike. At the very least, this minimal construction should always be specified for the all-metal fume hood exhaust fan.

Type of Fan

Fume hood exhaust fans should be of industrial quality, except for light-duty applications such as fume hoods used for teaching (not research) purposes. If the fan is properly maintained, this will generally guarantee protection against shaft and bearing problems.

Where one or two light-duty fume hoods are handled, roof-top, upblast fans are excellent. American fan manufacturers offer these fans in a plastic construction which guarantees longevity as well as good performance.

When more hazardous or toxic fumes are involved, it is essential to use a centrifugal fan of industrial quality in order to meet the higher static pressure requirements which usually derive from the high exhaust upblast velocities required at the roof for good fume dispersal. Most authorities require that these velocities be between 3000 to 4000 fpm. In addition, static pressure is often increased due to the requirement of scrubbers.

If the fan has a constant volume requirement,

its drive may be either a direct or vee-belt drive. However, the recent advent of volumetric control, or static pressure control, requires that fans be equipped with variable-speed drives or other techniques to change fan speed or characteristics. While variable inlet vanes are a generally accepted method for commerical systems, they are not recommended for fume hood fans due to poor efficiency and the need to actuate the vanes through an external damper motor. For this reason, variable-speed drives are the best solution to meet this requirement.

These variable-speed drives include several viable types, some of which are excellent but expensive. Currently, the following drives enjoy favor:

- Standard A.C. motors with variable frequency drive.
- Variable pitch belt drives.
- Direct current motors coupled to an M-G set.

A word of caution about variable-speed drives is necessary: Do not select a fan without checking its surge characteristics. Some fans will surge badly at low flow rates, even at modest static pressure requirements.

Finally, the type of centrifugal fan selected for fume hood exhaust should be carefully checked for efficiency and stability in the proposed operating range. "Paddle-wheel" industrial fans, for example, are almost never required for fume hood exhaust systems and should therefore not be used due to their inefficiency.

4.5.6 Exhaust System Design

Fume hood exhaust system design is well documented in various texts, handbooks, and standards, hence no real need exists to repeat their contents in this book. A few design hints are, however, in order:

1. Maintain, if possible, a duct velocity of 2000 fpm for fume hood exhaust systems.
2. Pay particular attention to good aerodynamics and avoid unnecessary turbulence in this design. When more than one fume hood is ganged onto a duct system, its branch duct should enter the main trunk duct at an angle to assure good confluence of the two air streams.

3. Provide adequate cleanout doors in the exhaust duct.

4. If at all possible, do not use remote balancing dampers in a fume hood exhaust duct. Dampering should be achieved in or at the hood and by duct sizing.

5. The discharge duct from the exhaust fan should be upblast, through the roof (preferably, a minimum of 4 to 6 feet above the roof), with a terminal velocity of 3000 to 4000 fpm. This duct should be as short as possible from the fan to the roof, and should be well constructed. The fan should be equipped with a drain in the bottom so that rain water can be drained through a small copper tube to the nearest floor drain.

6. The supply air system outlet to the laboratory should not be located close to the front of the fume hood. This is important to prevent an accidental blowout of the hood fumes into the room.

7. Do not locate the hood next to a door which is frequently used or next to a pedestrian traffic corridor, to preclude unnecessary turbulence in front of the hood. However, hoods should not be located where a scientist might be trapped in case of an explosion.

8. It may be necessary to raise the total exhaust air flow through the fume hood when final fume hood performance tests are made in the field, because one or more of the grid points test too low. For this reason, both the exhaust duct size and fan capacity should have some spare capacity for this additional flow requirement. Experience suggests that this safety factor need not exceed 15% of the design flow of the system. In any event, the air balancing specifications must clearly spell out the methodology to be used by the air balancer when the hood performance tests are made, including checkout of the hood baffles.

A recent paper by Caplan and Knutson* clearly demonstrates the acute need for an ASHRAE standard that would take into account room buildup of contaminants, and require a time duration testing element (say two hours). This paper concludes that, at best, the scientist is only safe when the hood is per-

*K. J. Caplan and G. W. Knutson, "The Effect of Room Air Change on the Efficiency of Laboratory Fume Hoods," ASHRAE *Transactions* (1977), Part I.

forming "very well" under steady-state conditions. Unfortunately, these ideal conditions may obtain only for limited periods of time. The practical conclusion is simply that hood performance tests may, in the future, require the expertise of an industrial hygienist, rather than an air balancer, to assure the safety of the user where hazardous contaminants are involved.

4.5.7 Volumetric Control Systems for Fume Hoods

In any laboratory facility the major energy consumer is the thermal energy needed to cool or temper outside air for makeup to fume hood exhaust systems. To reduce this significant waste of energy, two basic strategies have emerged: heat recovery of the thermal energy in the exhaust air, and volumetric control of the laboratory's fume hood exhaust air flow, leading to reduction in the room supply. Volumetric control is associated with fume hoods because it is directly related to fume hood operation.

Usually, the fume hood air exhaust requirement to maintain thermal comfort is greater than the supply air requirement. Since recirculation of fume hood exhaust is prohibited by codes, the supply air to the laboratory must essentially equal that exhausted, the difference being a small quantity of infiltration air to keep the laboratory room at negative pressure in relation to the adjacent areas. This room air balance invariably results in overcooling of the space or reheating the supply air to maintain thermal comfort.

Further, most fume hoods are essentially constant volume devices, whether the sash is open or closed. This derives from the fact that vertical sliding sash hoods are usually built with a full air flow bypass feature, while horizontal sash hoods take in about 95% of the rated air flow through the airfoil opening under the sash when the sash is closed. This is clearly wasteful of energy, since the protection for the scientist requires only a small air flow into the fume hood when the sash is closed, sometimes for several hours at a time.

The principal objective of a volumetric control system is to reduce the hood exhaust air flow drastically when the sash is closed. Several such systems are now commercially available (some however, are proprietary). Most of the major vendors of automatic temperature controls have developed these systems and will customize them for particular laboratory facilities.

A secondary reason for the volumetric control system for laboratories is to maintain a defined pressure relationship between the laboratory and its adjacent spaces; usually, the laboratory is held negative relative to its surrounding areas to preclude chemical fumes from penetrating into pedestrian corridors, etc.

To achieve these objectives, the state-of-the art for these volumetric systems has developed into two distinct methodologies, volumetric controls and space pressurization controls. Both yield substantial energy savings and good fume control for laboratories. (See Fig. 4.1 for a description of the evolution of fume hood control systems.)

Volumetric Controls

Generally, volumetric controls are based on a "tracking" system in which the supply air lags the fume hood exhaust air by a given cfm. When the sash of the hood is in the operating (open) position, the exhaust air is maintained at a preset volume to produce a safe velocity across the face of the hood sash opening. Supply air "tracks" the exhaust air to insure the negative pressure relationship desired for the laboratory.

When the sash is closed, the exhaust air is reduced to the minimum possible to maintain space thermal conditions and to assure good fume dilution inside the laboratory. The supply air accordingly tracks the exhaust air to generate the desired pressure relationship indicated above.

During unoccupied hours, the sash of each hood is kept closed to reduce fan and thermal energy. This all results in substantial annual energy savings.

Space Pressurization Controls

Largely as a result of the secondary aim of volumetric control, a new mode of tracking operation was developed by Honeywell, Inc. This uses a through-the-wall pressure sensor, called a "Velocitrol," which will induce through exhaust-supply air tracking, permitting just enough air infiltration into the laboratory to maintain it at the given negative pressure, generally 0.03" to 0.05" water gauge.

Furthermore, this system can maintain hood face velocity at any given flow rate by use of a "Velocitrol" sensor in the front face of the hood above

the sash. This assures that the minimum energy will always be used for fume hoods regardless of sash opening.

Honeywell has generated a whole series of volumetric control systems (based on the patented "Velocitrol"), all of which conserve energy for the laboratory air system and guarantee good pressure relationships with adjacent spaces.

4.6 SANITARY AND FIRE PROTECTION SYSTEMS

Sanitary and Storm Drainage Systems

Laboratories like all buildings, require complete sanitary and storm water drainage systems. Additional types of sanitary systems that may be required include garbage disposal, normal kitchen wastes, and sterilizers requiring vapor vents.

As a matter of economy, or where there are limitations on the storm water flow allowed to public sewer systems, controlled-flow roof drains should be considered, if they are permitted by local codes.

Materials for these systems include cast iron, galvanized steel, copper, and polyvinyl chloride (PVC), and are governed by local codes.

Laboratory Waste Water and Vent Systems

Wastes from all fixtures and equipment where acids are or may be used must be neutralized prior to discharge to the sanitary drainage system.

A comprehensive report on each laboratory function should be developed to determine the types of chemicals to be wasted. Waste piping can then be selected as the most appropriate to handle these chemicals.

Piping materials for these systems include high silicone iron, borosilicate glass, and plastics, including polypropelene, polyethylene, and PVC.

High silicone iron and borosilicate glass are the perferred materials for acid systems. Careful consideration must be given to expansion and contraction, supports, and to the temperature of the waste, if plastic piping systems are selected as an alternative.

Neutralization must be accomplished by chemical reaction. Wastes are normally discharged to sumps filled with limestone chips which raise the PH level of the waste to make it suitable for discharge into the sanitary sewer.

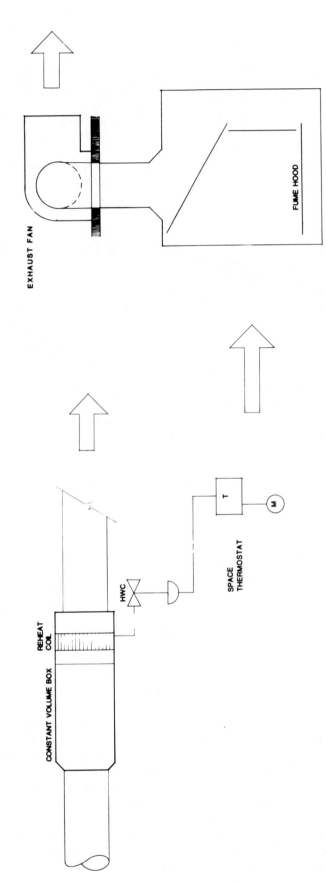

Figure 4.1 Fume hood control systems. (a) 1973—prior to the energy shortage.

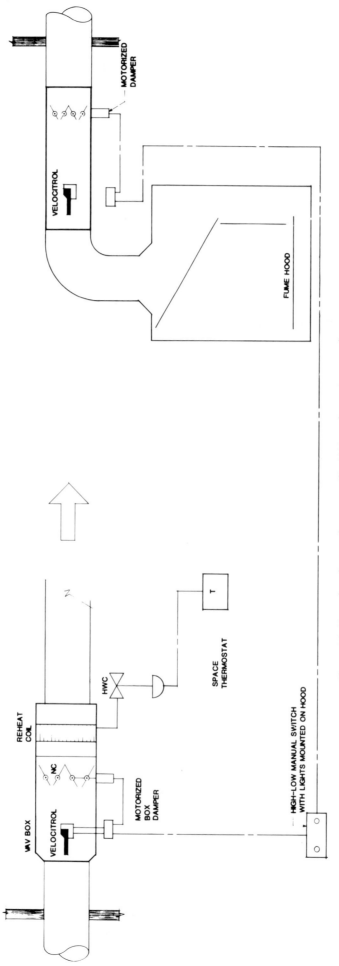

Figure 4.1 Fume hood control systems. (*b*) 1980—volumetric control system.

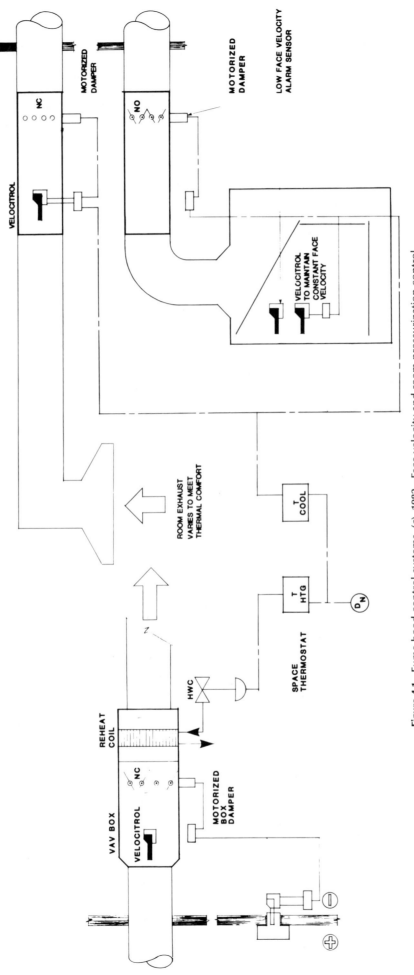

Figure 4.1 Fume hood control systems. (c) 1982—Face velocity and room pressurization control.

Central acid neutralizing sumps should be provided for areas containing numerous sinks, and these must be accessibly located for recharging. Individual acid neutralizing sumps must be provided for isolated sinks and individual neutralizing sumps must replace the fixture trap.

In the case of extremely large laboratories and industrial facilities, careful consideration should be given to discharge of acids into a treatment tank using injected sodium hydroxide (NaOH) solution as the neutralizing agent. This system requires control equipment, feeder pumps, alarms, etc.

Radioactive Waste Water and Drainage Vent Systems

Waste water drainage from fixtures or equipment which may be radioactive must be run separately from all other drainage systems.

The treatment and/or disposal of radioactive wastes will be based on the degree of radiation and quantities involved. Approval of the design of the system and disposal of its effluent should be approved by the owner and local authorities. The collection of the radioactive waste to holding tanks is one method of handling these wastes.

Horizontal drainage piping carrying radioactive waste must not be run on or in ceilings of occupied rooms, kitchens, food preparation or food serving areas, unless adequate lead shielding is provided in the ceiling construction.

Piping materials for radioactive wastes should be black steel, galvanized steel, or copper with welded or brazed joints.

Highly Infectious Waste Drainage and Vent Systems

Waste water drainage from fixtures and equipment which might have a highly infectious content must be run separately from all other drainage systems and be decontaminated before disposal into the sanitary drainage system.

Treatment and/or disposal of highly infectious wastes, based on the degree of contamination and the quantities involved, can only be determined after consultation with the owner and approval by the local authorities. Generally, high-temperature heating followed by cooling is required for the effluent, and electric incineration of the vapors in the vent terminal for the vent system. Depending on

the degree of contamination, wastes can be decontaminated by sanitizing (heating to 200°F) or sterilizing (heating to 280°F).

Stainless steel piping should be used for highly infectious wastes.

Water

Systems usually encountered in a laboratory are as follows:

1. Potable water consisting of cold water, hot water of various temperatures, and controlled temperature water.
2. Nonpotable water consisting of cold water and hot water.

Water conservation should be part of the standard design practice.

Excessive water pressure fluctuations are undesirable in research facilities. When such laboratories are supplied from a street pressure system where fluctuations occur, provide pressure reducers on branch lines or provide a gravity tank system for any potentially affected areas.

Extreme care must be taken to protect the potable water supply from contamination. Vacuum breakers should be provided for every below-rim connection hose and outlet. Vacuum breakers for fume hood outlets should be located outside the hood. Backflow preventors should be provided for all connections to equipment.

A separate nonpotable water system should be used for areas where water requirements may contaminate the potable water supply; such a system is preferable even when local requirements permit the use of backflow preventors on vacuum breakers. Areas served by such a system include animal drinking water systems, flushing rim floor drains in animal rooms, and all outlets in infectious disease and tissue culture research rooms.

Water for this system is provided through a break tank. Hot water when required is provided by a separate generator supplied from the nonpotable water system.

Piping material for water systems should be as follows:

- Underground: 3 inches and smaller: Type "K" copper tubing; 4 inches and larger: ductile iron cement lined.

- Interior Piping: 5 inches and larger: galvanized steel pipe; 4 inches and smaller: Type "L" copper tubing.

Pure Water Systems

Pure water systems consist of distilled water, deionized water, or demineralized water.

There are two basic types of pure water: *bio-pure* water, which is free from particular matter, minerals, bacteria, pyrogens, organic matter, and most dissolved gases; and *high purity* water, which is free from minerals, dissolved gases, and most particular matter.

The four basic methods of producing pure water are distillation, demineralization, reverse osmosis, and filtration. Depending on the type of pure water required, one or more of these methods will be needed, and under certain conditions a combination of several.

It is very important to take a raw water analysis before selecting equipment to produce pure water.

Piping methods for a pure water system can be PVC, polypropylene, stainless tubing, aluminum pipe, block tin-lined copper tubing, and block tin-lined brass pipe. The owner should be consulted regarding the selection of piping material for the pure water system.

Compressed Air Systems

There are two types of compressed air system: the laboratory system and the general building system. Each must be completely separate.

The laboratory system must provide absolutely oil-free dry air to laboratory outlets and laboratory equipment. The pumps should be of the rotary liquid ring type. Compressor receivers, filters, constant pressure valve, and piping must be completely packaged as integrated systems on a common base for a single point field installation. Liquid ring pumps must be provided with 100% recirculation systems. The system should deliver relatively dry, clean, oil-free air at a minimum of 55 psi. Lower pressure requirements should be met by the provision of pressure reducing valves. Non-lubricated, oil-less piston-type compressors are acceptable for laboratory air systems, but are not recommended. If used, this type of compressor must be located at the lowest level due to its excessive vibration.

General building systems include compressed air for HVAC pneumatic controls and for pneumatically operated doors. Although not commonly used, it is recommended that these systems be provided with liquid ring compressors. In common use are non-lubricated, oil-less, piston-type compressors for HVAC pneumatic controls, and an oil-lubricated, piston-type compressor for pneumatically operated doors—either air-cooled or water-cooled depending on size. After-coolers are generally required to cool the air, especially for oil-cooled pumps.

Coalescent oil filters must be provided in an accessible location for all types of non-lubricated compressors as a precautionary measure to trap any oil that might seep into the piping system.

Air Dryers

Refrigerated air dryers giving a pressure dew point of 35°F are normally used. With higher air pressure, a lower dew point can be achieved.

When a lower dew point is required, dessicant air dryers are necessary. The "Twin Tower" method should be used so that as one dryer becomes saturated with moisture, an automatic switch-over to the other dryer occurs. A dew point as low as −40°F can be achieved.

Piping materials for a compressed air system should be Type "L" copper tubing. For general building systems, small piping may be galvanized steel or black steel, except for HVAC pneumatic controls, where copper tubing should be used.

Vacuum Systems

The central vacuum air plant should be located below the areas served, and vacuums provided to all laboratory outlets at 15″ Hg. High vacuum can be provided to all outlets at 26″ Hg. Consult the owner about pressure needs.

The vacuum pumps may be of the rotary or liquid ring type. Vacuum pumps with controls, receivers, piping valves, etc., should be a completely integrated package system on a common base for single point field installation. Liquid ring pumps should be provided with a 100% water recirculation system, and the vacuum pump discharge should be run up through the roof, remote from compressed air and all other intakes.

Piping materials for a vacuum system should be

Type "L" copper tubing. For larger piping systems, use galvanized steel pipe with threaded or welded fittings.

Plugged cleanout connections must be strategically located throughout the system, preferably at all points where piping changes direction, to allow a means for removing stoppages.

Gases

Gases in a laboratory are used for a wide variety of applications. They can be categorized as carrier gases, treatment gases, chemical reaction processing gases, combustion gases, and equipment operating gases.

Gases most frequently used in laboratories are argon, acetylene, butylene, carbon dioxide, hydrogen, helium, oxygen, nitrogen, propylene, hydrogen sulfide, propane, and natural gas. The sources of the various gases can be broken down as follows:

1. Liquified gas.
2. Compressed gas.
3. Public utility.

Gas installation is governed by local and national codes and fire department criteria.

Proper regulation of these gases is essential. With the exception of combustion gases, all other types of gases can fluctuate from approximately 50 psi to 1000 psi operating pressures.

Before selecting piping material for these various gases, consult the owner and obtain a set of all available standards governing these systems.

Selected flammable gas piping running within the building must be encased within another pipe, which should be vented to the atmosphere.

Fire Protection

Fire protection must be provided in accordance with local codes; N.F.P.A. Life Safety Code 101; fire department regulations; and fire insurance underwriters.

The fire insurance underwriters will dictate the type of coverage, whether light, ordinary, or extra hazard, required for the building. Laboratory buildings must be protected by a combined fully automatic wet pipe sprinkler system and complete fire standpipe system for fire department use only. The system should be hydraulically designed. (In certain localities, combined systems are not permitted for laboratory buildings.)

Certain rooms require special types of fire suppression systems, as follows:

1. *Cold rooms, cold labs, and freezers.* Dry pipe sprinkler system. It is recommended that the sprinkler piping heads for these rooms be fabricated as part of the rooms, with a single point of connection for the contractor at the exterior of the room. Dry pendant-type sprinkler heads attached to the wet pipe system should be considered.

2. *Computer rooms.* Halon system below the raised floor and a preaction sprinkler system above the raised floor.

3. *Loading dock areas.* Dry pipe sprinkler system or antifreeze solution system.

4. *Fume hoods.* Sprinkler protection. A connection to the automatic wet pipe system must be provided. The head for the hood should be part of its basic fabrication.

Fire extinguishers must be provided throughout in accordance with N.F.P.A. requirements.

Piping materials for a sprinkler system should be as follows:

- Underground piping: ductile iron cement-lined pipe with mechanical joints and 250 psi mechanical joint fittings. Pipe and fittings must be cement lined. All joints and fittings should be restrained.

- Aboveground piping: scheduled 40 black steel pipe with threaded malleable iron fittings, cast iron flanged fittings, or mechanical cut or roll-groove couplings. Lightwall steel pipe and fittings with roll-groove couplings can be considered to reduce costs.

5

LABORATORY LIGHTING

Newton F. Watson, RIBA
Edward Rowlands, MIEE, FCIBS
David L. Loe, MCIBS

Illuminance, sometimes called illumination, (luminous flux per unit area) will be expressed in the derived SI unit lux (lx), which is a special name for the lumen per square meter (lm/m^2). The lux (lx) and kilolux (klx) replace the footcandle, which is also known as the lumen per square foot.

Similarly, the SI unit of luminance, the candela per square meter (cd/m^2), replaces the candela per square foot, the lambert, and the footlambert. Conversion factors are:

$$1 \text{ lx} = 0.092 \text{ footcandle}$$
$$1 \text{ footcandle} = 10.7639 \text{ lx}$$
$$1 \text{ klx} = 92.903 \text{ footcandles}$$
$$1 \text{cd/m}^2 = 0.092\ 903 \text{ cd/ft}^2$$
$$= 0.291\ 964 \text{ footlambert}$$
$$1 \text{ cd/ft}^2 = 10.7639 \text{ cd/m}^2$$
$$1 \text{ footlambert} = 3.426\ 259 \text{ cd/m}^2$$

5.1 LIGHTING THE TASK AND THE SPACE*

The correct lighting of a laboratory demands a careful analysis of the use of the space, which is best accomplished by identifying the types of task, their relative difficulty and complexity, whether they are to be carried out for long or short periods of time, whether errors would have serious consequences, and whether the tasks involve a degree of color discrimination. Other questions may arise depending on the type of laboratory under design, particularly in relation to possible future changes of use and work patterns and the scale of the work undertaken.

In general, the more visually demanding a task, the higher the illuminance required to perform it with comfort and efficiency. However, research has shown that even for the most demanding tasks a level of illuminance in excess of 1000 lux is rarely required. However, for elderly people and others with deteriorating eyesight, a higher level of illuminance than the recommended standard is usually necessary.

For guidance on the illuminance and type of

*The SI units for luminous intensity (the light-emitting power of a source), the candela (cd),and for luminous flux, the lumen (lm), are already in general use in the United States.

lighting for particular tasks, the national or appropriate international standards of codes of practice should be consulted—for example, those published by the Illuminating Engineering Society (IES) of North America [5-1], the Chartered Institution of Building Services (CIBS) of Great Britain [5-2], and the Commission Internationale de l'Éclairage (CIE) [5-3]. In general, the various codes give recommendations for illuminance relative to a grade of task of a particular visual difficulty (see Table 5.1). Recommendations may be given in the form of a range, or as an absolute level with modifying increments. These recommendations are the result of many research programs. The codes of practice will usually give recommendations for limiting discomfort glare. If these recommendations are followed, they will ensure that the lighting scheme does not provide a pattern of luminance uncomfortable for the task in hand. Since the recommendations are differently formulated from country to country, it is important to ensure that the appropriate ones are followed in every individual case.

The working illuminance can be provided over the whole of the working plane or just in the immediate work area, depending on whether the exact work area is known when the lighting is being planned. It is expected that for most types of task done in a laboratory, a minimum task illuminance of 500 lux will be appropriate, but it may be necessary to provide higher levels for particularly demanding tasks. While the task illuminance can be provided in a number of ways, it will probably be

TABLE 5.1 Recommended Illuminance for Different Grades of Visual Task

Grade of Visual Task	Recommended Illuminance
	(lux)
High Contrast Large Detail (Rough Work)	200–300–500
Medium Contrast Medium Detail (Routine Work)	300–500–750
Low Contrast Small Detail (Demanding Work)	500–750–1000
Very Low Contrast Fine Detail (Fine Work)	750–1000–1500

best achieved by providing a general level of illuminance across the working plane of between 300 and 500 lux, supplementing this with local lighting as required. However, the luminance of the task area should not be considerably higher than the general adaptation level or visual discomfort may result.

In addition to lighting the task, lighting of the space itself should be considered. To give this the appearance of being well lit, there should be a reasonable level of light on the vertical surfaces, and the CIBS Interior Lighting Code [5-2] recommends an illuminance of between 0.5–0.8 of the task illuminance.

The artificial light source to be used should have a solar rendering and color appearance appropriate to the task. If a lamp of good color is required, one of the lamps with a CIE color rendering index (Ra) of at least 85 should be used [5-3]. However, if the laboratory is attached to a hospital or other establishment where the correct identification of color is important, special lamps may be necessary. Further, if artificial lighting is to be used to supplement natural light, this should also be considered when choosing the light source. Usually, this will mean using a light source with a correlated color temperature of at least 4000°K. But, because the color of daylight is always changing, whatever lamp is chosen will be something of a compromise.

If there is to be a useful amount of daylight, then it will be necessary to ascertain the level and distribution of natural light by calculating the values of daylight factor. If an overcast sky is the most likely sky condition for the locality of the laboratory, it is usual to use the CIE standard overcast sky distribution [5-4]. The daylight factors can then be converted to typical illuminance levels for different times of the day and year by consulting the predicted unobstructed sky illuminance for the particular locality [5-1, 5-5], and it may also be necessary to consider the orientation of the window. If it is not appropriate to consider an overcast sky as the typical natural lighting condition, then the sky condition for the locality should be used: normally this will be some form of clear sky, probably with direct sunlight.

It may be that the tasks of a particular laboratory will have other special considerations, such as optical aids—for example, magnifiers or microscopes—though today these often include built-in lighting equipment. The task may also create some

form of hazard that will require the use of special "proof" type luminaires, and in this case expert guidance should be obtained.

5.2 NATURAL LIGHTING

The provision of natural light in a space from conventional vertical glazing will provide the users with a view out and contact with the outside, with its changing light conditions—frequently a long-distance view which will provide relaxation of the ocular muscles. It can also provide sufficient lighting to yield considerable saving in electrical energy and, because of its directional nature, good modelling of three-dimensional objects. Because of high thermal transmittance, windows will be a source of heat loss in winter and possible heat gain in summer, but these losses and gains should be studied carefully, because it may be that the cost of the heat energy lost is less than that of light energy gained. Thermal transmittance can be improved by using double glazing and some of the solar control glasses, though these latter may be counter-productive, since in improving the thermal conditions there may be a reduction in light transmission, and thus in the amount of useful natural light.

The size and shape of a window for an acceptable view out has been the subject of much research, and though the results have varied it would seem that a window area of between 20 and 30% of the external wall is generally considered to be the most acceptable. Whether the window should be horizontal or vertical depends on many considerations outside the control of the lighting designer, and therefore no positive advice can be given here: however, low window heads which obstruct the view can be annoying, The size, and to some extent the shape of the window will also determine the level and distribution of natural light within the space, as will the reflection values of the internal surfaces and the transmission factors of the glazing material and the degree of obstruction of objects outside the window.

The illuminance from natural light is continually changing, due to the position of the sun (its altitude and azimuth angles) and to the degree of diffusion within the sky owing to the degree and depth of cloud cover. Because of this, it is impossible to design natural lighting on a simple basis of illuminance, as is the case for artificial lighting, and a unit of "Daylight Factor" is required.

The daylight factor (DF) is the ratio of the illuminance on a surface in a room to the illuminance on a horizontal plane from a totally unobstructed overcast sky at the same point in time. The daylight factor is used in temperate regions of the earth where overcast skies are the most likely condition, as in Northern Europe and North America. For convenience of calculation the luminance distribution has been standardized by the CIE [5-4], and it is on this basis that the daylight factor is normally calculated. Direct sunlight is excluded from the calculation, and any light from the sun is considered to be a bonus.

The daylight factor at a point within a room will depend on three components of illuminance relating to the total illuminance from an unobstructed overcast sky (Fig. 5.1). They are:

1. Sky Component (SC): that is, the light falling on the point directly from an area of unobstructed sky.
2. Externally Reflected Component (ERC): that is, the light falling on a point having been reflected from an external obstruction (e.g., buildings, trees, etc.).
3. Internally Reflected Component (IRC): that is, the light that enters the space and arrives at the point after reflection from one or more of the internal surfaces.

$$DF = SC + ERC + IRC$$

The daylight factor can be calculated in a number of ways using tables, protractors, and other calculation aids [5-4, 5-6] but nowadays it can most easily be calculated using a computer or programmable calculator [5-7].

The daylight factor can be converted to an illuminance value by multiplying the DF by the estimated unobstructed illuminance for a particular locality and time of year. The orientation of the window will also affect the level of illuminance (windows facing towards the equator will provide higher levels of light than those facing towards the poles [5-8]).

It will be useful, if possible, to calculate the proportion of the working year that a particular unobstructed illuminance is likely to occur. This will enable the designer to predict the minimum natural lighting conditions, and thus how much artificial light will be required to create a particular lighting condition within the design. Table 5.2 shows the conditions for London. These are based on measurements made over a 10-year period [5-5].

The distribution and levels of daylight within the space will depend on the window size relative to the depth of the space from the window and the distribution of windows along the window wall together with the degree of external obstruction. Fig. 5.2 indicates the distribution and levels of daylight factor and their corresponding illuminance values based on an unobstructed sky illuminance of 5000 lux for a regular array of windows of a particular size relative to the depth. For example, it can be seen that with a window head height of 2 m ($6\frac{1}{2}$ ft) above the sill at a distance of approximately 6 m (20 ft) from the window, the level of natural light is very low and artificial light will be necessary to provide adequate illuminance for most tasks.

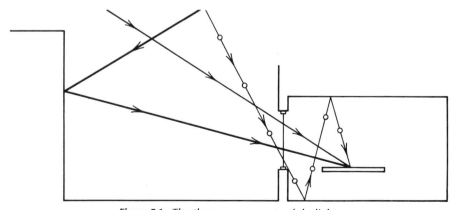

Figure 5.1 The three components of daylight.

TABLE 5.2 Percentage of Working Year (09.00 – 17.30) When Illuminance Values for Particular Daylight Factors Will Occur [a]

Unobstructed Diffuse Illuminance (lux)	Percentage of Year Illuminance Level Exceeded	Daylight Factors and Their Respective Illuminance Values (lux)			
		2%	5%	10%	20%
5,000	84	100	250	500	1,000
10,000	73	200	500	1,000	2,000
15,000	55	300	750	1,500	3,000
20,000	42	400	1,000	2,000	4,000

[a] These values are based on measurements made in London (Kew) [5-5]. For other localities, modifications may be necessary.

Though the daylight factor at a given point is a useful measure to calculate the likely working illuminance at that point, it does not give much indication of the general brightness within the whole space, and another useful measure is the "average daylight factor"; that is, the arithmetic mean of the daylight factors across the horizontal working plane. This gives some indication of the general lightness or darkness of the space. For example, a space with an average DF of 5% will appear generally light, while a space with an average DF of 2% will appear dull and rather dim.

The methods of calculating average DF vary, depending on the source of the equation; they enable a designer to determine the approximate amount of glazing that will be necessary to achieve a particular average daylight factor [5-9].

The natural light design should also take account of discomfort glare from the sky. This in general will depend on the luminance of the sky seen through the window in contrast with the luminance of the interior space [5-10]. The discomfort glare can be reduced by controlling the sky luminance with the provision of diffusing or venetian blinds to be used when there is a problem, by increasing the reflectance of the room surfaces to increase the luminance of the interior, and by orientating the work stations so that the occupants are not usually facing the windows.

In addition to designing the level of natural light and its distribution, it may be necessary to predict the amount of direct sunlight entering the space and therefore whether some form of sun control device is necessary. A computer can be used to calculate the sun position relative to the window and the degree of penetration, or sunpath diagrams can be used [5-6, 5-11].

In single-story buildings and the top floors of multistory buildings, use can be made of skylights. Similar considerations to the above will apply,

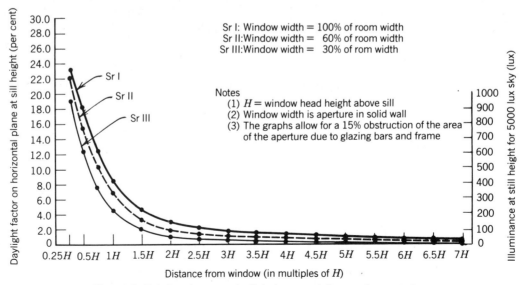

Sr I: Window width = 100% of room width
Sr II: Window width = 60% of room width
Sr III: Window width = 30% of rom width

Notes
(1) H = window head height above sill
(2) Window width is aperture in solid wall
(3) The graphs allow for a 15% obstruction of the area of the aperture due to glazing bars and frame

Figure 5.2 Relations between daylight factor and distance from window.

though generally a more uniform illuminance can be provided. However, heat gain will often be a problem in the summer months unless sun control is provided. When sun control devices are necessary, it is preferable for these to be installed outside the building, to prevent the heat energy from actually entering the building and creating the greenhouse effect.

As has been shown, the natural light conditions can be determined by calculation, but the range of numbers achieved will rarely indicate the visual effect of the lighting. An accurately-constructed model of the space using surfaces of the correct reflectance and studied in an artificial sky will show the effect that is likely to be achieved, and has the added advantage that measurements can also be made [5-6].

The model can also be used with a heliodon (Sun Model) to study the sunlight penetration and also any sun control devices required to limit the sun penetration for thermal and discomfort glare problems [5-6].

5.3   ARTIFICIAL LIGHTING

As discussed earlier, in a laboratory situation the main criterion to be used in the lighting design is the recommended illuminance for the satisfactory performance of the task. This is usually provided by general lighting for a large work area or by task lighting for local areas, with building lighting which can serve as a supplement.

5.3.1   General Lighting

For the design of lighting to provide a relatively uniform illuminance on a horizontal working plane throughout an interior by a regular array of overhead luminaires, the "lumen method" is most commonly used [5-1, 5-2]. Computer-based calculations similar to the lumen method can provide accurate simultaneous calculations of point and average illuminance. This determines the total lamp luminous flux required to provide the specified illuminance over the working area by the application of the utilization factor of the luminaire. This is dependent on the proportions of the interior, the reflectances of its surfaces, and the flux distribution and light output ratio of the luminaires.

The utilization factor can usually be obtained from manufacturers' data or reference books [5-1,

5-2], or by calculation from basic data [5-12, 5-13]. It is common practice to incorporate a maintenance factor to allow for typical soiling of the installation in use. The luminaire layout can be determined by considering the specified maximum spacing/mounting height ratio for the luminaire distribution to obtain an acceptable illuminance uniformity. But manufacturers' recommendations must be carefully reviewed, as they do not always provide the best design layout.

In addition to utilization factors for the illuminance on a horizontal working plane, similar CIE and CIBS factors are published [5-12, 5-13] for wall and ceiling surfaces. These enable the illuminance on these surfaces to be calculated and compared with the recommendations, based on research and experience, to achieve a satisfactory overall visual environment. The IES and CIE guides [5-2, 5-3] state that compared with the horizontal illuminance, the wall illuminance should be between 0.5 and 0.8, and the ceiling illuminance between 0.3 and 0.9. In addition, the recommendations state that the wall average reflectance should preferably lie between 0.3 and 0.8 and the ceiling reflectance should be as high as possible—above 0.6.

5.3.2   Task and Building Lighting

Task lighting is used where it is necessary to provide high illuminance on a restricted area, and also where directional lighting is an advantage to reveal form and texture and to overcome veiling reflections. This form of lighting is usually provided by a luminaire placed at a small distance from the task. The illuminance at a point can be calculated from a knowledge of the intensity distribution of the source using the inverse square and cosine laws if the source dimensions are less that 1/5 of the distance from the point. For larger sources or shorter distances, other methods are applicable [5-1, 5-2]: for linear sources a method using aspect factors based on the angular coordinates of the source is suitable. Frequently, manufacturers publish illuminance charts and tables for luminaires, often as isolux diagrams for various planes.

The building lighting usually takes the form of the general lighting described above. For an acceptable visual appearance, it is recommended that the illuminance of the building lighting should not be less than 1/3 of the task illuminance.

This form of lighting is very useful and satisfactory in a laboratory situation.

5.3.3 Discomfort Glare

The avoidance of discomfort glare in a lighting installation is one of the prime features in the design process. Discomfort glare occurs when there are areas of high luminance in the field of view compared with the adaptation luminance level of the eyes. Its effect is largely determined by the luminance, size, and number of glare sources, their locations in the field of view, and the background luminance (which affects eye adaptation). Generally speaking, direct discomfort glare increases with the luminance, size, and number of luminaires in a lighting installation, with their closeness to the line of sight, and with a decrease in the background luminance. Various systems have been developed for evaluating direct discomfort glare; the three most common are as follows:

1. *VCP Method* [5-1, 5-3]. The Visual Comfort Probability method gives ratings in terms of the percentage of people who will consider a given lighting system to be acceptable from the aspect of visual comfort. Direct glare will not be a problem if the VCP is 70 or higher and if certain luminaire luminances are not exceeded.

2. *Glare Index System* [5-3,5-14]. This is based on a formula which incorporates all the above main parameters to provide a measure of the discomfort glare in terms of a glare index. This is compared with a recommended limiting glare index for the particular type of interior or occupation under study.

3. *Luminaire Luminance Limiting System* [5-3]. Here the luminaire luminance is compared with limiting luminance distributions which are specified for different quality classes. This type of system is not usually as comprehensive in its scope as the other two.

It should be noted that in addition to the reduction of discomfort glare by the control of the luminaire parameters (luminance and size), improvement can often be achieved by an alteration in the visual environment, particularly by the increase of room surface reflectances.

5.3.4 Contrast Rendering Factor

As mentioned earlier, bright veiling reflections in the task must be avoided because not only do they produce discomfort but they reduce the task con-

trast and therefore its visibility. They can thus nullify any improvement in visual performance achieved by an increase in the illuminance level. This matter is particularly important with tasks which have specular (glossy) parts. It has been proposed that the effect be evaluated by means of a Contrast Rendering Factor (CRF) [5-1, 5-2]—a relative measure of the ability of the lighting to produce high contrast. In order to obtain a high CRF, probably the most important consideration is the relative positions of the light source, task, and viewer to avoid specular reflection—see Fig. 5.3. The task lighting must therefore be positioned carefully and in some situations the selection of a suitable luminaire light distribution, possibly with the use of polarizing diffusers, can be beneficial. In this context, it should be noted that tasks in laboratory spaces are often in planes other than horizontal (e.g., the screens of instruments incorporating visual displays [5-15]—see Fig. 5.4). The best relationship between light and task in this situation is indicated in Fig. 5.5).

5.3.5 Selection of Lamps

The selection of the type of lamp to be used in a given situation is influenced by a number of pa-

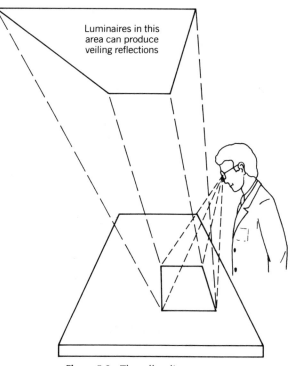

Figure 5.3 The offending zone.

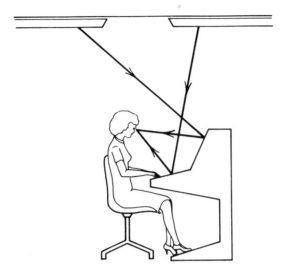

Figure 5.4 Veiling reflections on vertical and horizontal surfaces.

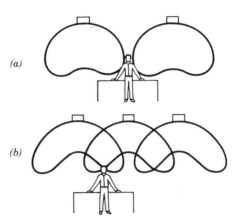

Figure 5.6 Luminous intensity distributions: (*a*), ''batwing''; (*b*) ''trouser-leg.''

rameters. The most important of these are:

- Efficacy (i.e., the ratio of the light output to the total power consumed).
- Life (in hours).
- Color appearance and color rendering.

5.3.6   Selection of Luminaires

One of the most important properties of a luminaire is its light output ratio. This can be considered in a limited way as a measure of its efficiency—it is the ratio of the total light output of a luminaire to that of the lamp or lamps with which it is

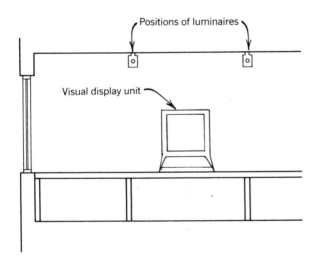

Figure 5.5 Best positions for viewing VDUs minimizing reflections from artificial lights and windows.

equipped. However, the highest light output ratio does not necessarily result in the best lighting environment. The type of light distribution produced by control methods, such as reflection, refraction, diffusion, and louvers, also needs careful selection (e.g., proportion up/down and broad/narrow). It is necessary to consider its suitability to produce the desired high utilization factor, low discomfort glare, and illuminance values on vertical surfaces mentioned earlier in this section. Two intensity distributions which can be particularly useful are illustrated in Fig. 5.6. These are commonly known as ''bat-wing'' and ''trouser-leg'' distributions. The spacing/mounting height ratios at which they can be used are higher than those applicable to the more conventional distributions.

Many general lighting installations use a form of specialized ceiling system in which there is integration with the structure of the ceiling and with the other services. Laboratories, on the other hand, often have no ceilings. Experience with the use of overall luminous ceilings has been disappointing from the visual aspect, but there are recent interesting developments in uplighting techniques—using high pressure discharge lamps above a cut-off height of about 1800 mm (about 5 ft 11 ins) to light the ceiling, and thus the remainder of the interior by indirect means.

5.4   INTEGRATED LIGHTING

As has been emphasized earlier, as well as providing the light pattern and illuminance levels required for the particular uses of the laboratory, the lighting system should form an integrated part of the overall design of the space and not appear as an appendage added toward the end of the building process. To achieve this design unity the lighting design should be considered early in the design program.

How this integration will be achieved will depend very much on the building techniques and the overall design concept. Laboratories often require a high degree of cleanliness, in which case exposed fittings could raise the question of maintenance—how to keep the item clean. A suspended ceiling can be used to conceal the electrical wiring and duct work. The suspended ceiling can be flat or coffered, giving an interesting sculptured effect. Coffers, in addition to housing luminaires, will themselves provide some light control features and, incidentally, depending on the materials used, will contribute to the acoustic characteristics of the space. Coffers can also be formed within the structure itself where a cast concrete ''waffle'' system is used.

In addition to the physical integration of structure and lighting, the elements of the lighting system itself should be integrated: that is, the natural and artificial lighting should be designed as one scheme, with the elements supplementing one another as required.

5.4.1 Switching and Control

In the past it has often been the practice for all the artificial lighting within a work space to be switched on first thing in the morning and left on until the end of the working day whether it was actually required or not. With careful planning of the lighting circuits and the incorporation of conveniently placed switches, supplemented with time switches and light-sensing switches, considerable savings of energy can be made. Some work [5-16, 5-17] has suggested that savings of up to 40% of the energy used in lighting can be made by incorporating efficient forms of automatic control. Normally these control systems will restrict the use of the lighting equipment to those areas where there is insufficient natural light, but with some form of individual manual override if required. The individual control can be achieved by pull-switches, or by infrared and ultrasonic activated switches. There are also occupancy detective devices to switch off equipment when a space is empty, and even full microprocessor control.

One important criterion of automatic control systems is that the system should not be so sensitive that the lights switch on and off with such frequency as to distract the staff. But since one of the pleasing aspects of natural light is its changing quality, the automatic system should not be such that this element of change is eliminated.

A further consideration is whether the use of the space is likely to change during the life of the installation and, if it is, whether the change be such that the lighting system will need radical alternatives. If this is thought likely, then it may be appropriate to design the integrated system to provide general lighting only, with the main task lighting being portable or integrated into the laboratory furniture. It should be borne in mind, however, that designing a multipurpose space rarely provides ideal conditions for any one of its uses.

5.5 SURFACE REFLECTANCE AND COLOR

The reflectance and color of the various surfaces and objects within a space will have considerable effect on the quality of the visual environment. Initially it may be useful to consider them separately, though inevitably they will affect one another.

Surface reflectance will largely affect the degree of lightness or darkness of the space and to some extent will affect the subjective size (e.g., a light-painted space will generally appear more spacious than a dark-painted space of the same size). It will also have a bearing on the effectiveness of the lighting, since the utilization factor of the scheme is much affected by the reflectance of the major surfaces, as is the internally reflected component of the natural light. The choice of colors will also affect the subjective assessment of the thermal quality of the space: for example, a space colored with predominately warm colors will generally seem warmer than a space colored with predominately cool colors, a fact which could be used to moderate ambient temperature conditions.

The choice of reflectance for laboratory work spaces should generally be on the high side to make the most use of interreflected light. For this type of space, the CIBS [5.2] recommends that the ceiling reflectance should be not less than 0.6. Generally speaking, the higher the reflectance of the ceiling, the lower the level of discomfort glare: there is a reduction in contrast between the luminance of the ceiling and the luminance of the light fittings. The wall surfaces should also be relatively light, which will help to maximize the interreflected light and will also help to reduce the contrast between the luminance of the view through the window and the window surround. The reflectance can, however, be too high, particularly if "brilliant" white paint is used and there is a high level of vertical illuminance, because the wall itself can become glaring: the CIBS [5-2] recommends a reflectance of between 0.3 and 0.8. The floor reflectance should be as high as is practical, though it is unlikely that the overall reflectance of the floor cavity will exceed 0.3.

The process of designing a color scheme is often a daunting task, mainly because there are no firm rules or formulas on which to base the decision. Since a laboratory is likely to be used for long periods of time and the aim will be to make it as visually comfortable as possible, it will be important not to use a highly colored design which may become overpowering and visually tiring, though initially stimulating. This does not mean that dominant (high chroma) colors should not be used in small areas, where they will considerably improve the visual quality of an interior; but they must be thought of as part of the overall design. High chroma colors can also be used to draw attention to a particular area (e.g., a fire assembly point, some form of hazard, or a reception desk). The eye is inevitably drawn to bright, colorful areas.

In choosing the combination of colors to be used, one of the simplest and often most successful ways is to choose colors of the same basic hue (Munsell Hue) and vary the lightness and saturation (Munsell Value and Chroma); this will provide a scheme where the colors go naturally together. An alternative is to use colors of the same hue as before but to add a small amount of a complementary color from the opposite side of the hue circle. This method of choosing colors is described by Gloag [5.18].

The choice of colors should be made using samples of the proposed materials, placing them together to see how they appear as a whole scheme, remembering that adjacent colors will affect the appearance of one another. The samples should also be studied under the light source and the illuminance to be used to see that no problems will arise due to the color rendering effect of the light source, and to make sure that the level of light is sufficient to create the effect required. Care should

also be taken to ensure that the color scheme does not create any visual distortion in the laboratory tasks (e.g., by reflecting light of a dominant color onto the task from a surface of a strong hue), perhaps causing errors of visual judgment.

In choosing a color scheme, it is important that not only the main surfaces of the space should be considered, but also the furniture and equipment used in the space, so that a coordinated visual effect is achieved.

The specification of colors must be very accurately expressed to ensure that the exact colors chosen are actually used. Wherever possible, the particular national color specification system should be used (e.g., that of the national standards institution), or, alternatively, the Munsell system [5.18].

5.6 ANCILLARY SPACES

In addition to the main laboratory spaces, the building will almost certainly contain other types of work space (e.g., offices, libraries, workshops). Though these spaces will perhaps house different tasks from those carried on in the laboratories, the technique of planning the lighting will be the same, but with variations for the different tasks. For example, in a library the lighting of vertical surfaces will need to be planned with bookstacks in mind, whereas in private offices it may be appropriate to provide a working illuminance on the desk, with the remainder of the room lit by wall-washing luminaires, uplights, or some form of cornice lighting. The main building will probably have a reception/entrance area where visitors will be received and gain their first impressions. This will need to be eye-catching in order to present the appropriate image of the organization, as well as providing comfortable conditions for the receptionist. In this type of situation, areas of light and shade will be important, as will the choice of colors and textures.

Restaurants, cafeterias, and rest rooms should be considered separately, since they require an atmosphere different from that of work spaces. In general, the levels of light will be important, but it will be the pattern of light that will create effect.

Throughout the building there should be enough variety in the lighting of the different types of space to help generate a feeling of well-being among the users. Light and color are important ingredients in creating pleasant, efficient spaces.

Finally, consideration should be given to lighting the exterior of the building and its immediate surroundings (e.g., service roads, pedestrian walkways, car parks), and also to the possible floodlighting of the building or the provision of illuminated signs.

It is impossible to consider all situations here, and it is suggested that other publications be consulted [5-1, 5-2] or, probably more important, that a qualified lighting consultant be appointed for this part of the building design.

5.7 EMERGENCY AND SECURITY LIGHTING

As part of the lighting scheme, or as an addition to it, it will be necessary to provide sufficient light for the occupants to evacuate the building in the case of a fire or other emergency. This is required by code, which usually indicates specific locations. The equipment providing the lighting on these occasions will need to be divorced from the normal electrical supply, since in the case of an emergency it is likely that the latter will be inoperative. The luminaires should be placed to illuminate the designated escape route, especially where the route changes direction. The actual lighting conditions will probably be specified in the local fire codes, which should be consulted. Following experiments, present recommendations in the UK specify a minimum illuminance along the center of the escape route at floor level of not less than 0.2 lux, and a diversity of illuminance not exceeding 40:1 [5-19]. This is very much a minimum condition, and if possible a higher level should be provided. It is possible that illuminated "Exit" signs could be designed to contribute to the lighting of the escape route as well as indicating door positions.

Since emergency lighting luminaires need to be able to operate independently of the main electrical supply, they are normally specially designed for that purpose and run from some form of battery supply or emergency generator. The battery supply can either be within the luminaire, referred to as "contained," or from a central battery unit supply. Luminaires will usually be one of two types: maintained or nonmaintained. Maintained luminaires normally operate from the electrical mains supply, but in the case of an emergency they are switched automatically to a battery supply of one of the two types mentioned. Nonmaintained luminaires are separate fittings which automatically come into operation only when there is a mains supply failure, and they are normally battery-operated. Whichever system is used, it is important that the equipment be regularly maintained, and it should be of the fail/safe type.

It should be stressed again that local regulations concerning fire and other emergencies must be consulted and complied with; if none exist, the CIE Publication No. 49 [5-20] will give some guidance.

In addition to the emergency lighting, it may be necessary to have a separate system of lighting for security purposes. This will often make use of some of the luminaires used for the normal lighting scheme, but supplied from a separate security lighting circuit. This will mean that only the light necessary for the security staff to make its patrol is provided, and thus minimum energy is used (unless of course TV monitors are involved). In the case of closed circuit television security surveillance systems, the manufacturer of the equipment should be consulted.

5.8 DESIGN DATA GUIDANCE FOR RESEARCH LABORATORIES (GENERAL)

Artificial Lighting

Illuminance		
Task	500 lux	750–1000 lux if work is very demanding with small detail and low contrast
Building	200 lux	300–400 lux if higher task illuminance used
Discomfort Glare		
Visual Comfort Probability (VCP)	70	with some luminaire luminance restriction

Artificial Lighting (*Continued*)

or

Limiting Glare Index	19	16 if work is very demanding
Lamps		
Color Appearance	Cool, intermediate, or warm	Intermediate for supplement to daylight where also used for night lighting
Color Rendering	$R_a \geqslant 70$	(CIE Color Rendering Index). Type of laboratory may dictate color rendering requirements and higher Ra

Natural Lighting

Daylight Factor		
Average	5%	2% for supplemented daylighting
Minimum	2%	
Discomfort Glare		
Limiting Daylight Glare Index (Windows)	22	20 if work is very demanding

REFERENCES

1. *IES Lighting Handbook*, Illuminating Engineering Society of North America, 1981.

2. *IES Code for Interior Lighting*, Illuminating Engineering Society, London (now Lighting Division, CIBS—Chartered Institution of Building Services), 1977.

3. *Guide on Interior Lighting*, Publication CIE No. 29, Commission Internationale de l'Éclairage, 1975.

4. *Daylight: International Recommendations for the Calculation of Natural Daylight*, Publication CIE No. 16, Commission Internationale de l'Éclairage, 1970.

5. D. R. G. Hunt, *Availability of Daylight*, Building Research Establishment, 1979.

6. R. G. Hopkinson, P. Petherbridge, and J. Longmore, *Daylighting*, Heinemann, 1966.

7. H. J. Bryan and R. D. Clear, "Calculating Interior Daylight Illumination with a Programmable Hand Calculator," *Journal of the IES* **10**, 4 (1981), 219–227.

8. D. R. G. Hunt, "The Use of Artificial Lighting in Relation to Daylight Levels and Occupancy," *Building and Environment* **14**, 1 (1979), 21–33.

9. Draft for Development—*Basic Data for the Design of Buildings: Daylight*, DD73, 1982, British Standards Institution, London.

10. *Daytime Lighting in Buildings*, IES Technical Report No. 4, 1972. *Control of Discomfort Sky Glare from Windows*, Supplement to IES Technical Report No. 4, 1977. Illuminating Engineering Society, London (now Lighting Division, CIBS—Chartered Institution of Building Services).

11. P. Petherbridge, "Sunpath Diagrams and Overlays for Solar Heat Gain Calculations," *Building Research Current Paper*, Research Series 39, Building Research Station, 1965.

12. *Calculations for Interior Lighting—Basic Method*, Publication CIE No. 40, Commission Internationale de l'Éclairage, 1978.

13. "The Calculation and Use of Utilization Factors," *Technical Memorandum No. 5*, Chartered Institution of Building Services, London, 1980.

14. *Evaluation of Discomfort Glare: the IES Glare Index System for Artificial Lighting Installations*, IES Technical Report No. 10, Illuminating Engineering Society, London (now Lighting Division, CIBS—Chartered Institution of Building Services), 1967.

15. "Lighting for Visual Display Units," *Technical Memorandum No. 6*, Chartered Institution of Building Services, London, 1981.

16. D. R. G. Hunt, "Simple Expressions for Predicting Energy Savings from Photo-Electric Control of Lighting," *Lighting Research and Technology* **9**, 2 (1977), 93–102.

17. V. H. C. Crisp, "The Light Switch in Buildings," *Lighting Research and Technology* **10**, 2 (1978), 69–82.

18. H. L. Gloag, and M. J. Gold, "Color Coordination Handbook," *BRE Report*, Building Research Establishment, 1978.

19. *Code of Practice for the Emergency Lighting of Premises other than Cinemas*, BS 5266, Part 1, 1975, British Standards Institution, London.

20. *The Emergency Lighting of Building Interiors*, Publication CIE No. 49, Commission Internationale de l'Éclairage, 1981.

6

DESIGN IN PRACTICE

SIX LABORATORIES

Susan Braybrooke

ARCO CHEMICAL COMPANY RESEARCH AND ENGINEERING CENTER, NEWTOWN SQUARE, PENNSYLVANIA

ARCHITECTS: Davis, Brody & Associates
                      Llewelyn-Davies Associates
                      Art and Design Consultant:
                      Herbert Bayer

The challenge of placing a very large high-tech laboratory building in a parklike setting (formerly the grounds of a girls' school) was met by a horizontal, glass-walled solution that hovers among clumps of fine trees. The profile of the 1100-ft-long blue-green solar-tinted glass curtain wall is softened by rounded grey-tinted canopies or sun visors of extruded plastic. (Fig. 6.1) These absorb and reradiate over a million BTU's per hour and reduce the solar load by an amount equal to 100 tons of refrigeration.

Consolidating key research, development, and engineering functions, The Meadows "campus" brings together for the first time some 800 chemists, engineers, and other personnel previously scattered in several locations.

The building is divided into east and west laboratory wings flanking a central element containing lobby, dining room, library, and storage. There is a smaller office building in front of the west wing, and there are several backyard structures for pilot manufacturing and large-scale testing.

The beauty of the site influenced the configu-

Figure 6.1   ARCO Research and Engineering Center exterior showing perimeter circulation and sunshades. (Robert Gray photo)

ration of the plan, which places major circulation along the outside walls to give everyone the benefit of attractive views as they travel to and from their daily tasks (see Fig. 6.1). Skylit atria were introduced between the major groups of laboratories with colored tile pavements designed by former Bauhaus teacher and artist Herbert Bayer.

The long walls of the laboratories which abut the atria have transparent acrylic glazing from a height of 5 ft to the underside of the ceiling, thereby giving outside awareness to all lab occupants. Offices for research professionals and senior technicians, immediately adjacent to the laboratories, are enclosed by 5-ft-high acoustical panels, allowing them to share as well in the ambience of the atria. With their brightly colored floors—echoing Pennsylvania Dutch motifs—plants, trees and benches, these indoor courtyards create a sense of place and community and establish an atmosphere for quiet contemplation (Fig. 6.2). Bold primary colors applied to laboratory furniture engender an added feeling of optimism and human warmth.

Standard fume hood dimensions were the basis of the 10-ft module employed throughout the lab areas. Within this module, three different laboratory configurations were developed to accommodate the varying needs of chemical and polymer researchers. The chemical staff (in the west wing) preferred labs without doors to minimize spills and breakages as they moved from room to room. Their laboratories are thus large, open spaces, some separated by storage into 500 sq ft modules, others, on the upper level, completely open (Fig. 6.3 and 6.4). Since polymer experiments carry some risk of explosion, each lab in the east wing is a self-contained unit with closing door and its own separate preparation room. The prep room, which contains oven, sink, and storage, is essentially for messy work, and leaves the lab itself relatively clean and uncluttered. In both wings, labs are grouped around service corridors, which supply then with air, nitrogen, hot and cold water, steam, and gaseous hydrocarbons (Fig. 6.5). Hazardous waste is collected from these corridors by a disposal firm.

Some labs have highly specialized analytical instrumentation or large walk-in fume hoods. All laboratories are at slightly negative air pressure compared to the rest of the building to make sure that no fumes or exhausts can drift into the hallways or offices. Since 80% of the heating and cooling load of the building is expended conditioning air that is ultimately exhausted through the hoods, energy conservation is achieved by limiting the size of the hood openings. Consequently, hood-sash openings are configured so that only one-third of the opening actually passes air when the hood is in operation. When the hood is not in operation, the variable volume air supply system reduces the flow of air and further conserves energy.

Behind the laboratories at the back of each wing are the applications areas where promising ideas are actually put to the test (Fig. 6.6). Also in back are machine and electrical shops and the boiler plant which feeds steam and compressed air to the entire facility. The high-pressure laboratory at the rear of the west wing includes 22 containment cells—small enclosed rooms with 14-inch-thick reinforced concrete walls, where chemical reactions are carefully studied. In the rare possibility of an explosion, these cells can contain blowouts equivalent to one-quarter-pound of TNT. Two larger cells, with 18-inch walls, interlaced with extra heavy-gauge steel reinforcing rods are capable of containing blowouts equal to ten pounds of TNT.

The pilot plant located behind the east wing can produce as much as 300 gallons of material in one continuous production process. A high-bay applications area which includes commercial size extruders, film rollers, blow molders, and other equipment enables ARCO researchers to explore the efficiency of various manufacturing processes and show potential customers how their particular polymer material will handle on an industrial scale.

The entire center is fully sprinklered. Safety showers are located within each laboratory, and eyewash stations, fire blankets, emergency air packs, and fire extinguishers are provided throughout.

Detailed plans and sections are given in Figs. 6.7, 6.8, and 6.9.

Figure 6.2 ARCO Research and Engineering Center interior courtyard. (Robert Gray photo)

Figure 6.3 Typical open lab in the chemical (west) wing. (Robert Gray photo)

Figure 6.4 Another typical open lab in the chemical (west) wing. (Robert Gray photo)

Figure 6.5 Service corridor. (Robert Gray photo)

Figure 6.6 "Backyard" structures for large-scale testing and pilot plant. (Robert Gray photo)

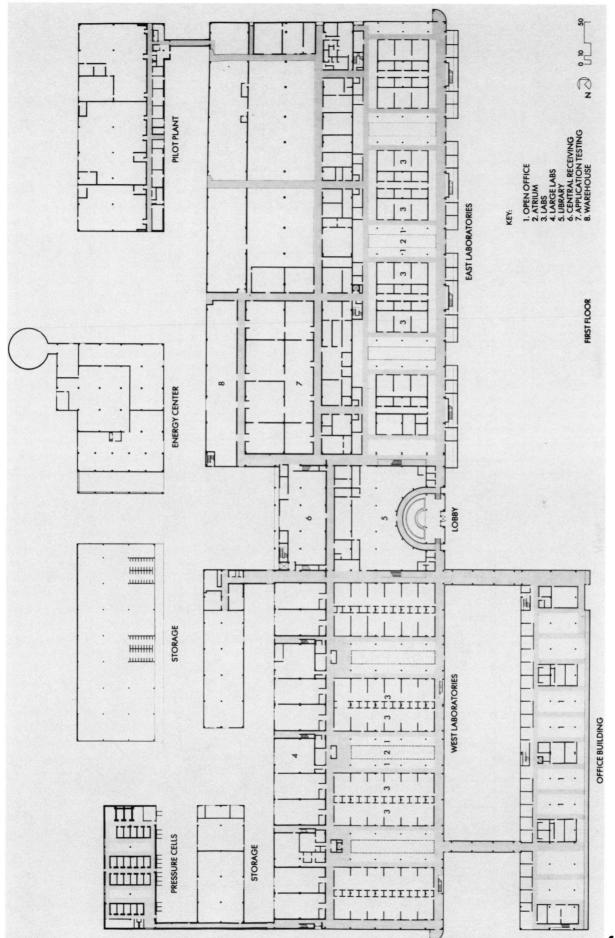

KEY:
1. OPEN OFFICE
2. ATRIUM
3. LABS
4. LARGE LABS
5. LIBRARY
6. CENTRAL RECEIVING
7. APPLICATION TESTING
8. WAREHOUSE

FIRST FLOOR

PILOT PLANT

ENERGY CENTER

STORAGE

PRESSURE CELLS

STORAGE

EAST LABORATORIES

WEST LABORATORIES

OFFICE BUILDING

LOBBY

N

0 10   50

Figure 6.7 First floor plan.

111

112

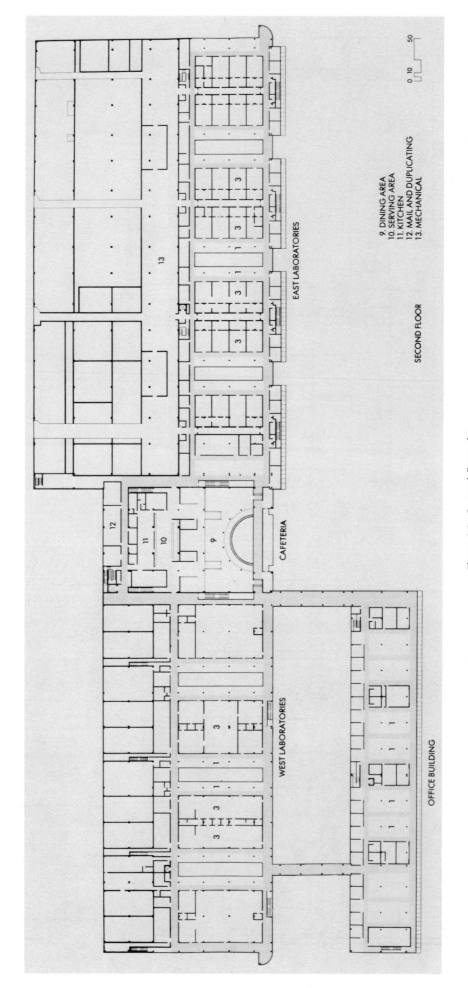

9. DINING AREA
10. SERVING AREA
11. KITCHEN
12. MAIL AND DUPLICATING
13. MECHANICAL

EAST LABORATORIES

SECOND FLOOR

CAFETERIA

WEST LABORATORIES

OFFICE BUILDING

Figure 6.8 Second floor plan.

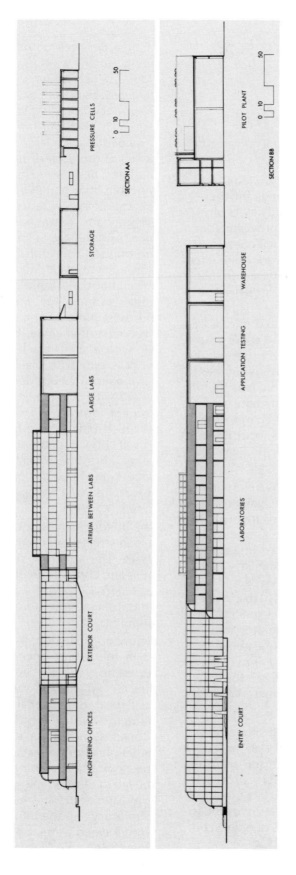

Figure 6.9 Sections AA, BB.

113

THE ROWLAND INSTITUTE FOR SCIENCE, CAMBRIDGE, MASSACHUSETTS

ARCHITECTS: The Stubbins Associates

The Rowland Institute for Science (Fig. 6.10 and 6.11) is dedicated to pure research of all kinds and therefore required great flexibility, not only in its physical space and equipment, but in provisions for special present and future services. Scientists from a variety of disciplines, invited to work there, are encouraged to have much closer interaction than is common in typical university or industrial situations.

The initial program was formulated jointly by the owner and the architect through a series of intimate discussions extending over a period of twelve months. The owner wanted an environment "to free the mind and spirit," and the labs themselves were to be "places in which anything can be done." Merle Westlake, principal-in-charge of the project for The Stubbins Associates, contributed the following "lab notes":

- The size of laboratory spaces was determined through familiarity with room sizes gained from past experience. It was agreed early in the planning stages that there would be a mixture of large "organic" laboratories (approximately 30′ × 30′) and smaller (15′ × 30′) chemistry laboratories. The larger rooms then could be equipped as physics labs, biology labs, a laser lab, or any other laboratory for a specific scientific endeavor. Two suites of laboratory rooms are provided on separate floors, one above the other. Centrally located on each floor is a supply room for equipment storage, solvents, glassware, and other necessary materials (Fig. 6.12).

- Vertical chases along the internal side of each laboratory contain main risers for all mechanical and electrical services. Office and artifacts rooms are located along the exterior wall of each lab. Initial staffing of the larger lab provides space for four persons and includes two offices plus an artifacts room for storage of objects on open shelves.

- Staffing may be increased 50% without physical

change. Services for the laboratories are racked along the side walls for easy access behind sectional bench units which are easily interchanged, removed, or adjusted in height. One laboratory, for example has become a laser lab. (Fig. 6.13) Two four-foot-wide fume hoods are provided in each large lab. All services are exposed at the underside of the ceiling slab, including a perimeter electric buss duct tray. Removable floor panels at the center of the large laboratories provide access to all services to accommodate central benches or special equipment as required. Suspended acoustic ceilings are omitted to avoid dust collection. In addition, electrostatic air cleaning is provided throughout the building. Laboratory lighting consists of four-foot fluorescent fixtures using Durotest lamps and no diffusers. Walls and ceiling are painted white. The floor is a white vinyl tile with a small black fleck. Laboratory case work is gray with black trim. (Fig. 6.14) Desks have natural wood tops and chairs are upholstered with bright-colored fabrics. Laboratory counter tops are charcoal-gray "colorceram". All finish materials were subjected to tests prior to selection to determine effects of super solvents, abrasion, impact damage, and appearance. Fume hood design was also meticulously researched (see Notes 1 and 2 supplied by Dr. James D. Foley).

- The building site is bounded on three sides by urban streets and on the fourth side by a tidal basin. The concrete structure is founded on piles and contains no basement areas. Since direct current was present within the subsoil strata, magnetic protection was required for the building.

- Before construction, tests were made to determine the extent of potential vibration transferred from the adjacent streets to the building site, and an analysis was made of the proposed structural and mechanical systems to determine the optimal locations for electron microscopes. Care was taken to locate the hydrogenation laboratory at an exterior corner of the top floor and to reinforce the interior walls of the lab in order to minimize damage should an explosion occur. The nuclear magnetic research laboratory and the infrared and ultraviolet lab were located at the opposite end of the floor from the chemical laboratories as additional insurance against any possible chemical vapors.

Figure 6.10 Rowland Institute for Science. (Edward Jacoby photo)

Figure 6.11 Another exterior view of Rowland Institute for Science. (Edward Jacoby photo)

- In order to encourage interdisciplinary communication, a large central landscaped, sky-lighted atrium is provided where the scientists may meet, stroll, or sit. All laboratories open directly upon the atrium. Laboratory offices are entered from within the lab and are located along the exterior wall. Communication between laboratories may be either directly through the secondary exit doors or via the atrium doors.

- Each chemical lab contains two eight-foot-wide fume hoods and adjacent mechanically exhausted storage cabinets centrally located back to back. This arrangement assures maximum protection to the companion researcher in the event of an explosion in one of the hoods. Since there is an exit at each end of the lab, no one is trapped.

- Laboratory dark rooms in some cases are also interconnected in order to extend or increase their usefulness. Entry vestibules to the dark rooms provide not only a light lock, but space for lightproof storage.

- The building contains a greenhouse, or botany laboratory, especially equipped with panels of pyrex glass which permit transmision of 100 percent of the ultraviolet light.

- To encourage interaction between the artist and the scientist, a painting studio with adjacent sculpture court is provided at the roof level of the building.

- The central, skylighted atrium, 40 feet wide by 140 feet long, was carefully designed to be a peaceful internal garden where one may meditate or communicate or repair from the technical environment of the laboratory. Plant materials were selected to suggest those of the New England woods, with ground cover to simulate the rolling hills and meadows. Moss is used extensively and moss-covered granite stones imported from the woods in Maine (Fig. 6.15).

- In addition to the laboratory facilities, special ancillary provisions were made for study or research.

- The archive/museum provides space for display of important artifacts or historical models.

- The interdisciplinary library provides reference materials of over 2000 curent world journals plus private reading areas and other areas to encourage discussions.

- The 40-seat conference/auditorium is equipped with front and rear projection facilities, capable of being controlled totally by one person from one point on the platform.

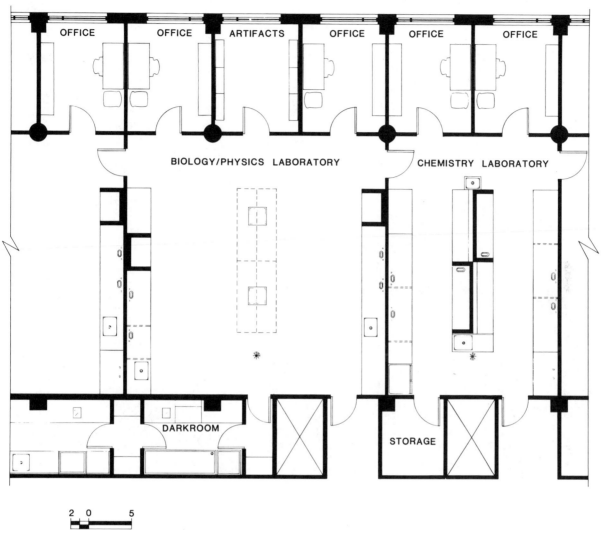

Figure 6.12 Plan of typical labs and ancillary spaces.

Note 1.   Floor Covering Resistance to Solvents*

Before deciding to use vinyl or epoxy flooring in the laboratories at The Rowland Institute for Science, we compared their relative resistance to commonly used organic solvents. Although literature was available describing the resistance of these materials to acids, bases, oils, etc., information pertaining to solvent resistance was not satisfactory for our purposes. We were concerned with solvent penetration of flooring for two reasons. The first, and most important, was that any

*Notes 1 and 2 Supplied by Dr. James D. Foley.

solvent (and chemicals dissolved in it) absorbed by the flooring material would slowly be released into the laboratory atmosphere as the flooring "dried." This low-level contamination by solvents and chemicals could constitute a health hazard over a long time period. A second concern was the fact that permanent stains result when flooring is penetrated by solvents containing dyes or other colored substances.

For the above reasons the following experiment was carried out. A water soluble dye, Malachite Green, was dissolved in a number of commonly used organic solvents. A twenty-microliter sample (about one drop) of each solution was placed on a flooring sample. After about five minutes the flooring was washed with a stream of warm water.

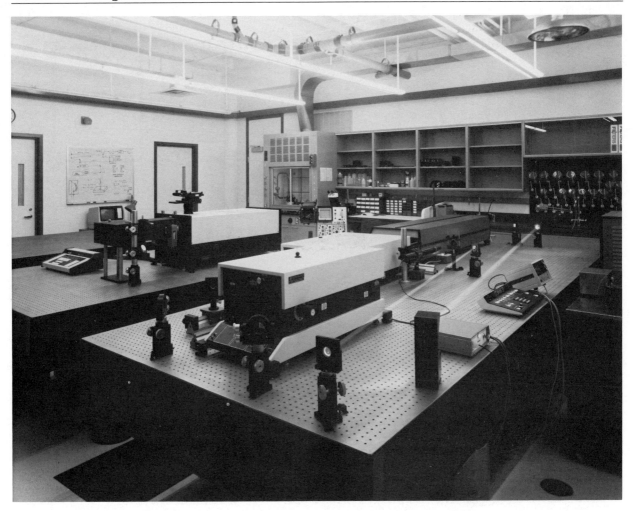

Figure 6.13 Laser lab. (Edward Jacoby photo)

It is noted that we were able to show that if the dye-solvent solution did not penetrate the flooring, the stream of water completely removed all of the dye from the surface of the sample. After towel-drying the samples, the relative degree of staining by each dye-solvent combination was *visually* observed and recorded. The samples were then washed with a sponge containing water and detergent. In general, this had at best a minimal effect of reducing the stains. We then scrubbed the stained areas with an abrasive cleaner. Although this procedure did substantially remove the stains, it also resulted in a scratched, dull surface.

As noted above, our original work was done with two samples, vinyl and epoxy. We recently repeated our work, using additional flooring materials supplied by The Stubbins Associates. The results of this study are recorded in Table 6.1. The detergent wash again did not reduce the stains sig-

nificantly except in the case of the water-malachite green spot observed on the polyacrylate sample, which was completely removed by this procedure.

Since our original study showed that both samples were penetrated by dye-solvent solutions, the final selection of our flooring material was based on other considerations, such as crack resistance and ease of repair and replacement. If one of the samples had been totally resistant to penetration by most solvents, it is my guess that we would have selected that material for the laboratory flooring.

Note 2.   Comments on Fume Hood Design*

Before deciding on the final fume hood design for The Rowland Institute for Science, I asked ten chemists to describe an "ideal" hood. They were

Figure 6.14 Typical lab, showing lighting and equipment and outlook to atrium. (Edward Jacoby photo)

Figure 6.15 Landscaped atrium. (Edward Jacoby photo)

instructed not to be constrained by financial or spatial consideration. The following comments represent the majority's view of what features are desirable and undesirable in fume hoods:

1. *Air Supply/Exhaust.* Each hood should have a separate exhaust fan which makes its use independent of all other hoods. The exhaust fan should be operated by an electrical switch located on or near the hood. The switch should have *OFF*, *LOW SPEED*, and *HIGH SPEED* (Normal) settings. It is also desirable to be able to control the required supplemental air supply with a switch on each hood.

2. *Size.*
   (a) Width: The hood should be at least four feet wide in laboratories where occasional work with toxic substances occurs.

   In laboratories where workers continually work with hazardous chemicals, an eight-foot-wide hood should be required for each worker.
   (b) Depth: A working depth of 26–28 inches was acceptable to most workers.
   (c) Height: The ceiling should be at least four feet above the work surface and this height should be maintained for as much depth as possible. An angled ceiling air baffle usually restricts the maximum height to the front 7–8 inches of the hood.

3. *Sash.* The sash should operate vertically and horizontally. This is easily accomplished by mounting 18–22-inch-wide pieces of safety glass in two tracks that are contained in a vertically operating frame.

TABLE 6.1 Malachite Green Staining of Floor Samples.[a]

Solvent	Water	Dimethyl-sulfoxide	Dimethyl-formamide	Methanol	Acetone	Methylene Chloride
Floor Covering						
Vinyl[g]	0	1–2	2	1	2	3
Polyacrylate[b]	1	1	2	3	2	2
Epoxy 1[c]	0	1–2	3	1	1	1
Epoxy 2[d]	0	0	0–1	0–1	0	1
Epoxy 3[e]	0	1	0–1	0–1	0	1–2
Epoxy 4[e,h]	0	1	2	—	3	3

[a]Staining values: "0"—no stain; "1"—slight stain; "2"—moderate stain; "3"—deep stain.
[b]Monile 200.
[c]Morritex (silica granules in epoxy matrix) with U-10 topcoat.
[d]Trafficote (silica aggregates in epoxy resin).
[e]Industrial Epoxy Topping #115.
[f]Morritex (Type K).
[g]100% Vinyl.
[h]Solvent washed away after 10 minutes, all other samples washed after about 5 minutes.

4. *Walls.* The walls should be smooth (easier to clean), chemically inert, crack-resistant, and durable. They should be white to maximize light levels in the hood. Most chemists wanted to have a grid of metal or fiberglass rods, attached to the back wall. These rods, which are used to support reaction vessels and equipment, should be at least eight inches above the working surface in order to maximize workspace.

   Most workers wanted to have small shelves mounted on the side walls for chemical storage.

5. *Work Surface.* The surface should be made of a chemically-inert, durable material. The surface should have a raised lip around its perimeter which helps contain chemical spills inside the hood. All holes that penetrate the working surface should be protected by a similar barrier.

   Each hood should have at least one small sink that is not protected by a raised barrier. The sink should have a recessed cover that is flush with the surface.

6. *Services.* All services should be mounted on the side walls or on the front exterior of the hood. This leaves the working area uncluttered.

7. *Lighting.* The lights should be mounted on the exterior of the hood ceiling. This allows burned-out bulbs to be replaced without disturbing hood contents.

8. *Cabinets.* It is most important that the cabinets under each hood be vented to the hood exhaust. This allows them to be used for chemical storage and provides a mechanism for expelling toxic fumes from vacuum pumps that are conveniently located in these spaces. The cabinets should contain electrical outlets that can be operated by switches mounted on the front of the hood. Most chemists wanted these cabinets lined with a soundproofing material in order to minimize the noise generated by pumps.

   It is noted that at RIS we have additional vented cabinets located next to our large hoods. These greatly increase our chemical storage capacity.

9. *Objectionable Features.*

   (a) Minimize service connections under hood work surface that invade the cabinet areas. This is especially important for waste connections from the sinks.

   (b) Front sashes should open high enough to prevent workers from constantly hitting their heads on them. Obviously, the bottoms of the sashes should not have sharp edges—a rubber bumper located on the bottom of the sash would be a nice safety feature.

   (c) The supplemental air supply for the hood should not blow directly on the worker standing in front of the hood. This is especially uncomfortable when unconditioned supplemental air is used.

NATIONAL HOSPITAL FOR NERVOUS DISEASES, LONDON

ARCHITECTS: Llewelyn-Davies Weeks

Forming part of the first phase of the combined development of the Hospital for Sick Children, Great Ormond Street, and the National Hospital, Queen Square, this 10-story tower provides approximately 10,000 square meters (107, 640 sq ft) of laboratory space for teaching, medical, and research activities.

The scheme is based on a laboratory bay serviced from vertical ducts at each of the four corners, offering maximum options for laboratory and environmental services. Each bay can be subdivided by the user as required. The modular laboratory furniture is also extremely flexible.

Pipe shafts are in opposite corners of each laboratory module so that each wall of a laboratory module can have piped supplies and drainage. Supply air shafts flank the double access corridors, bringing high-velocity supply air to velocity reducers in the corridor ceilings, and thence across the ceiling to ceiling-mounted air diffusers in each room.

The square module (Fig. 6-16) shows dimensions at intervals of 1.2 meters (3.937 ft). Thus each module is 3.6 meters (11.811 ft) wide and 8 meters (26.246 ft) long. On a typical floor (Fig. 6.17) various partition arrangements are possible and services available to meet changes in configuration. Because of budget restrictions, some of the labs are naturally ventilated, the number of these varying from floor to floor.

Inside the laboratories, all benches are mobile and can be moved about like tables, the pads on the feet being adjustable to take up any small irregularities. Under-bench cupboards and drawer units can be wheeled about to fit in anywhere (Fig. 6-18).

Services are provided through two spines fixed to vertical supports between the benches. The lower one, which is optional, carries all water and gas supplies and has drip cups built in where required. Drainage, which is in glass, runs above the floor to catchpots in the plumbing ducts. Connections in the drainage system can easily be made and unmade, and benches containing sinks can be moved as easily as those without. Electrical outlets may be provided in the distribution spine as frequently as is required, generally two per 1.2 meters (3.937 ft). This spine is about 500 mm (1'8") above the bench top so that it is easily accessible even if the bench is cluttered with equipment. Telephones are fixed where required to the modular vertical support system. All shelves are adjustable in height (Fig. 6.19).

The exterior view (Figs. 6.20, 6.21) shows alternate extract and plumbing ducts. All ducts incorporate structural members. Ducts are accessible from inside the building and air extract shafts have external removable panels. The structure is poured concrete with precast concrete panels below windows.

The building is on the corner of Queen Square and is a recent addition to a hospital complex that has gone on developing over the past eighty years. The town planning regulations imposed a height limitation and the client's program needs resulted in a very low floor-to-floor height. This prevented the use of a more relaxed air distribution system, since only minimal horizontal distribution was possible.

Typical floor plan

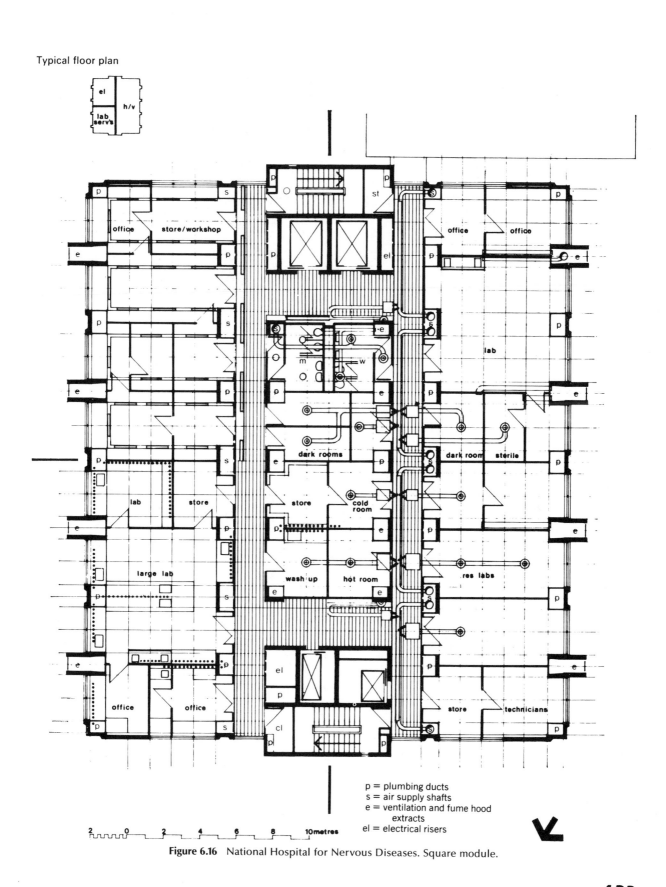

p = plumbing ducts
s = air supply shafts
e = ventilation and fume hood
     extracts
el = electrical risers

Figure 6.16 National Hospital for Nervous Diseases. Square module.

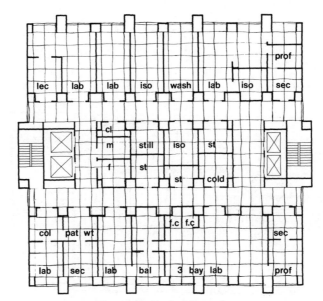

Figure 6.17 Typical floor plan.

Figure 6.18   Mobile benches. (John Dartnell photo).

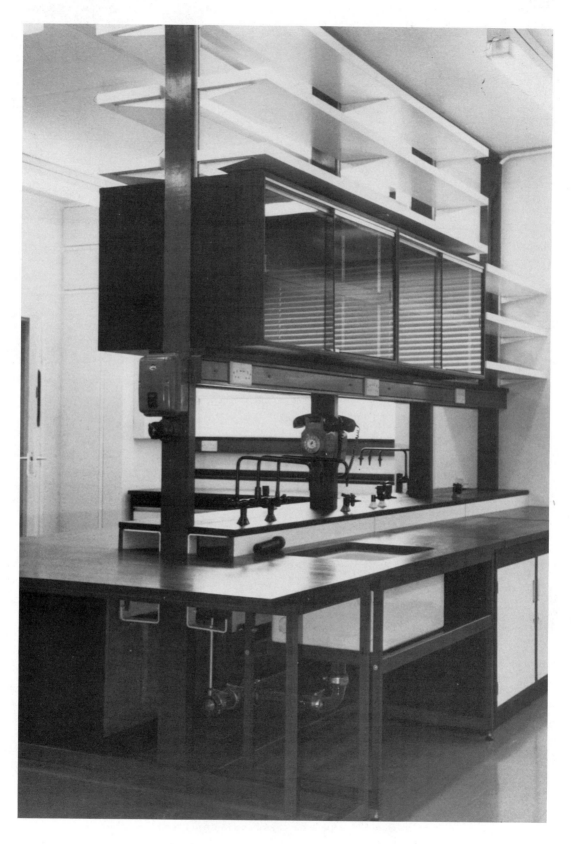

Figure 6.19 Service spines and vertical supports.

Figure 6.20 Exterior showing alternate extract and plumbing ducts. (Crispin Boyle photo).

Figure 6.21 Exterior view. (Crispin Boyle photo)

BROWN UNIVERSITY GEOLOGY AND CHEMISTRY LABORATORIES, PROVIDENCE, RHODE ISLAND

ARCHITECTS: Russo & Sonder Davis, Brody & Associates

Brown University's new laboratories for geology and chemistry were built to house the research activities of two distinguished faculties. It was important to design for state-of-the-art technology in the research of both disciplines while maintaining the distinct identity of each department. The aesthetic challenge was to place a large, new, technically sophisticated building within the context of an urban campus rich in architectural and historical significance (Fig. 6.22). At the eastern end of the

Brown campus, the laboratory site is bounded on two sides by university buildings four stories and taller, and on a third side by lower-scaled residential buildings (Figs. 6.23, 6.24). This meant that extremely careful attention had to be paid to the exhaust system to make sure that no toxic fumes would penetrate the campus under any weather conditions whatsoever.

The building contains approximately 7200 sq. ft. of laboratories, 100 offices for faculty and graduate students, seminar rooms, and a variety of storage and support spaces, distributed on five floors. Because of their greater fume hood requirements, the chemistry labs (Fig. 6.25) are placed on the top three floors, with the geology labs below. This arrangement also made sense in view of the vibration accompanying many of the geological experiments, which involve rock crushing and the like. While it was possible to employ a 20 by 30 ft lab module for

Figure 6.22   Brown University. Campus view. (Nick Wheeler photo)

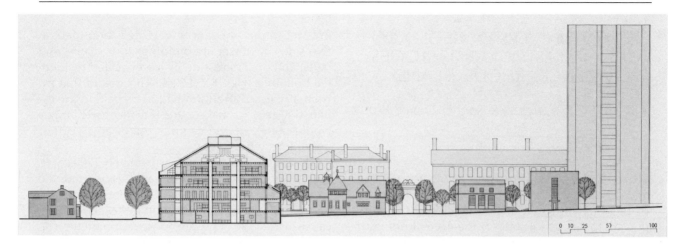

Figure 6.23   Section looking west.

the chemists, (Fig. 6.25) the more varied activities of the geologists precluded a tightly modular approach to their floors (Fig. 6.27). Two open stairways (supplementing code egress requirements) connect the floors of each department to encourage informal communication among researchers in each faculty (Fig. 6.28).

The laboratories are serviced from two parallel mechanical shafts, which supply piped services to lab benches and collect ducted exhausts from the fume hoods. Designed with narrow connections into the main exhaust duct, hoods do not pull air out of the labs themselves at high speeds, but maintain constant exhaust efficiency at lower speeds. In the mechanical attic under the sloped roof, variable speed fans propel laboratory fumes out through ducts clustered in the four brick roof stacks. The aerodynamic shape of the roof is itself a factor in the safe discharge of exhaust fumes into the upper air streams.

The principal structural frame of the building is poured-in-place reinforced concrete, a choice influenced by the need for vibration resistance. Inside, waffle slabs are exposed to view in the major laboratory and shop areas. Special attention was paid to exterior masonry detailing to give scale and texture to the building. The face bricks are nominally 4 by 12 inches, with special shapes and sizes used to form the bull-nosed window sills and the bands of rusticated masonry at the base of the

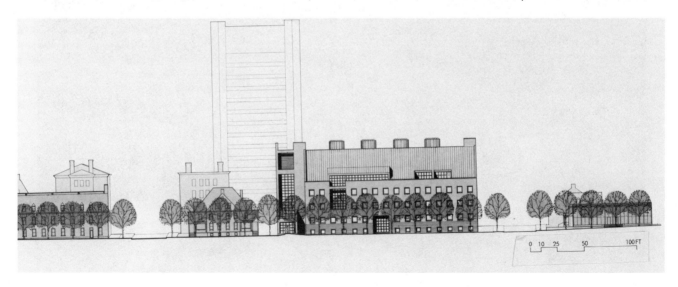

Figure 6.24   George Street elevation.

Figure 6.25   Chemistry lab interior. (Nick Wheeler photo)

south facade. The roof is constructed of precast planks on steel rafters and sheathed in natural copper which will oxidize green with age. In addition to its aerodynamic qualities, the shape of the roof also serves to reduce the building's apparent bulk and relate to the scale of the campus. Individual office windows facing George Street reinforce the scale of the older part of the campus (Fig. 6.29), but on the north side larger, industrial-type windows admit natural light to the labs and provide views out to what has now become the campus science quadrangle (Figs. 6.30, 6.31).

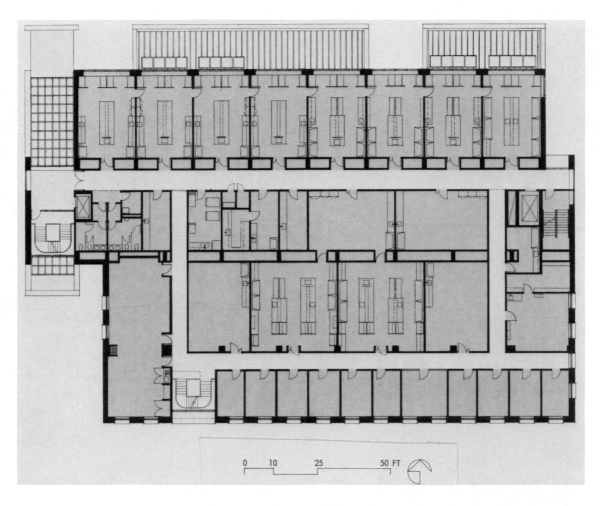

Figure 6.26   Chemistry lab floor plan.

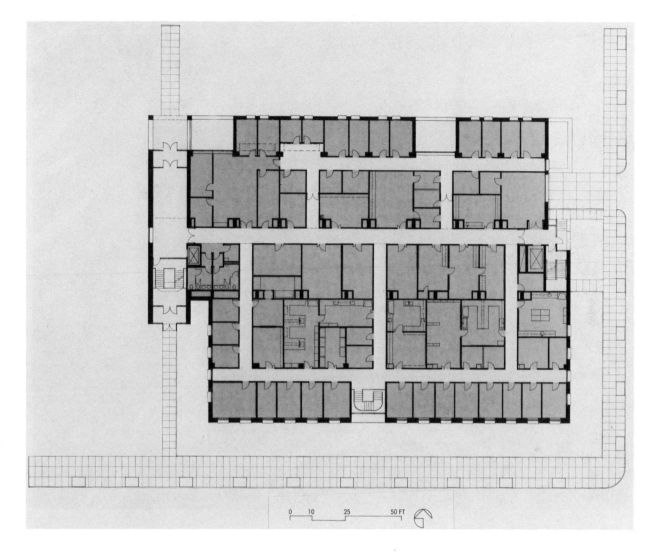

Figure 6.27 Geology lab floor plan.

Figure 6.28 Between-floor departmental stairs. (Nick Wheeler photo)

Figure 6.29 George Street elevation. (Nick Wheeler photo)

Figure 6.30 Industrial lab windows overlook science courtyard. (Nick Wheeler photo)

Figure 6.31 Science courtyard. (Nick Wheeler photo)

MEDICAL SCIENCE BUILDING, UNIVERSITY OF MEDICINE AND DENTISTRY OF NEW JERSEY AT NEWARK

ARCHITECTS: The Eggers Group, PC
The Grad Partnership
Gilbert L. Seltzer Associates

Forming the central portion of the 1,767,000-square-foot U-shaped campus megastructure (Fig. 6.32) (one of the largest projects ever constructed by the State of New Jersey), the Medical Science Building is composed primarily of laboratories serving the New Jersey Medical School and the entire complex as well. Linked on the eastern end to the Library via a two-level spine containing administrative offices, on the west its upper floors abut the University Hospital. It is connected through a lecture hall core on its lower floors to both the Hospital and the Dental School (Figs. 6.33, 6.34, 6.35).

Students and faculty enter the 683,000-square-foot building through a two-story lobby flanked by conference rooms, two 120-seat lecture halls, and a lounge (Figs. 6.36, 6.37, 6.38). The first two floors provide instructional facilities and faculty offices for the Medical School, while the five upper levels are devoted to laboratories. Basic science facilities are in the eastern portion of the building, near the library; clinical sciences are on the west to promote easy communication with the hospital, where faculty are actively engaged in medical practice.

Figure 6.32   University of Medicine and Dentistry of New Jersey at Newark. Aerial view of campus. (Otto Baitz photo)

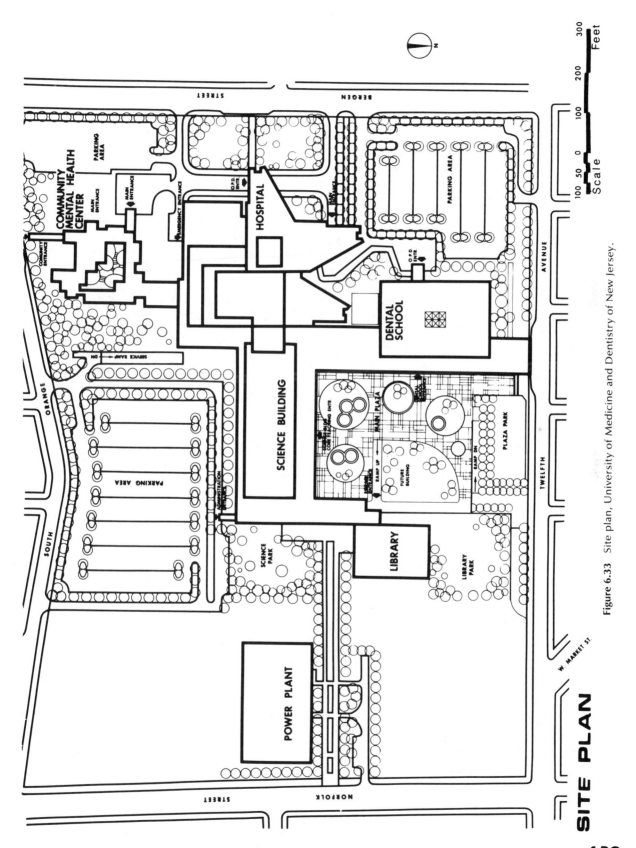

SITE PLAN

Figure 6.33 Site plan, University of Medicine and Dentistry of New Jersey.

139

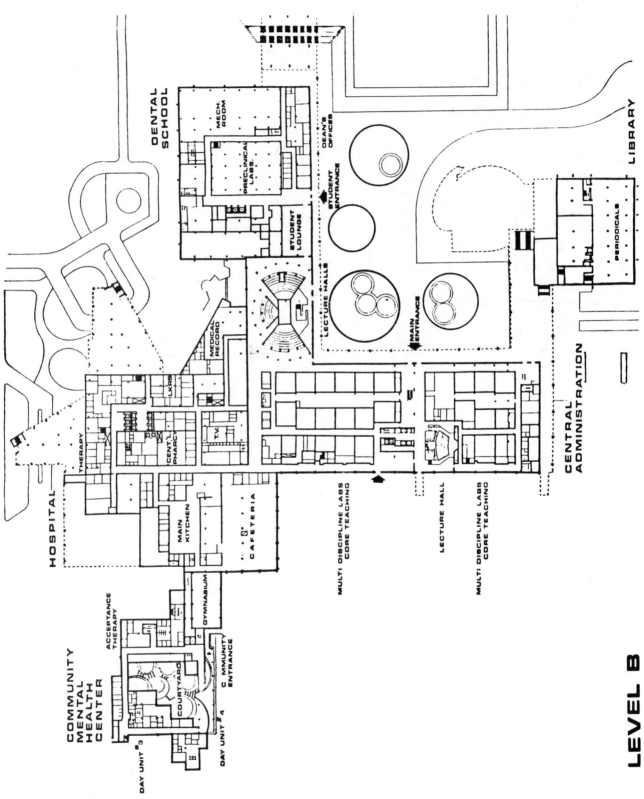

DENTAL SCHOOL

MECH. ROOM

PRECLINICAL LABS.

STUDENT LOUNGE

DEAN'S OFFICES

STUDENT ENTRANCE

LECTURE HALLS

MAIN ENTRANCE

LIBRARY

PERIODICALS

HOSPITAL

THERAPY

MEDICAL RECORD

LKRS

CENT'L PHARM

T.V.

MAIN KITCHEN

CAFETERIA

MULTI DISCIPLINE LABS CORE TEACHING

LECTURE HALL

MULTI DISCIPLINE LABS CORE TEACHING

CENTRAL ADMINISTRATION

COMMUNITY MENTAL HEALTH CENTER

ACCEPTANCE THERAPY

GYMNASIUM

COURTYARD

COMMUNITY ENTRANCE

DAY UNIT #3

DAY UNIT #4

LEVEL B

Figure 6.34 Plan, Level B.

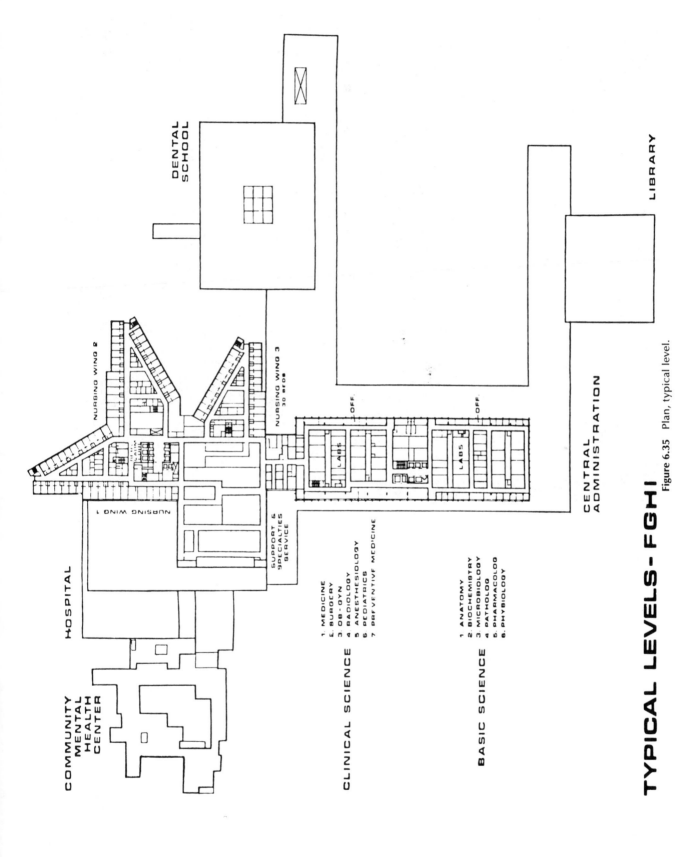

TYPICAL LEVELS-FGHI

Figure 6.35 Plan, typical level.

HOSPITAL

COMMUNITY MENTAL HEALTH CENTER

DENTAL SCHOOL

LIBRARY

CENTRAL ADMINISTRATION

NURSING WING 2

NURSING WING 1

NURSING WING 3
30 BEDS

SUPPORT & SPECIALTIES SERVICE

LABS

LABS

OFF.

OFF.

CLINICAL SCIENCE
1. MEDICINE
2. SURGERY
3. OB-GYN
4. RADIOLOGY
5. ANESTHESIOLOGY
6. PEDIATRICS
7. PREVENTIVE MEDICINE

BASIC SCIENCE
1. ANATOMY
2. BIOCHEMISTRY
3. MICROBIOLOGY
4. PATHOLOG
5. PHARMACOLOG
6. PHYSIOLOG

141

Figure 6.36 Lecture hall entrance. (Otto Baitz photo)

Each lab floor, therefore, accommodates the same discipline as its adjoining level in the hospital (Fig. 6.39). Central receiving, storage and HVAC monitoring system serving the entire complex, shops, a morgue, and a 10,000-square-foot animal quarters are housed in the basement.

The lecture hall core serves the Medical and Dental Schools and the Hospital. One 140-seat and two 270-seat halls are grouped in clover-leaf formation around a central rear projection and set-up facility.

All laboratories are planned according to consistent modules, coordinated with structural bays and building components. Teaching labs are generally based on the multidiscipline concept, and a 16-student instructional unit (Figs. 6.40, 6.41). Research labs for the basic and clinical sciences are placed back-to-back along mechanical shaftways to permit ease of servicing and potential flexibility. Perimeter corridors separate labs from faculty offices located at the exterior walls, but these are still conveniently close to the research areas. Support facilities include "interlab" preparation areas for the teaching laboratories, and spaces housing sophisticated equipment for research. Compressed air, vacuum, oxygen, nitrous oxide, and nitrogen are supplied to the labs from central stations.

The exterior mass of the building is visually reduced by alternating concrete bands with windows and by recessing the mechanical spaces on the third floor. This setback is faced with metal grillework, creating a transition between the glass-walled lower levels and the predominantly concrete upper stories (Figs. 6.42, 6.43).

Figure 6.37 Interior, lecture hall. (Otto Baitz photo)

Figure 6.38 Entrance circulation. (Otto Baitz photo)

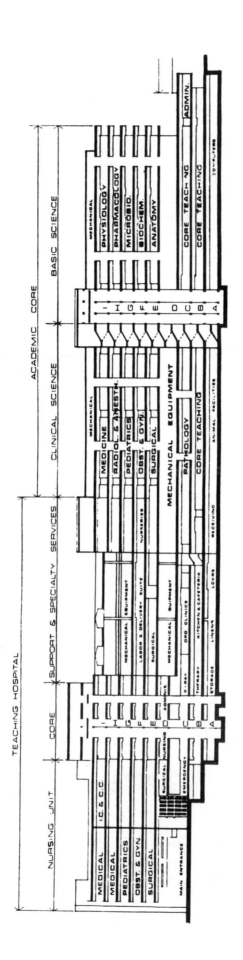

SECTION EAST-WEST

Figure 6.39   Section, University of Medicine and Dentistry of New Jersey.

Scale

100   0   100   200

Feet

145

Figure 6.40 Teaching lab. (Otto Baitz photo)

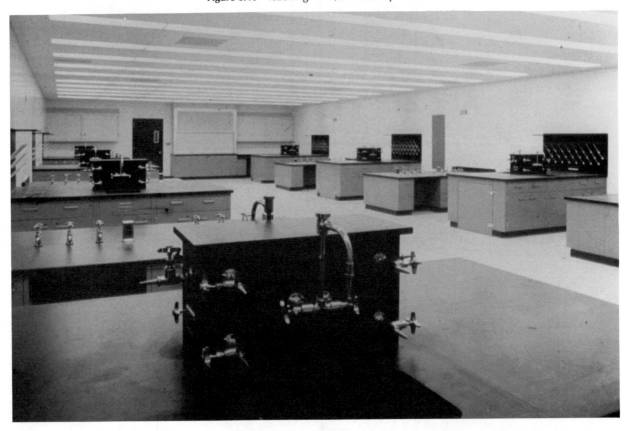

Figure 6.41 Teaching lab. (Otto Baitz photo)

Figure 6.42 Exterior view. (Otto Baitz photo)

147

Figure 6.43 Exterior view. (Otto Baitz photo)

E. R. SQUIBB & SONS, INC., WORLD HEADQUARTERS, PRINCETON, NEW JERSEY

ARCHITECTS: Hellmuth, Obata & Kassabaum
Laboratory Consultant: Earl L. Walls Associates

Completed in 1972, the research laboratories that form part of Squibb's worldwide headquarters on the outskirts of Princeton can be thought of as one of the seminal modern lab designs. They were named "Lab of the Year" by *Industrial Research* magazine; they are often visited and studied; and their basic plan configuration has worked so well that it is being applied again more than ten years later in the development of additional labs.

The Squibb research facilities form a series of interconnected modules at the northern end of the complex, (Fig. 6.44) which houses the multinational pharmaceutical company's administrative and marketing personnel, as well as some 500 scientists engaged in research in organic chemistry, microbiology, pharmacology, and biochemistry. The lab modules are interconnected by a glass-enclosed pedestrian spine, which links them to a lab support building, a library and research information center, the administrative office area, a dramatic skylit entry area, and an attractive lakeside dining room (Figs. 6.45, 6.46, 6.47, 6.48).

While the research modules share the basic limestone, brick, and bronze glass architectural vocabulary of the complex as a whole, their interior treatment responds to rigorous research demands. Labs, generally based on a 21 by 33 ft plan, are placed along outside walls, with office areas for scientists at the windows. Core areas contain instrument labs, environmental spaces and storage

Figure 6.44 Squibb World Headquarters. (Barbara Martin photo)

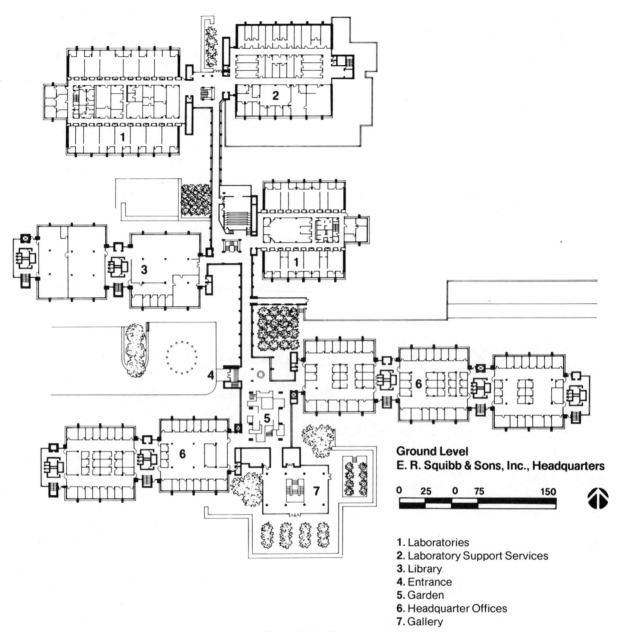

**Ground Level
E. R. Squibb & Sons, Inc., Headquarters**

0   25   0   75   150

1. Laboratories
2. Laboratory Support Services
3. Library
4. Entrance
5. Garden
6. Headquarter Offices
7. Gallery

Figure 6.45 Plan.

Laboratory
Building

Research
Administration

Headquarters
Offices

Figure 6.46 West elevation.

Figure 6.47 Dramatic skylit entry space, a focus for scientists and administrative personnel. (Alexandre Georges photo)

Figure 6.48 Dining room is right on the water. (George Cserna photo)

(Figs. 6.49, 6.50, 6.51). Multiple exits from each laboratory have been achieved through the planning device of running benches to the central corridor wall and leaving a fire lane by the perimeter windows.

Flexibility, a key concern, is attained through the service distribution pattern and a system of cast-stone-topped lab furniture, suspended from free-standing cantilevered structural frames, whose configurations can be readily changed to accommodate specific work patterns (Figs. 6.52, 6.53). Vertical service distribution shafts branch to acccessible, but not too conspicuous, in-the-wall pipe chases just outside lab doors, making it possible to add new outlets without disrupting the work of the department as a whole.

The built-in ceiling sprinkler system is backed up by fire extinguishers located in the corridors. There are safety showers and low-pressure eye washers. Emergency power generation covers all critical experimentation, ventilation to the animal rooms, and corridor lighting. Animals are housed in their own windowless block, and have fairly generous cages and exercise areas. Seamless urethane-coated floors and epoxy-painted walls make for easy maintenance in the animal building.

100% fresh air is provided to all lab and animal spaces, with sufficient air volume to operate at least two hoods per lab. Air in the animal housing is changed 12 to 15 times an hour, and individual temperature and humidity controls for each animal room permit each species to be kept in exactly the right conditions.

There is good use of color in the lab areas, and the whole environment feels bright and spacious. Some of the labs in the biology module, for example, are more open, with wider aisles and fewer offices. For safety reasons in the organic chemistry section, large glass panels were inserted in the doors to the corridor after the building was completed (Fig. 6.54). Directors' and administrative offices for each discipline are placed at the outer ends of the buildings. There are two central vacuum systems, one operating at 5 mm pressure and one at 50–100 mm, since the evaporation of solvents requires high vacuum to operate efficiently. Fume hoods have five horizontal doors, but only three can open at one time (Fig. 6.53). A warning system lights up if people are working on the roof.

The 273-acre site was carefully landscaped to provide a positive corporate image and give employees beautiful surroundings in which to work and pleasant views at all times. It was also a response to a high-class residential community's fears about having such a plant in its midst (Fig. 6.55).

Figure 6.49 Open lab area. (Barbara Martin photo)

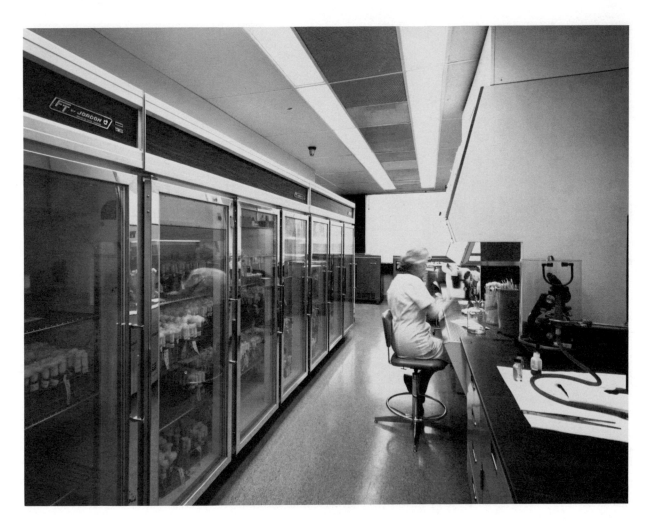

Figure 6.50 Environmental room.

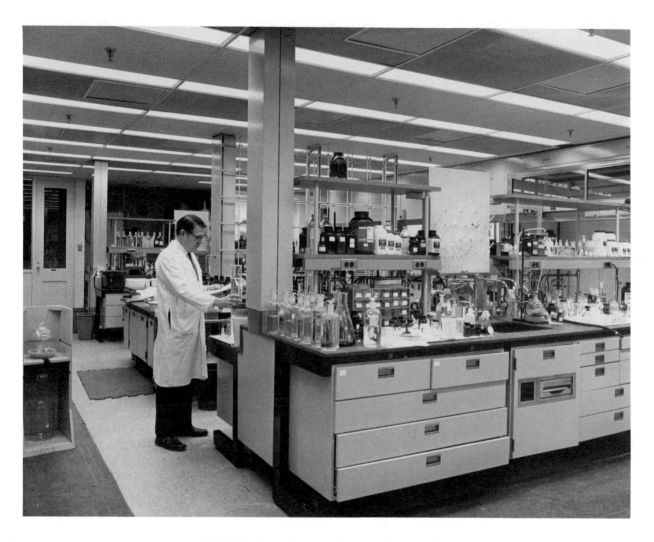

Figure 6.51 Open lab area. (Alexandre Georges photo)

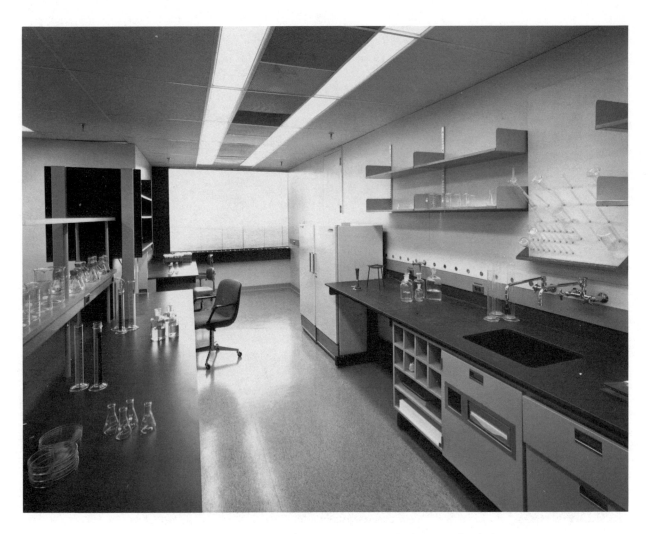

Figure 6.52 Furniture system has cast-stone tops. (Barbara Martin photo)

Figure 6.53 Open lab shows flexible furniture system. (Barbara Martin photo)

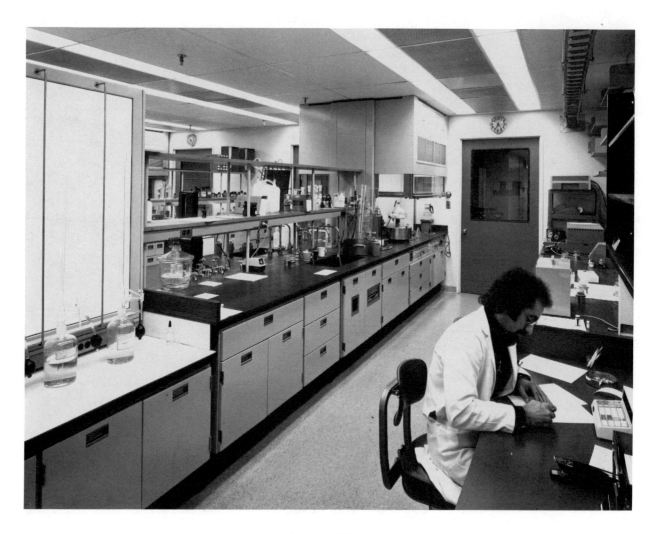

Figure 6.54 Organic chemistry lab with glass panel in door.

Figure 6.55   Squibb World Headquarters. (Barbara Martin photo)

EXXON RESEARCH AND ENGINEERING HEADQUARTERS, CLINTON, NEW JERSEY

COMPARATIVE ANALYSIS OF LABORATORY BUILDING SERVICE, PREPARED FOR HELLMUTH, OBATA & KASSABAUM, INC., ARCHITECTS

Joseph R. Loring & Associates, Inc., Consulting Engineers,

Distribution Study: *Service Corridor*
                       Interstitial Space
                       Vertical Distribution

- Availability of Services
- Accessibility of Services
- Headroom Conditions
- Space Available for Future Modifications

C. ASSUMPTIONS

The following assumptions have been made with respect to the physical characteristics of each scheme:

Service Corridor Scheme. Based upon a floor-to-floor height of 15 feet with a central service corridor 12 feet wide, serving a conventional stall arrangement of laboratory modules on either side of this corridor. The primary entrance to each laboratory module is from a small circulation corridor for pedestrian use only, located on the outboard side of each row of laboratory modules. Only the sprinkler piping and supply air ducts for each row of laboratory modules will run above the circulation corridors. The flow of all lab materials, etc., will be through the central service corridor. In this scheme, each fume hood exhaust duct and fan serves one-third of a floor (i.e., 12 laboratory modules out of a total of 36), or 24 fume hoods. This arrangement permits centralized exhaust fan units on the top floor, from which heat recovery of the thermal energy in the exhaust gases is feasible.

Interstitial Space Scheme. Based upon the elimination of the central service corridor and the conversion of that "cubage" into an additional 3.25 feet of floor-to-floor has been assumed to be divided as follows:

- Laboratory floor-to-floor height   10 feet
- Interstitial space height   8.25 feet

The width of each main circulation corridor must be expanded to accommodate the additional flow of lab materials, carts, gases, etc. The basic supply air and fume hood exhaust duct arrangement for this scheme is identical to that of the "Central Core." This scheme would also require some additional storage space on each floor to compensate for the shafts required by the plumbing stacks and for the space required for vented cabinets etc., all of which would be located in the service corridor under the "Central Core Scheme."

A. GENERAL

The purpose of this study is to examine and compare the advantages and disadvantages of providing environmental and service distribution systems to the laboratories on this project, based on the three following concepts:

I. SERVICE CORRIDOR (Referred to as "Central Core" in report of June 21, 1979)
II. INTERSTITIAL SPACE
III. VERTICAL DISTRIBUTION

B. BASIS OF COMPARISON

Each of these concepts will be evaluated with respect to:

1. *Flexibility:* Since each of the schemes will be developed, initially, to satisfy a particular laboratory and equipment layout, the true measure of the relative "flexibility" of each scheme will be the ability to accommodate changes to equipment within the individual laboratories as well as to changes in the number of modules per laboratory.
2. *Safety:* Comparative "safety" of each of the schemes will be evaluated in terms of personnel safety (laboratory and maintenance) and fire protection.
3. *Construction Implications and Cost:* The initial construction cost of each of the schemes will include architectural and structural implications, as well as mechanical and electrical.
4. *Maintenance and Relocation Costs:* The recommended scheme must permit maintenance and relocation operations to be conducted with minimum cost and disruption of services, in view of the life-cycle implications of these costs. Key factors involved in the determination of these maintenance and relocation costs are:

Vertical Distribution Scheme. Eliminates both the central service core and the interstitial space between floors; however, the main circulation corridors must be expanded to accommodate the additional flow of lab materials, carts, gas cylinders, etc. In addition, vertical shaft space on a modular basis must be provided for the various services to be distributed vertically to each of the labs. The top floor of each lab building will have to be increased in this scheme for the horizontal distribution of the various utilities. All fume hood exhaust duct risers will terminate at roof exhaust fans; each riser and its associated fan will serve six fume hoods. Because of the large number of fume hood exhaust fans and their dispersed locations on the roof, heat recovery from the exhaust air is precluded as an economically viable option.

Graphical Illustration of Each Scheme. Isometric and sectional drawings showing a typical section through a laboratory for each scheme are attached to the report; each of the three disciplines (HVAC, Plumbing, and Electrical) is depicted on a separate drawing for each scheme, for the purpose of clarity (see Figs. A.1–A.9). Structural framing has not been included on these drawings for the same reason; however, it was generally assumed that each laboratory (comprised of two laboratory modules) would be framed as a typical structural bay. The structure for the Interstitial Scheme is discussed below.

D. COMPARATIVE ANALYSIS

I. SERVICE CORRIDOR SCHEME

1. *Flexibility:* The main attribute of this scheme, in terms of flexibility, is the floor-to-floor height of 15' which is available in both the service corridor and the laboratories. This height will permit space to be reserved for the future addition of services not presently contemplated, and for the modifications and alterations to existing services within the service corridor, without major disruption of the laboratory functions.

   One foot of space has been left clear on either side of the service corridor for plumbing stacks; this also provides the flexibility for running individual exhaust ducts directly to the roof for any future labs on any floor which may use unusually hazardous chemicals.

   If several laboratory modules must be combined for a large laboratory, this scheme will readily permit the demounting of partitions and rearrangements of the lab furniture, as required for the new layout. Such modification will not interfere with the conduct of work in the adjacent modules. While such changes to the basic laboratory module layout, i.e., two laboratory modules per laboratory, are expected to be infrequent, this scheme has the advantage of such flexibility without a large pre-investment cost.

2. *Safety:* The presence of the service corridor between laboratories will provide a factor of safety which neither of the other schemes can offer; namely, a convenient location in which to place vented cabinets, storage racks, and/or various other pieces of equipment which would otherwise have to be accommodated within the confines of the laboratory. Gas cylinders with nontoxic gases can be placed in the corridor for special lab use; those with toxic gases would be put in vented cabinets.

   The presence of the sprinkler protected and ventilated service corridor offers an additional means of egress in the event of an emergency.

3. *Construction Implications and Cost:* The cost of this scheme will be discussed below, based upon the drawings included with this report. The presence of the service corridor permits the location of supporting columns within the service corridor without interfering with laboratory arrangements.

4. *Maintenance and Relocation Costs:* This scheme provides for the availability of services to each laboratory module via taps from mains run at ceiling or walls of the service corridor. The 12-foot corridor width combined with the 15-foot floor-to-floor height will permit full accessibility to all services, allow for future modifications and additions, and still maintain acceptable headroom conditions. Alterations

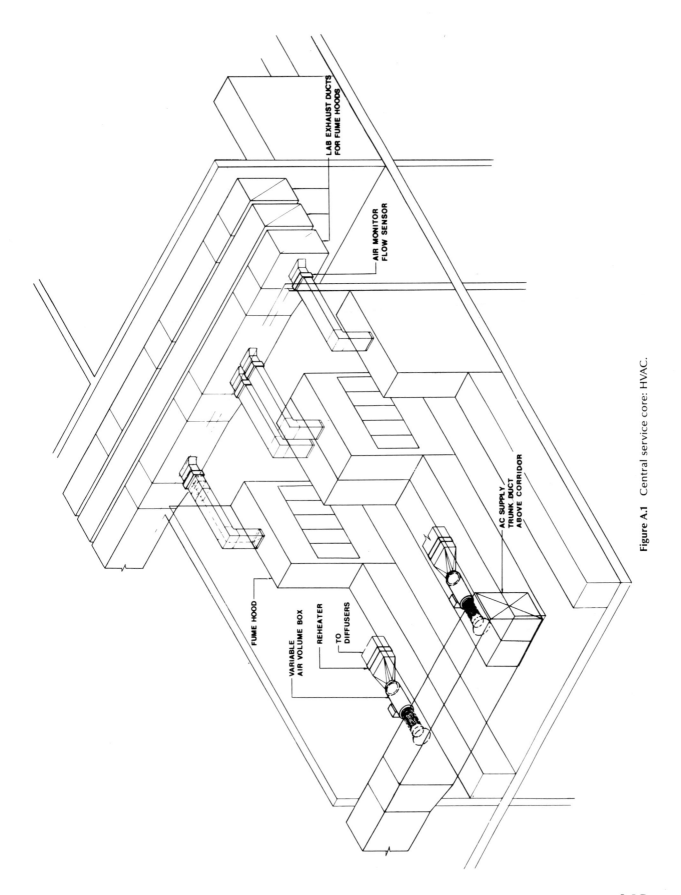

LAB EXHAUST DUCTS
FOR FUME HOODS

AIR MONITOR
FLOW SENSOR

FUME HOOD

VARIABLE
AIR VOLUME BOX

REHEATER

TO
DIFFUSERS

AC SUPPLY
TRUNK DUCT
ABOVE CORRIDOR

Figure A.1 Central service core: HVAC.

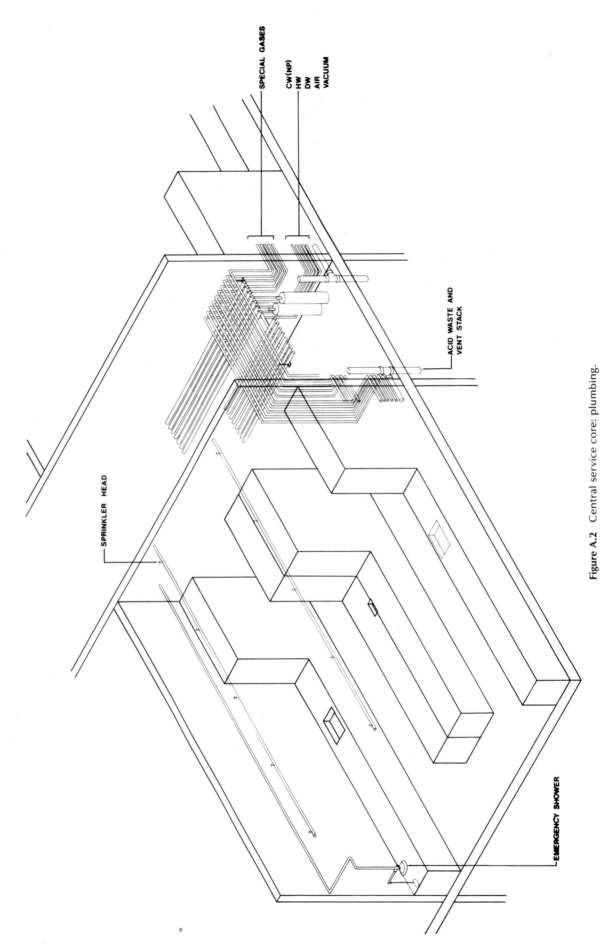

SPECIAL GASES

CW(NP)
HW
DW
AIR
VACUUM

ACID WASTE AND
VENT STACK

SPRINKLER HEAD

EMERGENCY SHOWER

Figure A.2 Central service core: plumbing.

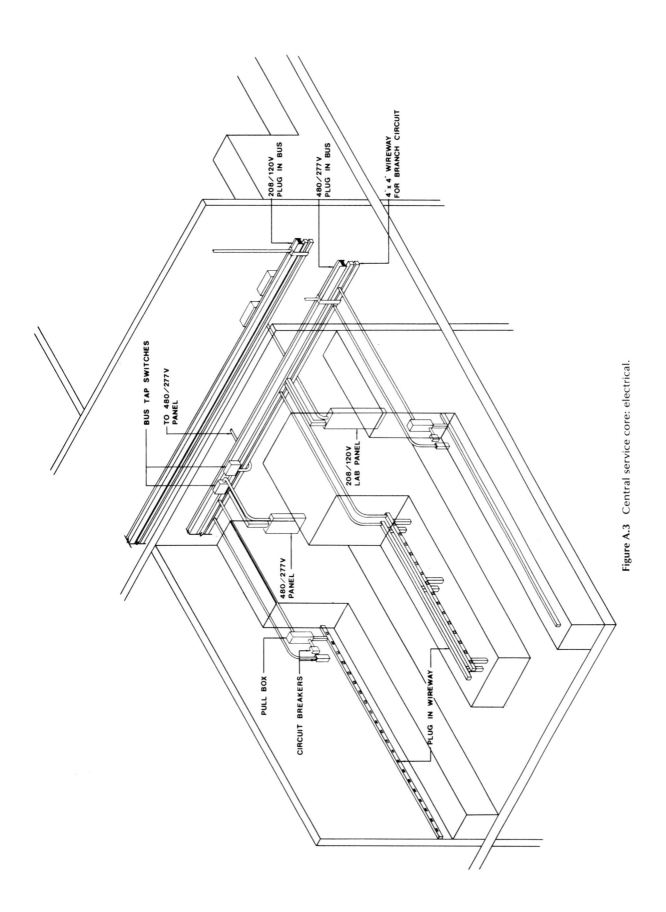

208/120V PLUG IN BUS

480/277V PLUG IN BUS

4' x 4' WIREWAY FOR BRANCH CIRCUIT

BUS TAP SWITCHES

TO 480/277V PANEL

208/120V LAB PANEL

480/277V PANEL

PULL BOX

CIRCUIT BREAKERS

PLUG IN WIREWAY

Figure A.3 Central service core: electrical.

165

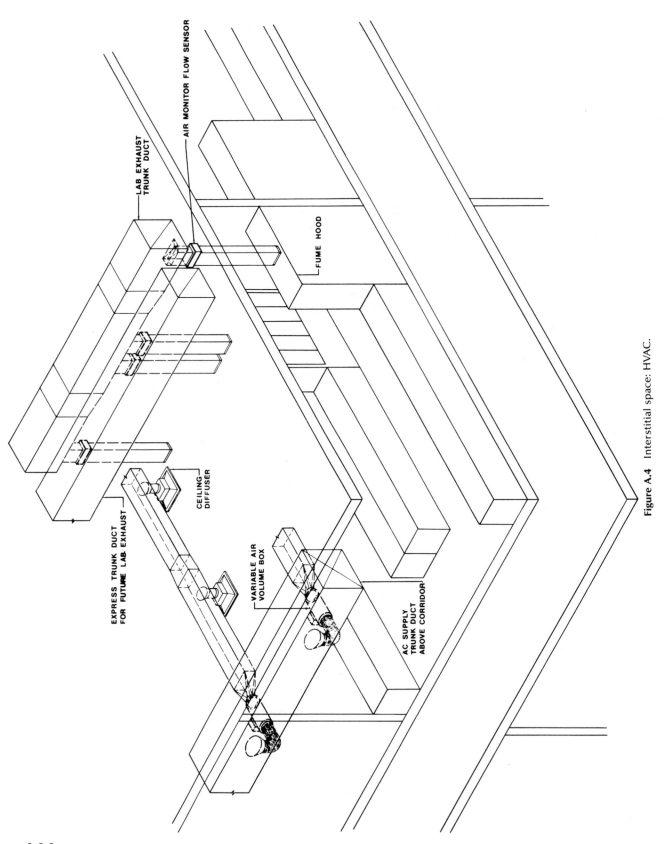

Figure A.4 Interstitial space: HVAC.

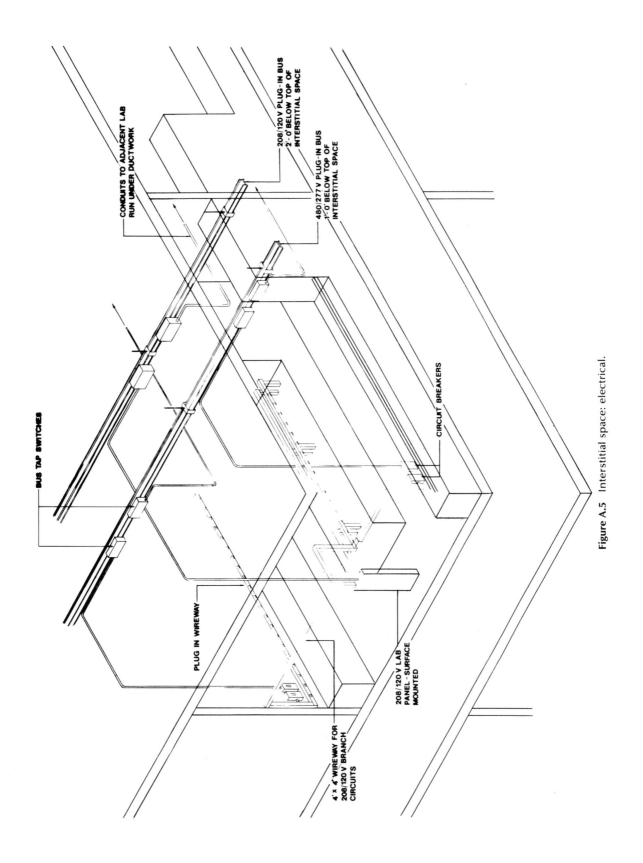

Figure A.5 Interstitial space: electrical.

BUS TAP SWITCHES

CONDUITS TO ADJACENT LAB RUN UNDER DUCTWORK

208/120 V PLUG-IN BUS 2'-0" BELOW TOP OF INTERSTITIAL SPACE

480/277 V PLUG-IN BUS 1'-0" BELOW TOP OF INTERSTITIAL SPACE

CIRCUIT BREAKERS

PLUG IN WIREWAY

208/120 V LAB PANEL - SURFACE MOUNTED

4' x 4' WIREWAY FOR 208/120 V BRANCH CIRCUITS

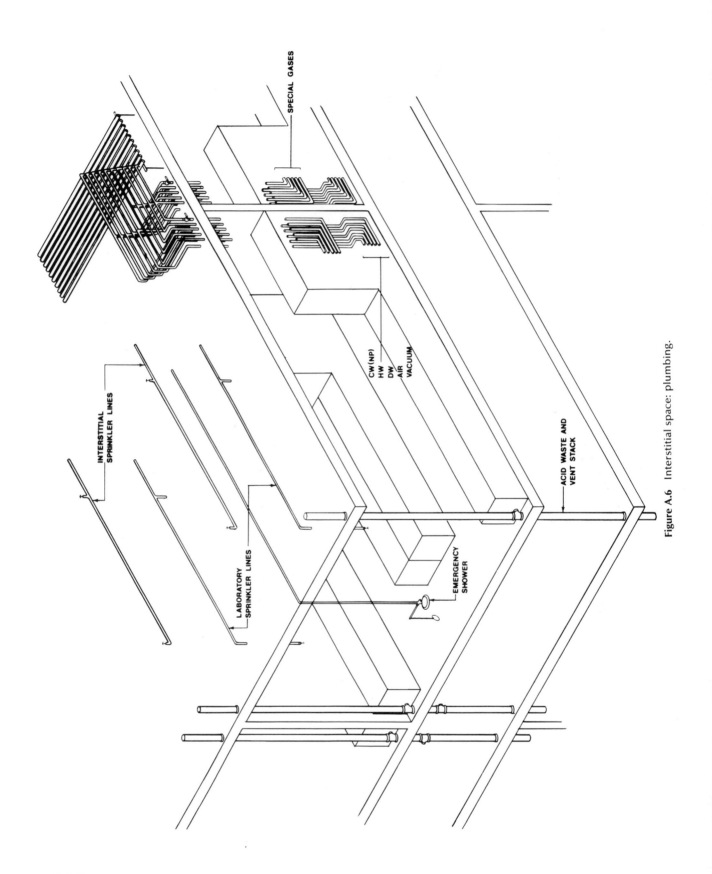

SPECIAL GASES

CW (NP)
HW
DW
AIR
VACUUM

INTERSTITIAL SPRINKLER LINES

LABORATORY SPRINKLER LINES

EMERGENCY SHOWER

ACID WASTE AND VENT STACK

Figure A.6 Interstitial space: plumbing.

168

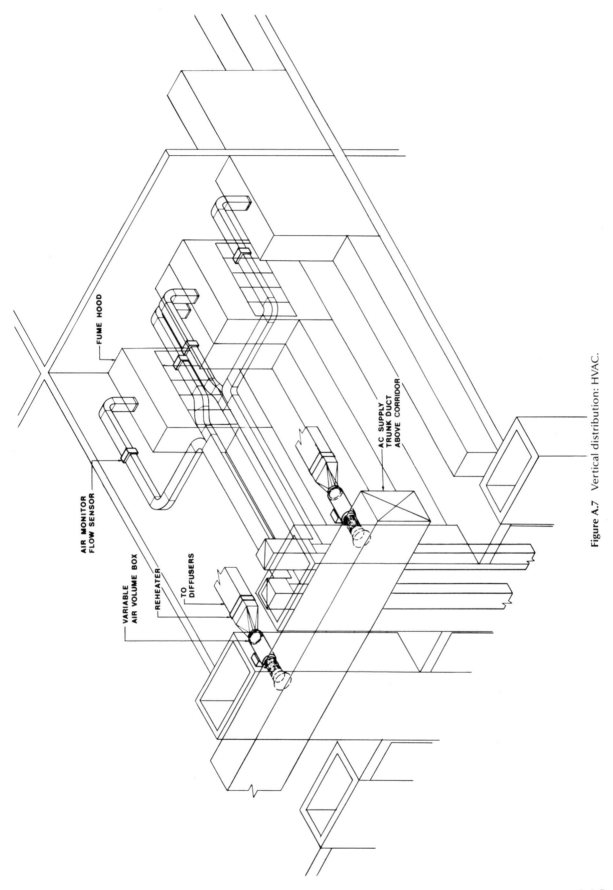

AIR MONITOR
FLOW SENSOR

FUME HOOD

VARIABLE
AIR VOLUME BOX

REHEATER

TO
DIFFUSERS

AC SUPPLY
TRUNK DUCT
ABOVE CORRIDOR

Figure A.7 Vertical distribution: HVAC.

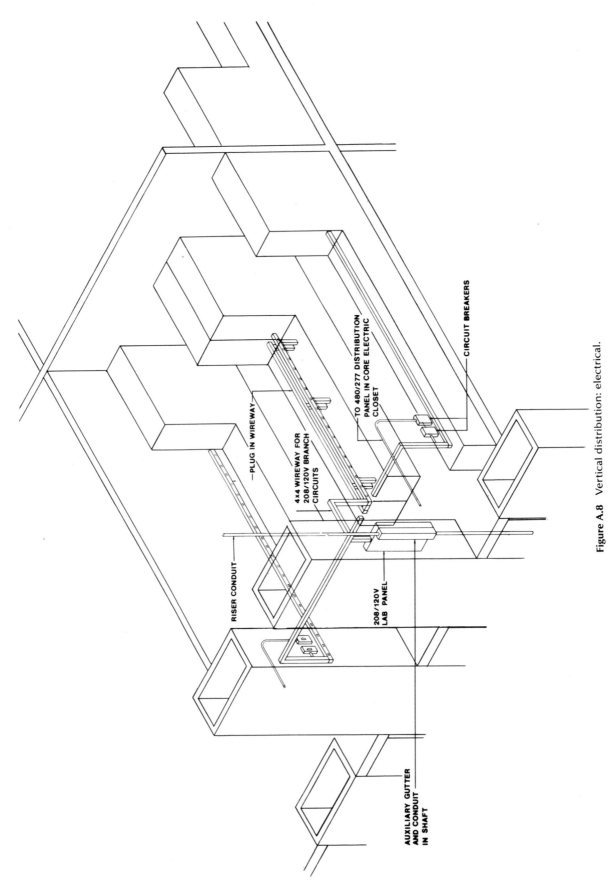

CIRCUIT BREAKERS

TO 480/277 DISTRIBUTION PANEL IN CORE ELECTRIC CLOSET

PLUG IN WIREWAY

4×4 WIREWAY FOR 208/120V BRANCH CIRCUITS

RISER CONDUIT

208/120V LAB PANEL

AUXILIARY GUTTER AND CONDUIT IN SHAFT

Figure A.8 Vertical distribution: electrical.

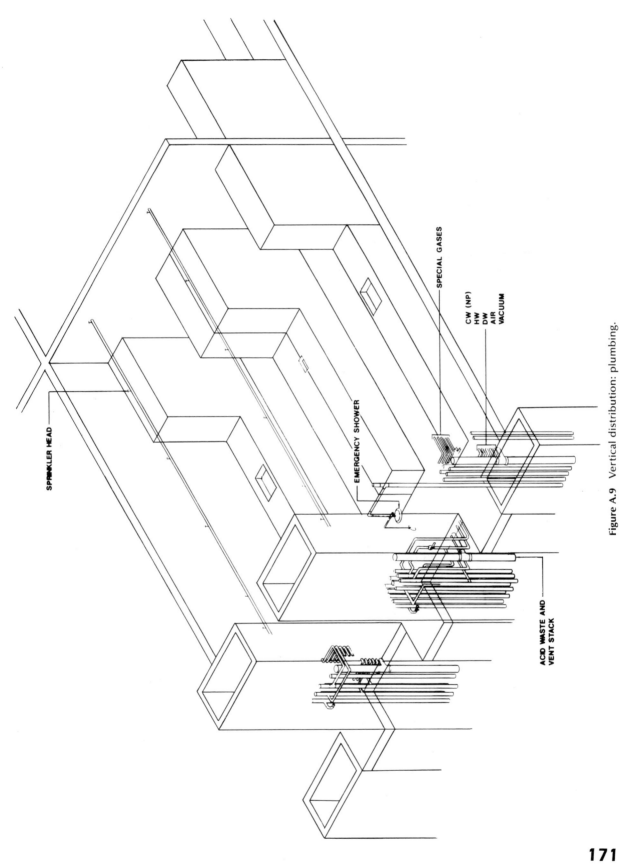

SPRINKLER HEAD

SPECIAL GASES

CW (NP)
HW
DW
AIR
VACUUM

EMERGENCY SHOWER

ACID WASTE AND
VENT STACK

Figure A.9 Vertical distribution: plumbing.

and additions to services will be made in a well-ventilated and lighted space with ample room in which to bring in and install construction materials.

II. INTERSTITIAL SPACE SCHEME

1. *Flexibility:* This method of providing for distribution of services was evolved to provide the "ultimate" in flexibility for hospitals and laboratories in terms of equipment location and the ability to make changes with a minimum disruption to the functioning of the space below. The suitability of applying a system of this type to a laboratory building in which the individual laboratory modules are generally well-defined, and in which future modifications will almost invariably occur within the predetermined modules, is questionable. Since "ultimate" flexibility is not required on an ongoing basis, the loss of usable floor-to-floor height in this concept becomes a major disadvantage. Future modifications could render significant portions of the interstitial space useless because of the limited space condition.

2. *Safety:* The Interstitial Space Scheme offers no apparent benefits from a safety standpoint, nor does it pose any special safety problems (except for the possibility of interference with pedestrian traffic while servicing the labs via the circulation corridors). The space will have to be sprinklered and provided with smoke exhaust ducts.

3. *Construction Implications and Cost:* While the Interstitial Space Scheme is based upon the conversion of the "cubage" of the service corridor into an additional 3.25 feet of floor-to-floor height (from 15 feet to 18.25 feet), the problem of how to handle the additional height over the circulation spaces and office spaces must be dealt with. From purely a structural viewpoint, this scheme would require the framing and pouring of six levels in lieu of three levels for the other two schemes. The structural system required to support the Interstitial Space Scheme will therefore impose significant cost penalties, in addition to the added cost for sprinkler protection, smoke venting, etc.

4. *Maintenance and Relocation Costs:* While this scheme, initially, provides for the greatest potential availability of services, experience has shown that availability and accessibility of these services degrade as the space is utilized. This is due largely to the constricted headroom conditions and the obstructions caused by the presence of structural members which are required for interstitial spaces. Future modifications, therefore, become costly due to rerouting of services around obstructions and the difficulty of working in tight space conditions.

The latest laboratory design manual published by the Federal Government is the *Design and Construction Guide for Cancer Research Facilities,* printed in 1976. It included the following about "Interstitial Space":

"Several major laboratory facilities have been built using an interstitial space above each laboratory floor for a walk-through utility floor. While there are beneficial features, the initial, very expensive costs have not justified the benefits. Therefore, NCI (National Cancer Institute) does not recommend using this building design except in very unusual situations."

III. VERTICAL DISTRIBUTION SCHEME

1. *Flexibility:* This method provides adequate flexibility as long as the experiments conducted within each laboratory do not involve dramatic changes in service requirements. This system, however, is not able to cope with unforeseen situations in which the need for one or more of the basic services increases significantly. It is the least flexible of the three schemes. As stated above, the fume hood exhaust system is not suitable for heat recovery.

2. *Safety:* This scheme offers no apparent benefits from a safety standpoint, nor does it pose any special safety problems (except for the possibility of interference with pedestrian traffic while servicing labs via the circulation corridors).

3. *Construction Implications and Cost:* This scheme contains approximately the same "cubage" as the service corridor scheme due to the widening of the main circula-

tion corridors and the added height of the top floor. Supporting columns will have to be located in the wall separating the back-to-back laboratories, limiting, to a certain extent, the location of doors, vertical risers, etc.

4. *Maintenance and Relocation Costs:* This scheme is least able to accommodate future changes or additions in a cost-effective manner. Since services are distributed vertically and are fixed rigidly in specific shafts, the necessity to make unforeseen additions or modifications to services will probably involve costly modifications to the space, or may eliminate the use of various laboratories, since it may not be feasible to make the changes.

E. COST COMPARISON

I. SERVICE CORRIDOR

1. *Architectural and Structural:* The cost comparison will assume the cost of this system as the base against which the other schemes will be evaluated.

2. *Mechanical/Electrical:* The cost comparison will assume the cost of this system as the base against which the other schemes will be evaluated.

II. INTERSTITIAL SPACE SCHEME

1. *Architectural and Structural:* The 1979 cost of the architectural and structural systems for this scheme is estimated to be $236,000 higher than that of the Service Corridor Scheme.

2. *Mechanical/Electrical:* The 1979 cost of the mechanical and electrical systems for this scheme is estimated to be $82,458 higher than that of the Service Corridor Scheme.

3. *Life-Cycle Cost Analysis:* A 15-year Life Cycle Cost Analysis shows that the Service Corridor Scheme is more cost-effective by a present cost worth of $401,650 than the

Vertical Distribution Scheme; see Cost Addenda.

III. VERTICAL DISTRIBUTION SCHEME

1. *Architectural and Structural:* The cost of the architectural and structural systems for this scheme is estimated to be $105,000 higher than that of the Service Corridor Scheme.

2. *Mechanical/Electrical:* The first cost of the mechanical and electrical systems for this scheme is estimated to be $100,305 higher than that of the Service Corridor Scheme.

3. *Life-Cycle Cost Analysis:* A 15-year Life Cycle Cost Analysis indicates that the Service Corridor Scheme is more cost effective by a present cost worth of $530,310 than the Interstitial Space Scheme; see Cost Addenda.

F. SUMMARY AND RECOMMENDATIONS

Of the three schemes studied, the Service Corridor Scheme is the best suited to serve the present and future requirements of the laboratory types and arrangements proposed for this project.

The primary drawback of the Interstitial Space Scheme is its initial cost. Its application to this type of laboratory arrangement is also questionable, since the ultimate flexibility implied (but often not realized) with this type of system is not required for this project. The elimination of the central service corridor imposes other operational drawbacks which render this scheme unsuitable.

The major shortcoming of the Vertical Distribution Scheme is lack of flexibility which would result in costly and time-consuming disruptions to the laboratories to accommodate future changes. Also, the tight space conditions for utilities and the large number of roof-mounted exhaust fans make maintenance more difficult, and heat recovery impractical.

COST ADDENDA

I. FIRST COST DIFFERENTIALS

1. First Costs

A. Scheme—Service Corridor versus Vertical Distribution

1. M/E   Cost Differential

HVAC	$ 23,400
Electrical	$ 24,962
Plumbing	$ 51,943
First Cost Differential	$ 100,305 (1979)

$100,305 \times 1.12^3 = \$140,430$ (1983) ECIP Infl. Rates*
$100,305 \times 1.075^3 = \$124,609$ (1983) Exxon Infl. Rates

2. Architectural

Cost Differential = [$1,767,000 − $1,662,000] = $105,000 (1979)

$105,000 \times 1.12^3 = \$147,517$ (1983) ECIP Rates
$105,000 \times 1.075^3 = \$130,441$ (1983) Exxon Rates

B. Scheme—Service Corridor versus Interstitial Space

1. M/E

HVAC	$ 3,920
Electrical	$ 2,860
Plumbing	$83,518
First Cost Differential	$82,458 (1979)

$82,458 \times 1.12^3 = \$115,430$ (1983) ECIP Rates
$82,458 \times 1.075^3 = \$102,437$ (1983) Exxon Rates

1. First Costs—Service Corridor versus Interstitial Space

A. Architectural

Cost Differential = ($1,898,000 − 1,662,000) = $236,000 (1979)

$236,000 \times 1.12^3 = \$331,563$ (1983) ECIP Rates

$236,000 \times 1.075^3 = \$293,182$ (1983) Exxon Rates

2. Electrical Cost Differential

A. Service Corridor versus Vertical Distribution

1. $4,930 annual (1979) $\times 1.075^4 = \$6,583$ (1983) Exxon Rates

*Energy Conservation Investment Program (ECIP) (a NAFAC
program which is no longer in use).

3. Operating Costs Differential (Annual)

A.   Service Corridor versus Vertical Distribution

1.   Fitting Up Cost Differential

$$\$10,200 \text{ (1983 ECIP)} \times \frac{(1.075)^4}{(1.12)^4} = 10,200 \times 0.912 = \underline{\$9,300} \text{ (1983) Exxon Factors}$$

2.   Maintenance Cost Differential

$$\$2,800 \text{ (1983 ECIP)} \times 0.912 = \underline{\$2,550} \text{ (1983) Exxon Factors}$$

3.   Major Alt. Cost Differential

$$\$39,600 \text{ (1983 ECIP)} \times 0.912 = \underline{\$36,120} \text{ (1983) Exxon Factors}$$

B.   Service Corridor versus Interstitial Space

$$(-)\$9,900 \text{ (1979 ECIP)} \times 0.912 = \underline{\$9,030} \text{ (1983) Exxon Factors}$$

II. FIRST COST DIFFERENTIALS—"ECIP" INFLATION RATES

Life cycle costs are essentially defined as the first cost differential between two or more economic options at a given starting date, plus the owning and operating cost differentials over the economic life of the analysis, converted to present worth at the time of the starting date.

Since the Bid price for the project is based on a construction period spanning 1980 to 1983, the first cost differentials in current dollars must be escalated to reflect the actual Bid costs. This means escalating these differentials to 1982 prices at 12% per annum, or by $1.12 \times 1.12 \times 1.12 = 1.40$ as the multiplier.

The beginning of occupancy is 1983, at which time the present worth for the life cycle costs will begin. While there is a 12% escalation in prices from 1982 (Bid price base) to 1983, the discount rate is also 12%; hence, the first cost dollars used for 1983 (at the beginning of the study's time frame) are the same as those in the Bid price.

The current first cost differentials for each scheme are based on the Service Corridor as the base price. When the costs of the other two schemes are greater than the Service Corridor, they are denoted with a plus sign (+); when less than the Service Corridor, they are indicated with a minus sign (−).

The summary of the current first cost differentials escalated to 1983 are given in these tables:

Service Corridor versus Vertical Distribution

Architectural and Structural Systems Cost Differential:

$\$105,000 \times 1.40 = +\$147,520$ Cost Differential

Mechanical and Electrical Systems Cost Differential:

HVAC:	+$23,400 × 1.40	=	+$ 32,760
Electrical:	+$24,962 × 1.40	=	+$ 34,950
Plumbing:	+$51,943 × 1.40	=	+$ 72,720

Total M/E Cost Differential   +$140,430

Service Corridor versus Interstitial Space Scheme

Architectural and Structural Cost Differential:

$\$236,000 \times 1.40 = +\$331,560$ Cost Differential

Mechanical and Electrical Cost Differential:

HVAC: +$ 3,920 × 1.40 = +$ 5,490
Electrical: +$ 2,860 × 1.40 = +$ 4,000
Plumbing: +$83,518 × 1.40 = +$116,920

Total M/E Cost Differential   +$115,430

Note: The reason for the lower first cost of HVAC for Interstitial lies in the fact that trunk ducts can be round for most of the run, thereby reducing their costs.

III. ANNUAL COSTS—"ECIP" INFLATION FACTORS

The annual costs which relate to the three utility distribution schemes are:

1. Fitting-up costs when a laboratory's function is changed, but the basic laboratory arrangement is maintained.
2. Major alterations of laboratories which involve both removal of partitions and large modifications to the services.
3. Routine maintenance.
4. Annual energy costs.

Each of these items is discussed below:

1. *Fitting-Up Costs*
   a. *Fitting-UP Costs: Service Corridor versus Vertical Distribution.* Currently, the Linden research laboratories undergo 40 to 45 major fitting-up changes per year and at least 50 minor ones annually.

   The modifications at Linden all occur on vertical distribution systems; hence there is no yardstick to measure how much easier it would be to perform comparable changes with a Service Corridor distribution.

   Since all experiences by other organizations, such as the NIH of the Federal Government, confirm that vertical distribution is more difficult to change than the Service Corridor, we can safely ascribe an average penalty of 30 manhours per major fitting-up change against the vertical scheme. In view of the fact that the new laboratory complex at Clinton will be about twice the size of that at Linden, the total number of major changes at Clinton per year is extrapolated to be 80, out which 15% would apply to the 24 lab module buildings under study, or 12 per year. This yields a total of 360 manhours per year required for the vertical distribution scheme in excess of those for the Service Corridor Scheme.

It is further assumed that minor changes, such as removing a single fume hood, will result in an average penalty of 10 manhours against the vertical distribution scheme. Using the same proportions as the major changes above, this results in 15% of 100 total changes per year for a 24 laboratory module building, or 15 changes per annum. This yields a total of 150 excess manhours per year required for the vertical distribution scheme.

Assuming the average cost per 1983 manhour (fringes included) of $20, the annual penalty against vertical distribution is 510 manhours × $20, or $10,200. This does not include material costs because it is impossible to quantify them.

Two concrete examples which demonstrate and confirm the added cost of fitting-up modifications of Vertical Distribution over Service Corridor and Interstitial are given in the Appendix.

1. Study based on bringing 200 ampere, 208 volt, 3 phase feeder into lab module from halfway down the corridor (approximately 100 feet).

   Service Corridor = $0; Vertical Distribution = $1,657; Interstitial = $290.

2. Adding a vented cabinet for a lab module:

   Service Corridor = $0; Vertical Distribution = $960; Interstitial = $420.

b. *Fitting-Up Costs: Service Corridor versus Interstitial.* No substantial difference in fitting-up time for either major or minor fitting-up changes is thought to exist between Service Corridor and Interstitial Schemes. Although Interstitial is more flexible, this is generally offset by having to perform the work on two floor levels, thereby offsetting any gains in flexibility.

2. *Major Alteration Costs: Service Corridor versus Vertical Distribution and Service Corridor versus Interstitial.* Major alteration modifications will occur very infrequently but when they do, they are very expensive. With the vertical distribution of utilities now at the Linden labs, the current average cost of converting laboratories is $105 per sq. ft. without air conditioning, and $150 per sq. ft. with air conditioning.

If it were assumed that only one pair of laboratories in each building underwent a major alteration every five years, the vertical distribution scheme would cost $198,000 in current dollars (1320 sq. ft. × $150). With the Service Corridor, this figure should be reduced by at least 20%, or $39,600. The Interstitial Scheme should be even more effective; if we assume a 25% savings over the Vertical Distribution Scheme, this amounts to $49,500 for Interstitial.

Since Service Corridor is taken as the base scheme major alteration costs each five years for the other two schemes would be:

Vertical Distribution:	+$39,600
Interstitial:	−$ 9,900

3. *Annual Maintenance Costs.* There is assumed to be no significant annual maintenance cost difference between the Service Corridor and Interstitial schemes.

In evaluating the annual maintenance cost difference between Service Corridor and Vertical Distribution, there is only one significant difference in maintenance costs; this lies in the number and type of fume hood exhaust fans for each scheme. For this item, the following annual costs are estimated:

a. Additional cost of Vee-Belts per year for 24 fans for Vertical Distribution versus only 6 fans for Service Corridor is +$1,800.

b. Additional yearly manhour cost for fan maintenance of Vertical Distribution over Service Corridor is 100 manhours (Vertical Distribution) − 50 manhours (Service Corridor) = 50 manhours × $20/manhour, or $1000 annually.

With Service Corridor as the base scheme, a summary of the maintenance cost differences for the other schemes is:

Interstitial:	$0
Vertical Distribution:	$2,800

4. *Annual Energy Costs.* To assure exhaust system stability, static pressure controllers for exhaust fans must be used for all three schemes. Because of the small size of the exhaust fans for Vertical Distribution, each static pressure controller maintains static pressure by an automatic damper in the exhaust duct, which results in no energy conservation. On the contrary, it is energy wasteful.

For Service Corridor and Interstitial, the static pressure controller changes the fan speed through a variable speed drive unit which assures both good system stability and energy conservation.

To quantify the precise amount of energy saved by the fan speed controller would depend on several variables: total exhaust air flow at any given time, hours of operation per year, and fan and fan motor characteristics at varying loads. A computerized system profile over the year's operation would yield the exact fan energy difference between Vertical Distribution and either of the other two schemes. This methodology, however, is not readily available; hence, manual calculations must be used to roughly estimate this difference. For the manual calculations required for this study, the following simplifying assumptions and calculations are made:

a. Hours of operation per year
4000 hours

b. Full-load fan horsepower (all schemes) for each building
   96HP

c. Average Percent of Full Load Volume
   80%

d. Average Percent of Rated HP for Damper Control (Vertical Distribution) at 80% load
   96%

e. Average Percent of Rated HP for Controlled Fan Speed Control—80% load (Service Corridor and Interstitial)
   65%

f. Energy Saved/Year = 4,000 hours × 96 HP × (0.96 − 0.65 = 0.31)
   119,040 HP-Hrs.

g. KWH Savings/Year (Based on 90% motor efficiency)
   98,670 KWH

h. Annual Savings @ $0.05/KWH (including demand and fuel adjustment) × 98,670 KWH
   $4930

i. Escalation of Savings to 1983 = $4930 × 2.07
   $10,200

IV. LIFE CYCLE COST ANALYSIS

The beginning of the "Life Cycle Cost Analysis" is 1983, and is based on a 15 year period for HVAC, Electrical and Plumbing costs.

The following economic parameters will be applied to this analysis:

- Discount rate (after taxes) 12%
- General rate of inflation for goods and services (after 1983) 10%
- Rate of inflation for electricity (to 1983) = 1.21 × 1.21 × 1.19 × 1.19 2.07
- Rate of inflation for electricity after 1983 per year 17%
- Income taxes rate 46%
- Architectural depreciation—150% declining balance with 40-year life. This yields 2.5/Year × 1.5 3.75%
- Equipment depreciation—Double Declining Balance based on 25-year life. This yields 2/25 8%
- Salvage value 0
- SPPW (Single Payment Present Worth) based on 12%

Since Service Corridor is the base scheme, savings in favor of the base scheme are denoted with a plus (+) sign, and those against the base scheme with a minus (−) sign.

Tables for Life Cycle Costing covering a 15-year period have been developed for the following cases:

Table A.1: Service Corridor versus Vertical Distribution—ECIP Inflation Factors.

Table A.2: Service Corridor versus Interstitial Space—ECIP Inflation Factors.

Table A.3: Service Corridor versus Vertical Distribution—Exxon Inflation Factors.

Table A.4: Service Corridor versus Interstitial Space—Exxon Inflation Factors.

All tables indicate that the Service Corridor Scheme is substantially more cost effective over 15 years than either the Vertical Distribution Scheme or the Interstitial Space Scheme.

TABLE A.1 15-Year Life Cycle Cost Analysis for Service Corridor versus Vertical Distribution—ECIP Inflation Rates

	Col. A			Col. B			Col. C	Col. D	Col. E	Col. F = C + D + E			Col. G
	Arch Depr. (150% Decl. Bal.)			M/E Depr. (200% Decl. Bal.)						Annual Labor Costs			
Year	Book Value	40 Year Factor	Arch. Depr.	Book Value	25 Year Factor	M/E Depr.	Fit-Up Cost Diff.	Major Alt. Cost Diff.	Maint. Cost Diff.	Subtotal Costs	Infl. Fact.		Escl. Cost Diff.
0	147,520			140,430									
1	147,520	× 0.0375 =	5,532	140,430	× 0.08 =	11,234	10,200		2,800	13,000	× 1.10	=	14,300
2	141,988	× 0.0375 =	5,325	129,196	× 0.08 =	10,336	10,200		2,800	13,000	× 1.21	=	15,730
3	136,663	× 0.0375 =	5,125	118,860	× 0.08 =	9,509	10,200		2,800	13,000	× 1.33	=	17,303
4	131,539	× 0.0375 =	4,933	109,351	× 0.08 =	8,748	10,200		2,800	13,000	× 1.46	=	19,033
5	126,606	× 0.0375 =	4,748	100,603	× 0.08 =	8,048	10,200	39,600	2,800	52,600	× 1.61	=	84,713
6	121,858	× 0.0375 =	4,570	92,555	× 0.08 =	7,404	10,200		2,800	13,000	× 1.77	=	23,030
7	117,288	× 0.0375 =	4,398	85,150	× 0.08 =	6,812	10,200		2,800	13,000	× 1.95	=	25,333
8	112,890	× 0.0375 =	4,233	78,338	× 0.08 =	6,267	10,200		2,800	13,000	× 2.14	=	27,867
9	108,657	× 0.0375 =	4,075	72,071	× 0.08 =	5,766	10,200		2,800	13,000	× 2.36	=	30,653
10	104,582	× 0.0375 =	3,922	66,306	× 0.08 =	5,304	10,200	39,600	2,800	52,600	× 2.59	=	136,431
11	100,660	× 0.0375 =	3,775	61,001	× 0.08 =	4,880	10,200		2,800	13,000	× 2.85	=	37,091
12	96,886	× 0.0375 =	3,633	56,121	× 0.08 =	4,490	10,200		2,800	13,000	× 3.14	=	40,800
13	93,252	× 0.0375 =	3,497	51,631	× 0.08 =	4,131	10,200		2,800	13,000	× 3.45	=	44,880
14	89,755	× 0.0375 =	3,366	47,501	× 0.08 =	3,800	10,200		2,800	13,000	× 3.80	=	49,367
15	86,390	× 0.0375 =	3,240	43,701	× 0.08 =	3,496	10,200	39,600	2,800	52,600	× 4.18	=	219,723

TABLE A.1 (Continued)

	Annual Energy Costs			Col. I = G + H	After Tax Costs				Col. L = J + K		Present Worth Factor		Present Worth	Cumul. Present Worth
Year	Energy Cost Diff.		Infl. Fact.		Escl. Cost Diff. (Col. H)	Net Cost Diff.		Tax Fact.		After Tax Cost (Col. J)	Depr. Savings (Col. K)	Total Cost				
0															287,950	287,950
1	10,200	×	1.17	=	11,934	26,234	×	0.54	=	14,166	(7,713)	6,454	×	0.8929 =	5,762	293,712
2	10,200	×	1.37	=	13,963	29,693	×	0.54	=	16,034	(7,204)	8,830	×	0.7972 =	7,040	300,752
3	10,200	×	1.60	=	16,336	33,639	×	0.54	=	18,165	(6,731)	11,434	×	0.7118 =	8,138	308,890
4	10,200	×	1.87	=	19,114	38,147	×	0.54	=	20,599	(6,293)	14,306	×	0.6355 =	9,092	317,982
5	10,200	×	2.19	=	22,363	107,076	×	0.54	=	57,821	(5,886)	51,935	×	0.5674 =	29,469	347,451
6	10,200	×	2.57	=	26,165	49,195	×	0.54	=	26,565	(5,508)	21,057	×	0.5066 =	10,668	358,120
7	10,200	×	3.00	=	30,613	55,946	×	0.54	=	30,211	(5,157)	25,054	×	0.4523 =	11,333	369,453
8	10,200	×	3.51	=	35,817	63,683	×	0.54	=	34,389	(4,830)	29,559	×	0.4039 =	11,938	381,391
9	10,200	×	4.11	=	41,906	72,559	×	0.54	=	39,182	(4,527)	34,655	×	0.3606 =	12,497	393,888
10	10,200	×	4.81	=	49,030	185,461	×	0.54	=	100,149	(4,244)	95,905	×	0.3220 =	30,879	424,767
11	10,200	×	5.62	=	56,365	94,455	×	0.54	=	51,006	(3,981)	47,025	×	0.2875 =	13,518	438,285
12	10,200	×	6.58	=	67,117	107,916	×	0.54	=	58,275	(3,737)	54,538	×	0.2567 =	13,999	452,284
13	10,200	×	7.70	=	78,527	123,406	×	0.54	=	66,639	(3,509)	63,131	×	0.2292 =	14,468	466,752
14	10,200	×	9.01	=	91,876	141,244	×	0.54	=	76,271	(3,296)	72,975	×	0.2046 =	14,932	481,684
15	10,200	×	10.54	=	107,495	327,218	×	0.54	=	176,698	(3,098)	173,599	×	0.1827 =	31,716	513,400

TABLE A.2   15-Year Life Cycle Cost Analysis for Service Corridor versus Interstitial Space—ECIP Inflation Rates

	Col. A			Col. B			Col. C	Col. D	Col. E	Col. F = C + D + E	Infl. Fact.	Col. G
	Arch. Depr. (150% Decl. Bal.)			M/E Depr. (200% Decl. Bal.)					Annual Labor Coss			
Year	Book Value	40 Year Factor	Arch. Depr.	Book Value	25 Year Facor	M/E Depr.	Fit-Up Cost Diff.	Major Alt. Cost Diff.	Maint. Cost Diff.	Subtotal Costs	Infl. Fact.	Escl. Cost Diff.
0	331,560			115,430								
1	331,560 ×	0.0375 =	12,434	115,430 ×	0.08 =	9,234	0		0	0	× 1.10 =	0
2	319,127 ×	0.0375 =	11,967	106,196 ×	0.08 =	8,496	0		0	0	× 1.21 =	0
3	307,159 ×	0.0375 =	11,518	97,700 ×	0.08 =	7,816	0		0	0	× 1.33 =	0
4	295,641 ×	0.0375 =	11,087	89,884 ×	0.08 =	7,191	0		0	0	× 1.46 =	0
5	284,554 ×	0.0375 =	10,671	82,693 ×	0.08 =	6,615	0	(9,900)	0	(9,900)	× 1.61 =	(15,944)
6	273,883 ×	0.0375 =	10,271	76,078 ×	0.08 =	6,086	0		0	0	× 1.77 =	0
7	263,613 ×	0.0375 =	9,885	69,992 ×	0.08 =	5,599	0		0	0	× 1.95 =	0
8	253,727 ×	0.0375 =	9,515	64,392 ×	0.08 =	5,151	0		0	0	× 2.14 =	0
9	244,213 ×	0.0375 =	9,158	59,241 ×	0.08 =	4,739	0		0	0	× 2.36 =	0
10	235,055 ×	0.0375 =	8,815	54,502 ×	0.08 =	4,360	0	(9,900)	0	(9,900)	× 2.59 =	(25,678)
11	226,240 ×	0.0375 =	8,484	50,141 ×	0.08 =	4,011	0		0	0	× 2.85 =	0
12	217,756 ×	0.0375 =	8,166	46,130 ×	0.08 =	3,690	0		0	0	× 3.14 =	0
13	209,590 ×	0.0375 =	7,860	42,440 ×	0.08 =	3,395	0		0	0	× 3.45 =	0
14	201,731 ×	0.0375 =	7,565	39,045 ×	0.08 =	3,124	0		0	0	× 3.80 =	0
15	194,166 ×	0.0375 =	7,281	35,921 ×	0.08 =	2,874	0	(9,900)	0	(9,900)	× 4.18 =	(41,355)

Annual Energy Costs | After Tax Costs

Year	Energy Cost Diff.		Infl. Fact.		Escl. Cost Diff. (Col. H)	Net Cost Diff. (Col. I = G + H)		Tax Fact.		After Tax Cost (Col. J)	Depr. Savings (Col. K)	Total Cost (Col. L = J + K)		Present Worth Factor		Present Worth	Cumul. Present Worth
0																446,990	446,990
1	0	×	1.17	=	0	0	×	0.54	=	0	(9,967)	(9,967)	×	0.8929	=	(8,899)	438,091
2	0	×	1.37	=	0	0	×	0.54	=	0	(9,413)	(9,413)	×	0.7972	=	(7,504)	430,587
3	0	×	1.60	=	0	0	×	0.54	=	0	(8,894)	(8,894)	×	0.7118	=	(6,330)	424,256
4	0	×	1.87	=	0	0	×	0.54	=	0	(8,408)	(8,408)	×	0.6355	=	(5,343)	418,913
5	0	×	2.19	=	0	(15,944)	×	0.54	=	(8,610)	(7,952)	(16,561)	×	0.5674	=	(9,397)	409,516
6	0	×	2.57	=	0	0	×	0.54	=	0	(7,524)	(7,524)	×	0.5066	=	(3,812)	405,704
7	0	×	3.00	=	0	0	×	0.54	=	0	(7,123)	(7,123)	×	0.4523	=	(3,222)	402,482
8	0	×	3.51	=	0	0	×	0.54	=	0	(6,746)	(6,746)	×	0.4039	=	(2,725)	399,757
9	0	×	4.11	=	0	0	×	0.54	=	0	(6,393)	(6,393)	×	0.3606	=	(2,305)	397,452
10	0	×	4.81	=	0	(25,678)	×	0.54	=	(13,866)	(6,060)	(19,926)	×	0.3220	=	(6,416)	391,036
11	0	×	5.62	=	0	0	×	0.54	=	0	(5,748)	(5,748)	×	0.2875	=	(1,652)	389,383
12	0	×	6.58	=	0	0	×	0.54	=	0	(5,454)	(5,454)	×	0.2567	=	(1,400)	387,984
13	0	×	7.70	=	0	0	×	0.54	=	0	(5,177)	(5,177)	×	0.2292	=	(1,186)	386,797
14	0	×	9.01	=	0	0	×	0.54	=	0	(4,917)	(4,917)	×	0.2046	=	(1,006)	385,791
15	0	×	10.54	=	0	(41,355)	×	0.54	=	(22,332)	(4,671)	(27,003)	×	0.1827	=	(4,933)	380,858

TABLE A.3 15-Year Life Cycle Cost Analysis for Service Corridor versus Vertical Distribution—Exxon Inflation Rates

	Col. A			Col. B			Col. C	Col. D	Col. E	Col. F = C + D + E		Col. G
	Arch. Depr. (150% Decl. Bal.)			M/E Depr. (200% Decl. Bal.)					Annual Labor Coss			
Year	Book Value	40 Year Factor	Arch. Depr.	Book Value	25 Year Facor	M/E Depr.	Fit-Up Cost Diff.	Major Alt. Cost Diff.	Maint. Cost Diff.	Subtotal Costs	Infl. Fact.	Escl. Cost Diff.
0	130,440			124,609								
1	130,440 × 0.0375 =		4,892	124,609 × 0.08 =		9,969	9,300		2,550	11,850 ×	1.065 =	12,620
2	125,549 × 0.0375 =		4,708	114,640 × 0.08 =		9,171	9,300		2,550	11,850 ×	1.13 =	13,441
3	120,840 × 0.0375 =		4,532	105,469 × 0.08 =		8,438	9,300		2,550	11,850 ×	1.21 =	14,314
4	116,309 × 0.0375 =		4,362	97,032 × 0.08 =		7,763	9,300		2,550	11,850 ×	1.29 =	15,245
5	111,947 × 0.0375 =		4,198	89,269 × 0.08 =		7,142	9,300	36,120	2,550	47,970 ×	1.37 =	65,723
6	107,749 × 0.0375 =		4,041	82,127 × 0.08 =		6,570	9,300		2,550	11,850 ×	1.46 =	17,291
7	103,709 × 0.0375 =		3,889	75,557 × 0.08 =		6,045	9,300		2,550	11,850 ×	1.55 =	18,415
8	99,820 × 0.0375 =		3,743	69,513 × 0.08 =		5,561	9,300		2,550	11,850 ×	1.65 =	19,612
9	96,076 × 0.0375 =		3,603	63,952 × 0.08 =		5,116	9,300		2,550	11,850 ×	1.76 =	20,886
10	92,474 × 0.0375 =		3,468	58,836 × 0.08 =		4,707	9,300	36,120	2,550	47,970 ×	1.88 =	90,046
11	89,006 × 0.0375 =		3,338	54,129 × 0.08 =		4,330	9,300		2,550	11,850 ×	2.00 =	23,690
12	85,668 × 0.0375 =		3,213	49,798 × 0.08 =		3,984	9,300		2,550	11,850 ×	2.13 =	25,230
13	82,456 × 0.0375 =		3,092	45,815 × 0.08 =		3,665	9,300		2,550	11,850 ×	2.27 =	26,870
14	79,363 × 0.0375 =		2,976	42,149 × 0.08 =		3,372	9,300		2,550	11,850 ×	2.41 =	28,616
15	76,387 × 0.0375 =		2,865	38,777 × 0.08 =		3,102	9,300	36,120	2,550	47,970 ×	2.57 =	123,371

Year	Energy Cost Diff.		Infl. Fact.		Escl. Cost Diff. (Col. H)	Net Cost Diff. (Col. I = G + H)		Tax Fact.		After Tax Cost (Col. J)	Depr. Savings (Col. K)	Total Cost (Col. L = J + K)		Present Worth Factor		Present Worth	Cumul. Present Worth
0																255,049	255,049
1	6,583	×	1.065	=	7,011	19,631	×	0.54	=	10,601	(6,836)	3,765	×	0.8929	=	3,362	258,411
2	6,583	×	1.13	=	7,467	20,907	×	0.54	=	11,290	(6,384)	4,905	×	0.7972	=	3,911	262,321
3	6,583	×	1.21	=	7,952	22,266	×	0.54	=	12,024	(5,966)	6,058	×	0.7118	=	4,312	266,633
4	6,583	×	1.29	=	8,469	23,713	×	0.54	=	12,805	(5,577)	7,228	×	0.6355	=	4,594	271,227
5	6,583	×	1.37	=	9,019	74,742	×	0.54	=	40,361	(5,216)	35,145	×	0.5674	=	19,942	291,169
6	6,583	×	1.46	=	9,606	26,896	×	0.54	=	14,524	(4,881)	9,643	×	0.5066	=	4,885	296,054
7	6,583	×	1.55	=	10,230	28,645	×	0.54	=	15,468	(4,569)	10,899	×	0.4523	=	4,930	300,984
8	6,583	×	1.65	=	10,895	30,507	×	0.54	=	16,474	(4,280)	12,194	×	0.4039	=	4,925	305,909
9	6,583	×	1.76	=	11,603	32,489	×	0.54	=	17,544	(4,011)	13,534	×	0.3606	=	4,880	310,789
10	6,583	×	1.88	=	12,357	102,403	×	0.54	=	55,298	(3,760)	51,538	×	0.3220	=	16,594	327,383
11	6,583	×	2.00	=	13,160	36,850	×	0.54	=	19,899	(3,527)	16,372	×	0.2875	=	4,707	332,090
12	6,583	×	2.13	=	14,016	39,246	×	0.54	=	21,193	(3,310)	17,882	×	0.2567	=	4,590	336,680
13	6,583	×	2.27	=	14,927	41,797	×	0.54	=	22,570	(3,108)	19,462	×	0.2292	=	4,460	341,140
14	6,583	×	2.41	=	15,897	44,513	×	0.54	=	24,037	(2,920)	21,117	×	0.2046	=	4,321	345,461
15	6,583	×	2.57	=	16,930	140,302	×	0.54	=	75,763	(2,745)	73,018	×	0.1827	=	13,340	358,801

TABLE A.4 15-Year Life Cycle Cost Analysis for Service Corridor versus Interstitial Space—Exxon Inflation Rates

Year	Arch. Depr. (150% Decl. Bal.) Col. A Book Value	40 Year Factor	Arch. Depr.	M/E Depr. (200% Decl. Bal.) Col. B Book Value	25 Year Facor	M/E Depr.	Col. C Fitt-Up Cos Diff.	Col. D Major Alt. Cos Diff.	Col. E Maint. Cost Diff.	Col. F = C + D + E Subtotal Costs	Infl. Fact.	Col. G Escl. Cost Diff.
0	293,182			102,437								
1	293,182 ×	0.0375 =	10,994	102,437 ×	0.08 =	8,195	0		0	0 ×	1.065 =	0
2	282,188 ×	0.0375 =	10,582	94,242 ×	0.08 =	7,539	0		0	0 ×	1.13 =	0
3	271,606 ×	0.0375 =	10,185	86,703 ×	0.08 =	6,936	0		0	0 ×	1.21 =	0
4	261,420 ×	0.0375 =	9,803	79,766 ×	0.08 =	6,381	0		0	0 ×	1.29 =	0
5	251,617 ×	0.0375 =	9,436	73,385 ×	0.08 =	5,871	0	(9,030)	0	(9,030) ×	1.37 =	(12,372)
6	242,182 ×	0.0375 =	9,082	67,514 ×	0.08 =	5,401	0		0	0 ×	1.46 =	0
7	233,100 ×	0.0375 =	8,741	62,113 ×	0.08 =	4,969	0		0	0 ×	1.55 =	0
8	224,358 ×	0.0375 =	8,413	57,144 ×	0.08 =	4,572	0		0	0 ×	1.65 =	0
9	215,945 ×	0.0375 =	8,098	52,573 ×	0.08 =	4,206	0		0	0 ×	1.76 =	0
10	207,847 ×	0.0375 =	7,794	48,367 ×	0.08 =	3,869	0	(9,030)	0	(9,030) ×	1.88 =	(16,951)
11	200,053 ×	0.0375 =	7,502	44,497 ×	0.08 =	3,560	0		0	0 ×	2.00 =	0
12	192,551 ×	0.0375 =	7,221	40,938 ×	0.08 =	3,275	0		0	0 ×	2.13 =	0
13	185,330 ×	0.0375 =	6,950	37,663 ×	0.08 =	3,013	0		0	0 ×	2.27 =	0
14	178,380 ×	0.0375 =	6,689	34,650 ×	0.08 =	2,772	0		0	0 ×	2.41 =	0
15	171,691 ×	0.0375 =	6,438	31,878 ×	0.08 =	2,550	0	(9,030)	0	(9,030) ×	2.57 =	(23,224)

Annual Labor Coss

		Annual Energy Costs		Col. H	Col. I = G + H		After Tax Costs		Col. J	Col. K	Col. L = J + K				
Year	Energy Cost Diff.		Infl. Fact.		Escl. Cost Diff.	Net Cost Diff.		Tax Fact.		After Tax Cost	Depr. Savings	Total Cost		Present Worth Factor	Present Worth	Cumul. Present Worth
0	0				0	0				0					395,619	395,619
1	0	×	1.065	=	0	0	×	0.54	=	0	(8,827)	(8,827)	×	0.8929	(7,881)	387,738
2	0	×	1.13	=	0	0	×	0.54	=	0	(8,336)	(8,336)	×	0.7972	(6,645)	381,092
3	0	×	1.21	=	0	0	×	0.54	=	0	(7,876)	(7,876)	×	0.7118	(5,606)	375,487
4	0	×	1.29	=	0	0	×	0.54	=	0	(7,445)	(7,445)	×	0.6355	(4,731)	370,755
5	0	×	1.37	=	0	(12,372)	×	0.54	=	(6,681)	(7,041)	(13,722)	×	0.5674	(7,786)	362,969
6	0	×	1.46	=	0	0	×	0.54	=	0	(6,662)	(6,662)	×	0.5066	(3,375)	359,594
7	0	×	1.55	=	0	0	×	0.54	=	0	(6,307)	(6,307)	×	0.4523	(2,853)	356,741
8	0	×	1.65	=	0	0	×	0.54	=	0	(5,973)	(5,973)	×	0.4039	(2,412)	354,329
9	0	×	1.76	=	0	0	×	0.54	=	0	(5,660)	(5,660)	×	0.3606	(2,041)	352,288
10	0	×	1.88	=	0	(16,951)	×	0.54	=	(9,153)	(5,365)	(14,519)	×	0.3220	(4,675)	347,613
11	0	×	2.00	=	0	0	×	0.54	=	0	(5,088)	(5,088)	×	0.2875	(1,463)	346,150
12	0	×	2.13	=	0	0	×	0.54	=	0	(4,828)	(4,828)	×	0.2567	(1,239)	344,911
13	0	×	2.27	=	0	0	×	0.54	=	0	(4,583)	(4,583)	×	0.2292	(1,050)	343,861
14	0	×	2.41	=	0	0	×	0.54	=	0	(4,352)	(4,352)	×	0.2046	(891)	342,970
15	0	×	2.57	=	0	(23,224)	×	0.54	=	(12,541)	(4,135)	(16,676)	×	0.1827	(3,047)	339,924

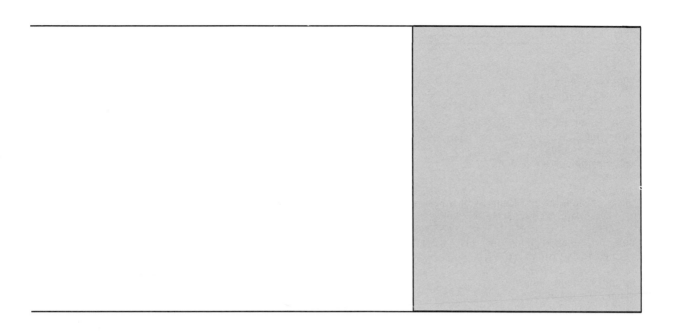

INDEX

SPM

FILLIW

.37